The History of the Pirates

Pirates

Biographies and Lives of noted Pirate Captains; Misson, Bowen, Kidd, Tew, Halsey, White, Condent, Bellamy etc. - and their several crews

By Thomas Carey

PANTIANOS
CLASSICS

Published by Pantianos Classics

ISBN-13: 978-1-78987-209-5

First published in 1825

Contents

The History of the Pirates

Captain Misson

CAPTAIN MISSON was born in Provence, of an ancient family. His father was master of a plentiful fortune; but having a great number of children, our rover had but little hopes of other fortune than what he could carve out for himself with his sword. His parents took care to give him an education equal to his birth, and upon the completion of it would have put him into the musketeers; but as he was of a roving temper, and much affected with the accounts he had read in books of travels, he chose the sea as a life which abounds with more variety, and would afford him an opportunity to gratify his curiosity, by the change of countries. Having made this choice, his father, with letters of recommendation, and everything fitting for him. sent him volunteer on board the Victoire, commanded by Monsieur Fourbin, his relation. He was received on board with all possible regard by the Captain, whose skip was as Marseilles, and was ordered to cruise soon after Misson's arrival. Nothing could be more agreeable to the inclinations of our volunteer than this cruise, which made him acquainted with the most noted ports in the Mediterranean, and gave him a great insight into the practical part of navigation. He grew fond of this life, and was resolved to be a complete sailor, which made him always one of the first on a yard arm, either to hand or reef, and very inquisitive in the different methods of working a ship: his discourse was turned on no other subject, and he would often get the boatswain and carpenter to teach him in their cabins the constituent parts of a ship's hull, and how to rig her, which he generously paid them for; and though he spent a great part of his time with these two officers, yet he behaved himself with such prudence that they never attempted any familiarity, and always paid the respect due to his family. The ship being at Naples, he obtained leave of his captain to go to Rome, which he had a great desire to visit. Hence we may date his misfortunes; for, remarking the licentious lives of the clergy, (so different from the regularity observed among the French ecclesiastics, the luxury of the Papal Court, and that nothing but hulls of religion were to be found in the metropolis of the Christian church, he began to figure to himself that all religion was no more than; a curb upon the minds of the weaker, which the wiser sort yielded to, in appearance only. These sentiments, so disadvantageous to religion and himself, were strongly riveted by accidentally becoming acquainted with a lewd priest, who was at his arrival (by mere chance) his confessor, and after that his procurer and companion, for he kept him company to his death.

Misson at length became so much attached to this man, that he advised him to go with him as volunteer, and offered him money to clothe him: the priest leaped at the proposal, and a letter coming to Mission from his captain, that he was going to Leghorn, and left it to him either to come to Naples, or go by land; he chose the latter, and the Dominican, whom he furnished with money, clothing himself very cavalierly, threw off his habit, and preceded him two days, staying at Pisa for Misson; from whence they went together to Leghorn, where they found the Victoire, and signior Caraccioli, recommended by his friend, was received on board. Two days after they weighed from hence, and after a week's cruise fell in with two Sallee-men, the one of twenty, the other of twenty-four guns; the Victoire had but thirty mounted, though she had ports for forty. The engagement was long and bloody, for the Sallee-men hoped to carry the Victoire; and, on the contrary, Capt. Fourbin, so far from having any thoughts of being taken, he was resolutely bent to make prize of his enemies, or sink his ship. One of the Sallee-men was commanded by a Spanish renegade, (though he had only the title of a lieutenant) for the captain was a young man who knew little of marine affairs.

This ship was called the Lion; and he attempted, more than once, to board the Victoire; but by a shot betwixt wind and water, he was obliged to sheer off, and running his guns, &c. on one side, to bring her on the careen to stop his leak; this being done with too much precipitation, she overset, and every soul was lost. His comrade, seeing this disaster, threw out all his small sails, endeavoured to get off, but the Victoire wronged her, and obliged her to renew the fight, which she did with great obstinacy, and made Monsieur Fourbin despair of carrying her if he did not board; he made preparations accordingly. Signior Caraccioli and Misson were the two first on board when the command was given; but they and their followers were beat back by the despair of the Sallee-men; the former received a shot in his thigh, and was carried down to the surgeon. The Victoire laid her on board the second time, and the Sallee-men defended their decks with such resolution, that they were covered with their own, and the dead bodies of their enemies. Misson seeing one of them jump down the main hatch with a lighted match, suspecting his design, resolutely leaped after him, and reaching him with his sabre, laid him dead the moment he was going to set fire to the powder. The Victoire pouring in more men, the Mahometans quitted the decks, finding resistance vain, and fled for shelter to the cook-room, steerage, and cabins, and some ran between decks. The French gave them quarters, and put the prisoners on board' the Victoire, the prize yielding nothing worth mention, except liberty to about fifteen Christian slaves; she was carried into and, sold with the prisoners at Leghorn. The Turks lost a great many men; the French not less than 35 in boarding, for they lost very few by the great shot, the Sallee-men firing mostly at the masts and rigging, hoping by disabling to carry her. The limited time of their cruise being out, the Victoire returned to Marseilles, from whence Misson taking his companion, went to visit his parents, to whom the captain sent a very advantageous character, both of his courage and conduct, lie was about a month at home when his captain wrote to him, that his ship was ordered to Rochelle, from whence he was to sail for the West Indies with some merchantmen. This was very agreeable to Misson and signior Caraccioli, who immediately set out for Marseilles. This town is well fortified, has four parish churches, and the number of inhabitants is computed to be about 120,000; the harbour is esteemed the safest in the Mediterranean, and is the common station for the French gallies.

Leaving this place, they steered for Rochelle, where the Victoire was docked, the merchant ships not being near ready. Misson, who did not care to pass so long a time in idleness, proposed to bis comrade the taking a cruise on board the Triumph, which was going into the English Channel; and the Italian readily consented to it.

Between the Isle of Guernsey and the Start Point, they met with the Mayflower, Capt. Balladine, commander,' a merchant ship of 18 guns, richly laden, and coming from Jamaica. The captain of the English made a gallant resistance, and fought his ship so long, that the French could not carry her into harbour, wherefore they took the money, and what was most valuable, out of her; and finding she made more water than the pumps could free, quitted, and saw her go down in less than four hours after. Monsieur Le Blanc, the French captain, received Capt. Balladine very civilly, and would not suffer either him or his men to be stripped, saying, *None but cowards ought to be treated after that manner; that brave men ought to treat such, though their enemies, as brothers; and that to use a gallant man (who does his duty) ill, speaks a revenge which cannot proceed but from a coward sold.* He ordered that the prisoners should have their chests; and when some of his men seemed to mutter, he bade them remember the grandeur of the monarch they served; that they were neither pirates nor privateers; and as brave men, they ought to show their enemies an example they would willingly have followed, and use their prisoners as they wished to be used.

They then run up the English Channel as high as Beachy Head, and, in returning, fell in with three fifty gun ships; which gave chase to the Triumph; but as she was an excellent sailor, she run them out of sight in seven glasses, and made the best of her way for the Land's-End. They here cruised eight days, then doubling Gape Cornwall, ran u the Bristol channel, near as far as Nash Point, an intercepted a small ship from Barbadoes, and stretching away to the northward, gave chase to a ship they saw in the evening, but lost her in the night. The Triumph then stood towards Milford, and spying a sail, endeavoured to cut her off the land, but found it impossible; for she got into the haven, though they came up with her very fast, and she had surely been taken had the chase been any thing longer.

Capt. Balladine, who took the glass, said it was the Port Royal, a Bristol ship, which left Jamaica in company with him and the Charles. They now returned to their own coast, and sold their prize at Brest, where, at his desire, they left Capt. Balladine, and Monsieur Le Blanc made him a present of a purse with 40 *louis* for his support. His crew were also left here.

At the entrance into this harbour the Triumph struck upon a rock, but received no damage. This entrance, called Gonlet, is very dangerous on account of the number of rocks which lie on each side under water, though the harbour is certainly the best in France. The mouth of the harbour is defended by a strong castle; the town is well fortified, and has a citadel for its farther defence, which is of considerable strength. In 1694 the English attempted a descent, but did not find their market, for they were beat off with the loss of their general, and a great many men. From hence the Triumph returned to Rochelle, and in a month after, our volunteers, who went on board the Victoire, took their departure for Martinico and Guadaloupe. They met with nothing in their voyage thither worth noting. I shall only observe, that signior Caraccioli, who was as ambitious as he was irreligious, had, by this time, made a perfect deist of Misson, and thereby convinced him, that all religion was no other than human policy. But his arguments on this head are too long, and too dangerous to translate; and as they are worked up with great subtlety, they may be pernicious to weak men, who cannot discover their fallacy; or who, finding them agreeable to their inclinations, would be glad to shake off the yoke of the Christian religion, which galls and curbs their passions, and would not give themselves the trouble to examine them to the bottom, but give it to what pleases, glad of finding some excuse to their consciences.

As he had privately held these discourses among the crew, he had gained a number of proselytes, who looked upon him as a new prophet risen up to reform the abuses in religion; and a great number being Rochellers, and, as yet, tainted with Galvanism, his doctrine was the more readily embraced. When he had experienced the affects of his religious arguments, he fell upon government, and showed, that every man was born free, and had as much right to what would support him, as to the air he respired. A contrary way of arguing would be accusing the deity with cruelty and injustice, for he brought into the world no man to pass a life of penury, and to miserably want a necessary support; that the vast difference between man and man, one wallowing in luxury, and the other in the most pinching necessity was owing only to avarice and ambition on the one hand, and a pusillanimous subjection on the other; that at first no other than a natural was known as eternal government, every father was the head, prince and monarch of his family, and obedience of such was both just and easy, for a father had compassionate tenderness for his children; but ambition keeping in by degrees, the stronger family set up and enslaved the weaker; and this additional strength over-run a third, by every conquest gathering force to make others, and this was the first foundation of monarchy. Pride increasing with power, man usurped the prerogative of God, over his creatures, that of depriving them of life, which was a privilege no one had over his own; for as he did not come into the world by his own election, he ought to stay the determined time of his creator; that indeed, death given in war, was by the law of nature

9

allowable, because it is for the preservation of our own lives; but no crime ought to be thus punished, nor indeed any war undertaken, but in defence of our natural right, which is such a share of earth as is necessary for our support.

These topics he often declaimed on, and very often advised with Misson about the setting up for themselves; he was as ambitious as the other, and as resolute. Caraccioli and Misson were by this, expert mariners, and very capable of managing a ship; Caraccioli had sounded a great many of the men on this subject, and found them very inclinable to listen to him. An accident happened which gave Caraccioli a fair opportunity to put his designs in execution, and he laid hold of it. They went off Martinico on a cruise, and met with the Winchelsea, an English man of war of 40 guns, commanded by Capt. Jones; they made for each other, and a very smart engagement followed; the first broadside killed the captain, second captain, and the three lieutenants, on board the Victoire, and left only the master, who would have struck, but Misson took up the sword, ordered Caraccioli to act as lieutenant, and encouraging the men fought the ship six glasses, when by some accident the Winchelsea blew up, and not a man was saved but Lieut. Franklin, whom the French boats took up, and he died in two days. None ever knew before this manuscript fell into my hands, how the Winchelsea was lost; for her head being driven ashore at Antigua, and a great storm having happened a few days before it was found, it was concluded, that she foundered in that storm. After this engagement, Caraccioli came to Misson and saluted him captain, and desired to know if he would choose a momentary or a lasting command, that he must now determine, for at his return to Martinico it would be too late; and he might depend upon the ship he fought and saved being given to another, and they would think him well rewarded if made a lieutenant which piece of justice he doubted; that he had his fortune in his hands, which he might either keep or let go; if he made choice of the latter, he must never again expect she would court him to accept her favours; that he ought to set before his eyes his circumstances, as a younger brother of a good family, but nothing to support his character; and the many years he must serve at the expense of his blood before he could make any figure in the world, and consider the wide difference between the' commanding and being commanded; that he might with the ship he had under foot, and the brave fellows under command, bid defiance to the power of Europe, enjoy every thing he wished, reign sovereign of the Southern Seas, and lawfully make war on all the world, since it would deprive him of that liberty to which he had a right by the laws of nature, that he might in time, become as great as Alexander was to the Persians: and by increasing his forces by captures, he would every day strengthen the justice of his cause, for who has power is always in the right. That Harry the fourth and Harry the seventh, attempted and succeeded in their enterprises on the crown of England, yet their forces did not equal his. Mahomet with a few camel drivers, founded the Ottoman empire; and Darius, with no more than six or seven companions, got possession of that of Persia.

In a word, he said so much that Misson resolved to follow his advice, and calling up all hands, he told them, "That a great number of them had resolved with him upon a life of liberty, and had done him the honor to create him chief; that he designed to force no man, and be guilty of that injustice he blamed in others; therefore, if any were averse to the following his fortune, which he promised should be the same to all, he desired they would declare themselves, and he would set them ashore, whence they might return with conveniency." Having made an end, they one and all cried, *"Vive le Capitain Misson et son Lieutenant le scavant Caraccioli"* — God bless Captain Misson and his learned Lieutenant Caraccioli. Misson thanked them for the honor they conferred upon him, and promised he would use the power they gave for the public good only, and hoped as they had the bravery to assert their liberty, they would be as unanimous in the preservation of it, and stand by him in what should be found expedient for the good of all; that he was their friend and companion, and should never exert his power, or think himself other than their comrade, but when the necessity of affairs should oblige him.

They shouted a second time, *Vive le Capitain:* he, after this, desired they would choose their subaltern officers, and give them power to consult and conclude upon what might be for the common interest, and bind themselves down by an oath to agree to what such officers and he should determine; this they readily gave in to. The schoolmaster they chose for second lieutenant, Jean Besace they nominated for third, and the boatswain, and a quarter master, named Mathieu le Tondu, with the gunner they desired might be their representatives in council. The choice was approved, and that every thing might pass methodically, and with general approbation, they were called into the great cabin, and the question put, *What course they should steer?* The captain proposed the Spanish coast as the most probable to afford them rich prizes. This was agreed upon by all. The boatswain then asked what colours they should fight under, and advised black as the most terrifying: but Caraccioli objected) "that they were no pirates, but men who were resolved to assert that liberty which God and nature gave them, and own no subjection to any, farther than was for the common good of all: that indeed obedience to governors was necessary, when they knew and acted up to the duty of their function; were vigilant guardians of the people's rights and liberties; saw that justice was equally distributed; were barriers against the rich and powerful, when they attempted to oppress the weaker; when they suffered none on the one hand to grow immensely rich, either by his own or his ancestor's encroachments: nor on the other, to be wretchedly miserable, either by falling, into the hands of villains, unmerciful creditors, or other misfortunes; while he had eyes impartial, and allowed nothing but merit to distinguish between man and man; and instead of being a burthen to the people by his luxurious life, he was by his care for, and protection of them, a real father, and in everything acted with the equal and impartial justice of a parent: but when a governor, who is the minister of the people, thinks himself raised to this dignity, that he may spend his days in pomp and luxury, looking upon his subjects as so many slaves, created for his use and pleasure, and therefore leaves them and their affairs to the immeasurable avarice and tyranny ot some one whom he has chosen for his favourite; when nothing but oppression, poverty and all the miseries of life flow from such an administration; that he lavishes away the lives and fortunes of the people, either to gratify his ambition, or to support the cause of some neighbouring prince, that he may in return, strengthen his hands should his people exert themselves in defence of their native rights; or should he run into unnecessary wars, by the rash and thoughtless councils of his favourite, and not able to make head against the enemy he has rashly or wantonly brought upon his hands, and buy a peace (which is the present case of France, as every one knows, by supporting King James, and afterwards proclaiming his son) and drain the subject; should the people's trade be wilfully neglected, for private interests, and while their ships of war lie idle in their harbours, suffer their vessels to be taken; and the enemy not only intercepts all commerce, but insults their coasts: it speaks a generous and great soul to shake off the yoke; and if we cannot redress our wrongs, withdraw from sharing the miseries which meaner spirits submit to, and scorn to yield to the tyranny. Such men as we, and, if the world, as experience may convince us it will, makes war upon us, the law of nature empowers us not only to be on the defensive, but also on the offensive part. As we then do not proceed upon the same ground with pirates, who are men of dissolute lives and no principles, let us scorn to take their colours; ours is a brave, a just, an innocent, and a noble cause; the cause of liberty. I therefore advise a white ensign, with liberty painted in the fly, and if you like the motto, *"a Deo a libertate"* for God and liberty, as an emblem of our uprightness and resolution."

The cabin door was left open, and the bulk-head, which was of canvass, rolled up: the steerage being full of men, who lent an attentive ear, they cried, *"Liberty, Liberty; we are free men: Vive the brave Capt. Misson and the noble Lieut. Caraccioli!"* This short council breaking up, everything belonging to the deceased captain, and the other officers, and men lost in the engagement, was brought upon deck and overhauled; the money ordered to be put into a chest, and the carpenter to clap on a padlock, and give a key to every one of the council; Misson telling them, all should be in common, and the particular avarice of no one should defraud the public.

When the plate Monsieur Fourbin had, was going to the chest, the men unanimously cried out "avast! keep that out for the captain's use, as a present from his officers and fore-mast men." Misson thanked them, the plate was returned to the great cabin, and the chest secured according to orders: Misson then ordered his lieutenants and other officers to examine who among the men, were in most want of clothes, and to distribute those of the dead men impartially, which was done with the general consent and applause of the whole crew. All but the wounded being upon deck, Misson from the barricade, spoke to the following purpose, "That since they had unanimously

12

resolved to seize upon and defend their liberty, which ambitious men had usurped, and that this could not be esteemed by impartial judges other than a just and brave resolution, he was under an obligation to recommend to them a brotherly love to each other; the banishment of all private piques and grudges, and a strict agreement and harmony among themselves; that in throwing off the yoke of tyranny, of which the action spoke an abhorrence, he hoped none would follow the example of tyrants, and turn his back upon justice; for when equity was trodden under foot, misery, confusion, and mutual distrust naturally followed!" He also advised them to remember there was a Supreme, the adoration of whom, reason and gratitude prompted us to, and our own interest would engage us (as it is best to be of the sure side, and after-life was allowed possible) to conciliate: that he was satisfied men who were born and bred in slavery, by which their spirits were broke, and were incapable of so generous a way of thinking who, ignorant of their birthright, and the sweets of liberty. dance to the music of their chains, which was indeed the greater part of the inhabitants of the globe, would brand this generous crew with the invidious name of pirates, and think it meritorious to be instrumental in their destruction. Self-preservation, therefore, and not a cruel disposition, obliged him to declare war against all such as should refuse him the entry of their ports, and against all, who should not immediately surrender and give up what their necessities required; but in a more particular manner against all European ships and vessels, as concluded implacable enemies. *And I do now,* said he, *declare such war, and, at the same time, recommend to you, my comrades, a humane and generous behaviour, towards your prisoners; which will appear by so much more the effects of a noble soul, as we are satisfied we should not meet the same treatment should our ill fortune, or more properly our disunion, or want of courage, give us up to their mercy.*

After this, he required a muster should be made, and there were able hands two hundred, and thirty-five sick and wounded. As they were mustered, they were sworn. After affairs were thus settled, they shaped their course for the Spanish West Indies, but resolved in the way, to take a week or ten days' cruise in the windward passage from Jamaica, because most merchantmen, which were good sailers, and did not stay for convoy, took this as the shorter cut for England.

Off St. Christopher's they took an English sloop becalmed, with their boats. They took out of her a couple of puncheons of rum, and half a dozen hogsheads of sugar. She was a New-England sloop, bound for Boston, and without offering the least violence to the men, or stripping them, they let her go. The master of the sloop was Thomas Butler, who owned he never met with so candid an enemy as the French man of war, which took him the day he left St. Christopher's. They met with no other booty in their way, till they came upon their station, when after three days, they saw a sloop which had the impudence to give them chase. Capt. Misson asked what could be the meaning of the sloop standing for them? One of the men who was acquainted with the West Indies, told him, it was a Jamaica privateer, and he should not wonder,

if he clapped him aboard. "I am," said he, "no stranger to their way of working, and this despicable fellow, as those who don't know a Jamaica privateer
may think him, it is ten to one will give you some trouble. It now grows towards evening, and you'll find as soon as he has discovered your force, he'll
keep out of the reach of your guns till the 12 o'clock watch is changed at
night, and he'll then attempt to clap you aboard, with hopes to carry you in
the hurry: wherefore, captain, if you will give me leave to advise you, let every man have his small arms; and at 12. let the bell ring as usual, and rather
more noise than ordinary be made, as if the one watch was turning in, and
the other out, in a confusion and hurry, and I'll engage he will venture to enter his men." The fellow's advice was approved and resolved upon, and the
sloop worked as he said she would; for upon coming near enough to make
out distinctly the force of the Victoire, on her throwing out French colours,
she, the sloop, clapped upon a wind, and the Victoire gave chase, but without
hopes of gaining upon her; she went so well to windward, that she could
spare the ship some points in her sheet, and yet wrong her: at dusk of the
evening, the French had lost sight of her, but about 11 at night, they saw her
hankering up on their weather bow, which confirmed the sailor's opinion,
that she would attempt to board them, as she did at the pretended change of
the watch; there being little or no wind, she lashed to the bowsprit of the Victoire, and entered her men, who were very quietly taken, as they entered,
and tumbled down the fore-hatch where they were received by others, and
bound without noise. Not one of the privateersmen was killed, few hurt, and
only one Frenchman wounded. The Victoire, seeing the better part of the
sloop's men secured, they boarded in their turn, when the privateersmen,
suspecting some stratagem, were endeavouring to cut their lashing and get
off. Thus the Englishmen caught a Tartar. The prisoners being all secured, the
captain charged his men not to discover, through a desire of augmenting
their number, the account they were upon.

The next morning Monsieur Misson called for the captain of the privateer,
and told him, he could not but allow him a brave fellow, to venture upon a
ship of his countenance, and for that reason he should meet treatment which
men of his profession seldom afforded the prisoners they made. He asked
him how long he had been out, what was his name, and what he had on
board? He answered he was but just come out, that he was the first sail he
had met with, and should have thought himself altogether as lucky not to
have spoke with him; that his name was Harry Ramsey, and what he had on
board were rags, powder, ball, and some few half ankers of rum. Ramsey was
ordered into the gun-room, and a council was held in the public manner
aforesaid, the bulk-head of the great cabin being rolled up. On their conclu-
sion, the captain of the privateer was called in again, when Capt. Misson told
him, he would return him his sloop, and restore him and his men to their liberty, without stripping or plundering them of anything, but what prudence
obliged him to, their ammunition and small arms, if he would give him his
word and honour, and his men take an oath, not to go out on the privateer

14

account in six months after they left him: that he did not design to continue on that station above a week longer, at the expiration of which time, he would let them go.

Ramsay, who had a new sloop, did not expect this favour which he thanked him for, and promised punctually to comply with the injunction, which his men as readily swore to, though they had no design to keep the oath. The time being expired, 1 he and his men were put on board their own sloop. At going over the ship's side, Ramsay begged Monsieur Misson would allow him powder for a salute, by way of thanks; but he answered him, the ceremony was needless, and he expected no other return than that of keeping his word, which indeed Ramsay did. Some of his men had found it more to their advantage to have been as religious.

At parting Ramsey gave the snip three cheers, and Misson had the complaisance to return one, which Ramsay answering with three more, made? the best of his way for Jamaica, and at the east end of the island met with the Diana, who, upon advice, turned back.

The Victoire steered for Carthagena, off which port they cruised some days, but meeting with nothing in those seas, they made for Porto Bello; in their way they met with two Dutch traders, who had letters-of-marque, and were just come upon the coast, the one had 20, the other 24 guns; Misson engaged them, and they defended themselves with a great deal of resolution and gallantry; and as they were manned apeak, he durst not venture to board either of them, for fear of being at the same time boarded by the other. His weight of metal gave him a great advantage over the Dutch, though they were two to one; besides, their business, as they had cargoes, was to get off, if possible, wherefore they made a running fight, though they took care to stick close to one another.

They maintained the fight for above six hours, When Misson, enraged at this obstinacy, and fearing, if by accident they should bring a mast, or topmast by the board, they would get from him, he was resolved to sink the larger ship of the two, and accordingly ordered his men to bring all their guns to bear a midship, then running close alongside of him, to raise their metal, his orders being punctually obeyed, he poured in a broadside, which opened such a gap in the Dutch ship that she went directly to the bottom, and every man perished.

He then manned his bowsprit, brought his spritsail yard fore and aft, and resolved to board the other, which the Dutch perceiving, and terrified with the unhappy fate of their comrade, thought a farther resistance vain, and immediately struck. Misson gave them good quarters, though he was enraged at the loss of thirteen men killed outright, beside nine wounded, of which six died. They found on board a great quantity of gold and silver lace, brocade silks, silk stockings, bales of broadcloth, baizes of all colours, and osnaburghs.

A consultation being held, it was resolved Capt. Misson should take the name of Fourbin, and returning to Carthagena, dispose of his prize, and set his prisoners ashore. Accordingly they plied to the eastward, and came to an anchor between Boca Chicea fort, and the town, for they did not think it expedient to enter the harbour. The barge was manned, and Caraccioli, with the name of D'Aubigny, the first lieutenant, who was killed in the engagement with the Winchelsea, and his commission in his pocket, went ashore with a letter to the governor, signed Fourbin, whose character, for fear of the worst was exactly counterfeited. The purport of his letter was, that having discretionary orders to cruise for three months, and hearing the English infested his coast he was come in search of them, and had met two Dutchmen, one of which he had sunk, the other he made prize of. That his limited time being near expired, he should be obliged to his excellency, if he would send on board him such merchants as were willing to take the ship and cargo off his hands, of which he had sent the Dutch invoice. Don Joseph de la Zerda, the then governor, received the lieutenant (who sent back the barge at landing) very civilly, and agreed to take the prisoners ashore, and do every thing that was required of him; and ordering fresh provisions and vegetables to be got ready as a present for the captain, he sent for some merchants, who were very ready to go on board, and agree for the ship and goods; which they did, for fifty-two thousand pieces of eight. The next day the prisoners were set ashore; a rich piece of brocade which was reserved, sent to the governor for a present, a quantity of fresh provision bought and brought on board, the money paid by the merchants, the ship and goods delivered, and the Victoire, at the dawn of the following day, got under sail. It may be wondered how such despatch could be made, but the reader must take notice, these goods were sold by the Dutch invoice, which the merchant of the prize affirmed was genuine. I shall observe, by the by, that the Victoire was the French man of war which Admiral Wager sent the Kingston in search of, and being afterwards falsely informed, that she was joined by another of 70 guns, and that they cruised together between the Capes, ordered the Severn up to windward, to assist the Kingston, which had like to have proved very fatal; for these two English men of war, commanded by Capt. Trevor and Capt. Pudnor, meeting in the night, had prepared to engage, each taking the other for the enemy. The Kingston's men not having a good look-out which must be attributed to the negligence of the officer of the watch, did not see the Severn till she was just upon them; but by good luck, to leeward, and plying up, with all the sail she could crowd, and a clear ship. This put the Kingston in such confusion, that when the Severn hailed, no answer was returned for none heard her. She was got under the Kingston's stern, and Capt. Pudnor ordered to hail for the third and last time, and if no answer was returned, to give her a broadside. The noise on board the Kingston was now a little ceased, and Capt. Trevor, who was on the poop with a speaking trumpet, to hail the Severn, by good luck heard her hail him, and answering the Kingston, and asking the name of the other ship, prevented the damage.

They cruised together some time, and meeting nothing which answered their information, returned to Jamaica, as I shall to my subject, begging pardon for this, as I thought, necessary digression.

Don Juan de la Zerda told the captain in a letter, that the St. Joseph, a galleon of 70 guns, was then lying at Porto Bello, and should be glad if he could keep her company till she was off the coast. That she would sail in eight or ten days for the Havana; and that; if his time would permit him, he would send an advice-boat. That she had on board the value of 800,000 pieces of eight in silver, and bar gold. Misson returned answer, that he believed he should be excused if he stretched his orders, for a few days; and that he would cruise off the Isle of Pearls, and Cape Gratias a Dios, and give for signal to the galleon, his spreading a white ensign in his fore-top-mast shrouds, the cluing up his fore-sail, and the firing one gun to windward, and two to leeward, which he should answer by hoisting his fore-top-sail three times, and the firing as many guns to leeward. Don Joseph, extremely pleased with this complaisance, sent a boat express to advise the St. Joseph, but she was already sailed two days, contrary to the governor of Carthagena's expectation, and this advice Capt. Misson had from the boat, which returning with an answer, saw the Victoire in the offing, and spoke to her. It was then resolved to follow the St. Joseph, and accordingly they steered for the Havanna, but by what accident they did not overtake her is unknown.

I forgot to tell my reader, that on board, the Dutch ship were fourteen French hugonots, whom Misson thought fit to detain. When they were at sea, he called them up, and proposed to them their taking on; telling them at the same time, he left it to their choice, for he would have no forced men; and that if they all, or any of them disapproved the proposal, he would either give them the first vessel he met that was fit for them, or set them ashore on some inhabited coast; and therefore bid them take two days for consideration before they returned an answer; and to encourage them, he called all hands up, and declared, that if any man repented of the course of life he had chosen, his just dividend should be counted to him, and he would set him on shore, either near the Havanna, or some other convenient place; but not one accepted the offer, and the fourteen prisoners unanimously resolved to join in with them; to which resolution, no doubt, the hopes of a good booty from the St. Joseph, and this offer of liberty, greatly contributed.

At the entrance of the Gulf they spied and came up with a large merchant ship bound for London, from Jamaica; she had 20 guns, but no more than thirty-two hands, so that it is not to be wondered at she made no resistance; besides, she was deep laden with sugars. Mons. Misson took out of her what ammunition she had, about four thousand pieces of eight, some puncheons of rum, and ten hogsheads of sugar; and, without doing her any further damage, let her proceed her voyage. What he valued most in this prize was the men he got, for she was carrying to Europe twelve French prisoners, two of which were necessary hands, being a carpenter and his mate. They were of Bordeaux from whence they came in the Pomechatraine, which was taken by the

Mermaid off Petit-Guave, after an obstinate resistance, in which they lost 40 men. These men very willingly came into Capt. Misson's measures. Having been stripped to the skin, they begged leave to make reprisals, but the captain would not suffer them, though he told the master of the prize, as he protected him and his men, he thought it reasonable these French should be clothed; upon this the master contributed of his own, and every man bringing up his chest, thought themselves very well off in sharing with them one half.

Though Misson's ship passed for a French man of war, yet his generosity in letting the prize go, gave the English grounds to suspect the truth, neither the ship nor cargo being of use to such as were upon the grand account.

When they had lost all hopes of the St. Joseph, they coasted along the north side of Cuba, and the Victoire growing now foul, they ran into a landlocked bay on the E. N. E. point, where they hove her down by boats and guns, though they could not pretend to heave her keel out; however, they scraped and tallowed as far as they could go; they, for this reason, many of them, repented they had let the last prize go, by which they might have careened,

When they had righted the ship, and put everything on board, they consulted upon the course they should steer. Upon this the council divided. The captain and Caraccioli, were for stretching over to the African, and the others for New England coast, alleging, that the ship had a foul bottom, and was not fit for the voyage; and that if they met with contrary? winds, and bad weather, their stock of provision might fall short; and that as they were not far from the English settlement of Carolina, they might either on that or on the coast of Virginia, Maryland, Pennsylvania, New York, or New England, intercept ships which traded to the islands with provisions and by that means provide themselves with bread, flour, and other necessaries. An account of the provisions was taken, and finding they had provisions for four months, Capt. Misson called all hands upon deck, and told them, as the council differed in the course they should steer, lie thought it reasonable to have it put to the vote of the whole company. That for his part, lie was for going to the coast of Guinea, where they might reasonably expect to meet with valuable prizes; but should they fail in their expectation one way, they would be sure of having it answered in another; for they could then throw themselves in that of East-India ships, and lie need not tell them, that the outward bound drained Europe of what money they drew from America. He then gave the sentiments of those who were against him, and their reasons, and begged that every one would give his opinion and vote according as he thought most conducive to the good of all. That he should be far from taking it ill if they should reject what he had proposed, since he had no private views to serve. The majority of votes fell on the captain's side, and they accordingly shaped their course for the coast of Guinea, in which voyage nothing remarkable happened. On their arrival on the gold coast, they fell in with the Nieuwstadt, of Amsterdam, a ship of 18 guns, commanded by Capt. Blaes, who made a running fight of five glasses: this ship they kept with them, putting on board

40 hands, and bringing all the prisoners on board the Victoire they were forty-three in number; they left Amsterdam with fifty-six: seven were killed in the engagement, and they had lost six by sickness and accidents, one falling overboard, and one being taken by a shark, going overboard in a calm.

The Nieuwstadt had some gold dust on board, to the value of about £2000 sterling and a few slaves to the number of seventeen, for she had but just begun to trade; the slaves were a strengthening of their hands, for the captain ordered them to be clothed out of the Dutch mariners' chests, and told his men "That the trading for those of our own species could never be agreeable to the eyes of divine justice: that no man had power over the liberty of another; and while those who professed a more enlightened knowledge of the Deity, sold men like beasts, they proved that their religion was no more than grimace, and that they differed from the barbarian in name only, since their practice was in nothing more humane: for his part, and he hoped he spoke the sentiments of all his brave companions, he had not exempted his neck from the galiing yoke of slavery, and asserted his own liberty to enslave others. That however these men were distinguished from the Europeans by their colour, customs, or religious rites, they were the work of the same omnipotent Being, and indued with equal reason, wherefore he desired they might be treated like freemen, (for he would banish even the name of slavery from among them) and divided into messes among them, to the end they might the sooner learn their language, be sensible of the obligation they had to them, and more capable and zealous to defend that liberty they owed to their justice and humanity."

This speech of Misson's was received with general applause, and the ship rang with *"Vive le Capitaine Misson"* Long live Capt. Misson. — The negroes were divided among the French, one to a mess, who, by their gesticulations showed they were gratefully sensible of their being delivered from their chains. Their ship growing very foul, and going heavily through the water, they run into the river Lagoa, where they hove her down, taking out such planks as had suffered most by the worms, and substituting new in their room.

After this they careened the prize, and so put out to sea, steering to the southward, and keeping along the coast, but met with nothing. All this while, the greatest decorum and regularity was observed on board the Victoire; but the Dutch prisoners' example began to lead them into swearing and drunkenness, which the captain remarking thought it was best to nip these vices in the bud; and calling both the French and Dutch upon deck, he addressed himself to the latter, desiring their captain, who spoke French excellently well, to interpret what he said to those who did not understand him. He told them, "before he had the misfortune of having them onboard, his ears were never grated with hearing the name of the great Creator profaned, though he, to his sorrow, had often since heard his own men guilty of that sin, which administered neither profit not pleasure, and might draw upon them a, severe punishment: that if they had a just idea of that great Being, they would never mention him, but they would immediately reflect on his purity and their own vileness. That we so easily took impressions from our company, that the Spanish proverb says, *Let a hermit and a thief live together, the thief would become hermit, or the hermit thief:* that he saw this verified in his ship, for he could attribute the oaths and curses he had heard among his brave companions, to nothing but the odious example of the Dutch: that this was not the only vice they had introduced, for before they were on board, his men were men, but he found by their beastly pattern they were degenerated into brutes, by drowning that only faculty which distinguishes between men and beasts, *reason.* That as he had the honour to command them, he could not see them run into these odious vices without a sincere concern, as he had a paternal affection for them; and he should reproach himself as neglectful of the common good, if he did not admonish them; and as by the post with which they had honoured him, he was obliged to have a watchful eye over their general interest; he was obliged to tell them his sentiments were, that the Dutch allured them to a dissolute way of life, that they might take some advantage over them: wherefore, as his brave companions, he was assured, would be guided by reason, he gave the Dutch notice, that the first whom he caught either with an oath in his mouth or liquor in his head, should be brought to the geers, whipped and pickled for an example to the rest of his nation; as to his friends, his companions, his children, those gallant, those generous, noble, and heroic souls he had the honour to command, he entreated them to allow a small time for reflection, and to consider how little pleasure and how much danger, might flow from imitating the vices of their enemies; and that they would among themselves, make a law for the suppression of what would otherwise estrange them from the source of life, and consequently leave them destitute of his protection."

It is not to be imagined what efficacy this speech had on both nations; the Dutch grew continent in fear of punishment, and the French in fear of being reproached by their good captain, for they never mentioned him without this epithet. Upon the coast of Angola, they met with a second Dutch ship, the cargo of which consisted of silk and woollen stuffs, cloth, lace, wine, brandy, oil, spice, and hardware: the prize gave chase and engaged her y but upon the coming up of the Victoire she struck. This ship opportunely came in their way, and gave full employ to the tailors, who were on board; for the whole crew began to be out at elbows; they plundered her of what was of use to their own ship, and then sunk her.

The captain having about ninety prisoners on board, proposed the giving them the prize with what was necessary for their voyage, and sending them away; which being agreed to, they shifted her ammunition on board the Victoire, and giving them provisions to carry them to the settlements the Dutch have on the coast, Misson called them up, told them what was his design, and asked if any of them was willing to share his fortune: eleven Dutch came in to him, two, of whom were sailmakers, one an armourer, and one a carpenter, necessary hands; the rest he let go, not a little surprised at the regularity, tranquility, and humanity, which they found among these new fashioned pirates.

They had now run the length of Saldanha bay, about ten leagues to. the northward of Table Bay. As here is good water, safe riding, plenty of fish and fresh provision, to be got of the natives for the merchandise they had on board, it was resolved to stay here some little time for refreshments. When they had the bay open, they spied a tall ship, which instantly got under sail, and hove out English colours. The Victoire made clear ship, and hove out her French ensign, and a smart engagement began. The English was a new ship built for 40 guns, though she had but 32 mounted, and 90 hands. Misson gave orders for boarding, and the number of fresh men he constantly poured in, after an obstinate dispute obliged the English to fly the decks, and leave the French masters of their ship, who promised, and gave them good quarters and stripped not a man.

They found on board the prize some bales of English broadcloth, and about £60,000 in English crown pieces, and Spanish pieces of eight. The English captain was killed in the engagement, and 14 of his men: the French lost 12, which was no small mortification, but did not however provoke them to use their prisoners harshly. Capt. Misson was sorry for the death of the commander, whom he buried on shore, and one of his men being a stone-cutter, he raised a stone over his grave with these words, *"Icy gist un brave Anglois,"* *Here lies a gallant Englishman.* When he was buried he made a triple discharge of fifty small arms, and fired minute guns.

The English, knowing whose hands they were fallen into, and charmed with Misson's humanity, 30 of them, in three days space, desired to take on with him. He accepted them, but at the same time gave them to understand, that in taking on with him they were not to expect they should be indulged in a dissolute and immoral life. He now divided his company between the two ships, and make Caraccioli captain of" the prize, giving him officers chosen by the public suffrage. The 17 negroes began to understand a little French, and to be useful hands, and in less than a month all the English prisoners came over to him, except their officers.

He had two ships well manned with resolute fellows: they now doubled the cape, and made the S. end of Madagascar, and one of the Englishmen Telling Capt. Misson, that the European ships bound for Surat, commonly touched at the island of Johanna, he sent for Capt. Caraccioli on board, and it was agreed to cruise off that island. They accordingly sailed on the West side of Madagascar, and off the bay de Diego. About half seas over, between that bay, and the island of Johanna, they came up with an English East-Indiaman, which made signals of distress as soon as she spied Misson and his prize: they found her sinking by an unexpected leak, and took all her men on board, though they could get little out of her before she went down. The English, who were thus miraculously saved from perishing, desired to be set on shore at Johanna, where they hoped to meet with either a Dutch or English ship in a little time, and the mean while they were sure of relief.

They arrived at Johanna, and were kindly received by the Queen Regent and her brother, on account of the English on the one hand, and of their strength on the other, which the queen's brother, who had the administration of affairs, was not able to make head against, and hoped they might assist him against the king of Mohila, who threatened him with a visit.

This is an island which is contiguous, in a manner, to Johanna, and lies about N. W. by N. from it. Caraccioli told Misson he might take his advantage in widening the breach between these two little monarchies, and, by offering his assistance to that of Johanna, in a manner rule both, for these would court him as their protector, and those come to any terms to buy his friendship, by which means he would hold the balance of power between them. He followed this advice, and offered his friendship and assistance to the queen, who very readily embraced it.

I must advise the reader, that many of this island speak English, and that the Englishmen who were of Misson's crew, and his interpreters, told them, their captain, though not an Englishman, was their friend and ally, and a friend and brother to the Johannamen, for they esteemed the English beyond all other nations.

They were supplied by the queen with all necessaries of life, and Misson married her sister, as Caraccioli did the daughter of her brother, whose armoury, which consisted before of no more than two rusty fire-locks and three pistols, he furnished with 30 fuzils, as many pair of pistols, and gave him two barrels of powder and four of ball.

Several of his men took wives, and some required their share of the prizes, which was justly given them, they designing to settle in this island; but the number of these did not exceed ten, which loss was repaired by thirty of the crew (they had saved from perishing) coming in to him.

While they past their time in all manner of diversions the place would afford them, as hunting, feasting, and visiting the island, the king of Mohila, made a descent, and alarmed the whole country. Misson advised the queen's brother not to give him. any impediment but let him get into the heart of the island, and he would take care to intercept their return; but the prince answered, should he follow this advice the enemy would do him and his subjects an irreparable damage, in destroying the cocoa walks, and for that reason he must endeavour to stop his progress. Upon this answer he asked the English who were not under his command, if they were willing to join him in repelling the enemies of their common host, and one and all consenting, he gave them arms, and mixed them with his own men, and about the same number of Johannians, under the command of Caraccioli and the queen's brother, and arming out all his boats, he went himself to the westward of the island, where they made their descent. The party which went by land, fell in with, and beat the Mohilians with great ease, who were in the greatest consternation, to find their retreat cut off by Misson's boats. The Johannians, whom they had often molested, were so enraged, that they gave quarter to none, and out of 300 who made the descent, if Misson and Caraccioli had not interposed, not a soul had escaped; 113 were taken prisoners, by his men, and carried on board his ships. These he sent safe to Mohila, with a message to the king, to desire he would make peace with his friend and ally the king of Johanna; but that prince, little affected with the service done him in the preservation of his subjects, sent him word he took laws from none, and knew when to make war and peace without his advice, which he neither asked nor wanted. Misson irritated by this rude answer, resolved to transfer the war into his own country, and accordingly set sail for Mohila, with about 100 Johanna men. The shore on sight of the ships, was filled with men to hinder a descent if intended, but the great guns soon dispersed this rabble, and under their cover he landed the Johannians, and an equal number of French and English. They were met by about 700 Mohilians, who pretended to stop their passage, but their darts and arrows were of little avail against Misson's fuzils; the first discharge made a great slaughter, and about 20 shells which were thrown among them, put them to a confused flight. The party of Europeans and Johannians then marched to their metropolis, without resistance, which they reduced to ashes, and the Johannians cut down all the cocoa walks that they could for the time, for towards evening they returned to their ships, and stood off to sea.

At their return to Johanna the queen made a festival, and magnified the bravery and service of her guests, friends, and allies. This feast lasted four days, at the expiration of which time the queen's brother proposed to Capt. Misson the making another descent, in which he would go in person, and did not doubt subjecting the Mohilians; but this was not the design of Misson, who had thoughts of fixing a retreat on the N. W. side of Madagascar? and looked upon the feuds between these two islands advantageous to his views, and therefore no way his interest to suffer the one to overcome the other; for while the variance was kept up, and their forces pretty much upon a level, it was evident their interest would make both sides caress him; he therefore answered, that they ought to deliberate on the consequences, for they might be deceived in their hopes, and find the conquest less easy than they imagined. That the king of Mohila would be more upon his guard, and not only intrench himself, but gall them with frequent ambuscades, by which they must inevitably lose a number of men; and, if they were forced to retire with loss, raise the courage of the Mohilians, and make them irreconcilable enemies to the Johannians, and entirely deprive him of the advantages with which he might now make a peace, having twice defeated them: that he could not be always with them, and at his leaving Johanna he might expect the king of Mohila would endeavour to take a bloody revenge for the late damages. The queen gave entirely into Misson's sentiments.

While this was in agitation, four Mohilians arrived as ambassadors to propose a peace. Finding the Johannians upon high terms, one of them spoke to this purpose: — *O ye Johannians, do not conclude from you late success, that fortune will be always favourable; she will not always give you the protection of the Europeans, and without their help it is possible you might now sue for a peace, which you seem averse to. Remember the sun rises, comes to its meridian height, and stays not there, but declines in a moment. Let this admonish you to reflect on the constant revolution of all sublunary affairs, and the greater is your glory, the nearer you are to your declension. We are taught by every thing we see, that there is no stability in the world, but nature is in continual movement. The sea, which overflows the sands, has its bounds set, which it cannot pass, which the moment it has reached, without abiding, returns back to the bosom of the deep. Every herb, every shrub and tree, and even our own bodies teach us this lesson, that nothing is durable, or can be counted upon. Time passes away insensibly, one sun follows another, and brings its changes with it. To-day's globe of light sees you strengthened by these Europeans elate with victory, and we, who have been used to conquer you, come to ask a peace. To-morrow's sun may see you deprived of your present succours, and the Johannians petitioning us: as therefore we cannot say what to-morrow may bring forth, it would be unwise on uncertain hopes to forego a certain advantage, as surely peace ought to be esteemed by every wise man.*

Having said this, the ambassadors withdraw, and were treated by the queen's orders. After the council had concluded., they were again called upon, and the queen told them, that by the advice of her good Friends, the Europeans, and those of her council, she agreed to make peace, which she wished might banish all memory of former injuries; that they must own the war was begun by them, and that she was far from being the aggressor; she only defended herself in her own kingdom, which they had often invaded, though, till within a few days, she had never molested their coasts. If then they really desired to live amicably with her., they must resolve to send two of the king's children, and ten of the first nobility, as hostages: that they might, when they pleased, return, for these were the only terms on which she would desist prosecuting the advantages she now had, with the utmost vigour.

The ambassadors returned with this answer, and, about ten days after, the two ships appearing upon their coasts, they sent off to give notice, that their king complied with the terms proposed, would send the hostages, and desired a cessation of all hostility, and, at the same time, invited the commanders on shore. The Johanna men on board dissuaded their accepting the invitation; but Misson and Caraccioli, fearing nothing, went, but armed their boat's crew. They were received by the king with demonstrations of friendship, and they dined with him under a tamarind tree; but when they parted from him, and were returning to their boats, they were inclosed by at least a hundred of the Mohilians, who set upon them with the utmost fury, and, in the first flight of arrows, wounded both the captains, and killed four of their boat's crew, of eight who were with them. They, in return, discharged their pistols with some execution, and fell in with their cutlasses; but all their bravery would have stood them in little stead, had not the report of their pistols alarmed and brought the rest of their friends to their assistance, who took their fuzils, and coming up while they were engaged, discharged a volley

24

on the back of the assailants, which laid twelve of them dead on the spot. The ships hearing this fire, sent immediately the yawls and long-boats well manned. Though the islanders were a little damped in their courage by this fire of the boat's crew, yet they did not give over the fight, and one of them desperately threw himself upon Caraccioli, and gave him a deep wound in the side with a long knife; but he paid for the rashness of the attempt with his life, one of the crew cleaving his skull. The yawls and long-boats now arrived, and being guided by the noise, reinforced their companions, put the traitors to flight, and brought off their dead and wounded. The Europeans lost by this treachery, seven slain outright, and eight wounded, six of which recovered.

The crew were resolved to revenge the blood of their officers and comrades the next day, and were accordingly on the point of landing, when two canoes came off with two men bound, the pretended authors of this treason, without the king's knowledge, who had sent them that they might receive the punishment due to their villany. The Johanna men on board were called for interpreters, who having given this account, added, that the king only sacrificed these men, but that they should not believe him, for he certainly had given orders for assassinating the Europeans; and the better way was to kill all the Mohillians that came in the canoes, as well as the two prisoners; go back to Johanna, take more of their countrymen, and give no peace to traitors; but Misson was for no such violent measures; he was averse to every thing that bore the face of cruelty, and thought a bloody revenge, if necessity did not enforce it, spoke a grovelling and timid soul: he, therefore, sent those of the canoes back, and bid them tell their king, if before the evening he sent the hostages agreed upon, he should give credit to his excuse; but if he did net, he should believe him the author of the late vile attempt on his life.

The canoes went off, but returned not with an answer; wherefore, he bid the Johanna men tell the two prisoners that they should be set on shore the next morning, and ordered them to acquaint their king, he was no executioner to put those to death whom he had condemned, but that he should find he knew how to revenge himself of his treason. The prisoners being unbound, threw them-! selves at his feet, and begged that he would not send them ashore, for they should be surely put to death, for the crime they had committed, was, the dissuading the barbarous action of which they were accused as authors.

Next day, the two ships landed 200 men, under the cover of their cannon; but that precaution of bringing their ships close to the shore, they found needless: not a soul appearing, they marched two leagues up the country, when they saw a body of men appear behind some shrubs. Caraccioli's lieutenant, who commanded the right wing, with fifty men, made up to them, but found he had got among pit-falls artificially covered, several of his men falling into them, which made him halt, and not pursue those Mohilians who made a feint retreat to ensnare him, thinking it dangerous to proceed farther; and seeing no enemy would face them, they retired the same way they came, and getting into their boats, went on board the ships, resolving to return with a strong reinforcement, and make descents at one and the same time in different parts of the island. They asked the two prisoners how the country lay, and what the soil was on the north side of the island; and they answered it was morass, and the most dangerous part to attempt, it being a place where they shelter on any imminent danger.

The ships returned to Johanna, where the greatest tenderness and care was shown for the recovery and cure of the two captains and of their men; they lay six weeks before they were able to walk the decks, for neither of them would quit his ship. Their Johanna wives expressed a concern they did not think them capable of; nay, a wife of one of the wounded men who died, stood some time looking upon the corpse as motionless as a statue, then embracing it, without shedding a tear, desired she might take it ashore to wash and bury it; and at the same time by an interpreter, and with a little mixture of European language, begged her late husband's friends would take their leave of him the next day.

Accordingly a number went ashore, and carried with them the dividend, which fell to his share, which the captain ordered to be given to his widow; when she saw the money, she smiled, and asked if all that was for her? — Being answered in the affirmative, "and what good will all that shining dirt do me? If I could with it purchase the life of my husband, and call him back from the grave, I would accept it with pleasure, but as it is not sufficient to allure him back to this world, I have no use for it; do with it what you please." Then she desired they would go with her and perform the last ceremonies to her husband's dead body, after their country fashion, lest he should be displeased; that she could not stay with them, to be a witness, because she was in haste to go and be married again. She startled the Europeans who heard this latter part of her speech, so dissonant from the beginning; however they followed her, and she led them into a plantain walk, where they found a great many Johanna men and women, sitting under the shade of plantains, round the corpse, which lay (as they all sat) on the ground, covered with flowers. She embraced them round, and then the Europeans, one by one, and after these ceremonies, she poured out a number of bitter imprecations against the Mohila men, whose treachery had darkened her husband's eyes, and made him insensible of her caresses, who was her first love, to whom she had given her heart with her virginity. She then proceeded in his praises, calling him the joy of infants, the love of virgins, the delight of the old; and the wonder of the young, adding, he was strong and beautiful as the cedar, brave as the bull; tender as the kid, and loving as the ground turtle. Having finished this oration, not unlike those of the Romans, which the nearest relation of the deceased used to pronounce from the rostrum, she laid down by the side of her husband, embracing him, and sitting up again, gave herself a deep wound under the left breast with a bayonet, and fell dead on her husband's corpse.

The Europeans were astonished at the tenderness and the resolution of the girl, for she was not, by what her mien spoke her, past seventeen; and they now admired, as much as they had secretly detested her, for saying she was in haste to be married again, the meaning of which they did not understand.

After the husband and wife were buried, the crew returned on board, and gave an account of what had passed; the captain's wives (for Misson and his were on board the Bijoux, the name they had given their prize from her make and gilding) seemed not in the least surprised, and Caraccioli's lady only said, she must be of noble descent, for none but the families of the nobility had the privilege allowed them of following their husbands, on pain if they transgressed, of being thrown into the sea, to be eat by fish; and they knew that their souls could not rest as long as any of the fish, who fed upon them, lived. Misson asked, if they intended to have done the same thing had they died? "We should not," answered his wife, "have disgraced our families; nor is our tenderness for our husband's inferior to hers whom you seem to admire,"

After their recovery, Misson proposed a cruise, on the coast of Zanguebar, which being agreed to he and Caraccioli, took leave of the queen and her brother, and would have left their wives on the island, but they could by no means be induced to the separation; it was in vain to urge the shortness of the time they were to cruise; they answered it was not farther than Mohila they intended to go, and if they were miserable in that short absence, they could never support a longer; and if they would not allow them to keep them company in the voyage, they must not expect to see them at their return, if they intended one.

In a word, they were obliged to yield to them, hut told them, if the views of their men should insist as strongly on following their example, their tenderness would be their ruin, and make them a prey to their enemies; they answered, the queen should prevent that, by ordering that no woman should go on board, and if any were in the ships, they should: return on shore: this order was accordingly made, and they set sail for the river Mozambique. In about ten days' cruise after they had left Johanna, and about 15 leagues to the eastward of this river, they fell in with a stout Portuguese ship of 60 guns, which engaged them from break of day till two in , the afternoon, when the captain being killed, and a great number of men lost, she struck; this proved a very rich prize, for she had the value of £250,000 sterling on board, in gold dust. The two women never quit the decks all the time of the engagement, neither gave they the least mark of fear except for their husbands, This engagement cost them 30 men, and Caraccioli lost his right leg; the slaughter fell mostly on the English, for of the above number, 20 were of that nation: the Portuguese lost double the number. Caraccioli's wound made them resolve to make the best of their way for Johanna, where the greatest care was taken of their wounded, not one of whom died, though their number amounted to 27.

Caraccioli kept his bed two months; but Misson seeing him in a fair way of recovery, took what hands could be spared from the Bijoux, leaving her sufficient for defence, and went out, having mounted ten of the Portuguese guns, for he had hitherto carried but thirty, though he had ports for forty. He stretched over to Madagascar, and coasted along this island to the north-ward, as far as the most northerly point, when turning back, he entered a bay to the northward of Diego Suares. He run ten leagues up this bay, and on the larboard side found it afforded a large, and safe harbour, with plenty of fresh water. He came to an anchor, went on shore and examined the nature of the soil, which he found rich, the air wholesome, and the country level. He told his men this was an excellent place tor an asylum, and that he determined here to fortify and raise a small town, and make docks for shipping, that they might have some place to call their own; and a receptacle, when age or wounds had rendered them incapable of hardship, where they might enjoy the fruits of their labour, and go to their graves in peace: that he would not, however, set about this, till he had the approbation of the whole company; and were he sure they would all approve this design, which he hoped, it be-ing evidently for the general good, he should not think it advisable to begin any works, lest the natives should, in his absence, destroy them; but, howev-er, as they had nothing upon their hands, if they were of his opinion, they might begin to fall and square timber, ready for the raising a wooden fort, when they returned with their companions.

The captain's motion was universally applauded, and in ten days they felled and rough hewed a hundred and fifty large trees, without any interrup-tion from or seeing any of the inhabitants. They felled their timber at the wa-ters' edge, so that they had not the trouble of hauling them any way, which would have employed a great deal more time: they returned again, and ac-quainted their companions with what they had seen and done, and with the captain's resolution, which they one and all came into.

Capt. Misson then told the queen, as he had been serviceable to her in her war with the island of; Mohila, and might continue to be of farther use, he did not question her lending him assistance in the settling himself on the coast of Madagascar, and to that end furnish him with 300 men, to help in his build-ings. The queen answered, she could do nothing without consent of council, and that she would assemble her nobility, and did not question their agree-ing to anything he could reasonably desire, for they were sensible of the obli-gations the Johannians had to him. The council was accordingly called, and Misson's demand being told, one of the eldest said, he did not think it expedi-ent to comply with it, nor safe to refuse; that they should in agreeing to give him that assistance, help to raise a power, which might prove formidable to themselves, by the being so near a neighbour; and these men who had lately protected, might, when they found it for their interest, enslave them. On the other hand, if they did not comply, they had the power to do them great damage: that they were to make choice of the least of two possible evils, for he could prognosticate no good to Johanna, by their settling near it. Another answered, that many of them had Johanna wives: that it was not likely they would make enemies of the Johanna men at the first settling, because their friendship might be of use to them; and from their children there was noth-ing to be apprehended in the next generation, for they would be half their own blood; that in the meanwhile, if they complied with the request, they might be sure of an ally and protector against the king of Mohila; wherefore, he was for agreeing to the demand.

After a long debate, in which every inconvenience and advantage was maturely considered, it was agreed to send with him the number of men he required, on condition he should send them back in four moons, make an alliance with them, and wax against Mohila. This being agreed to, they staid till Caraccioli was thoroughly recovered: then putting the Johannians on board the Portuguese ship, with forty French and English, and fifteen Portuguese to work her, and setting sail, they arrived at the place where Misson designed his settlement, which he called *Libertatia,* and gave the name of *Liberi* to his people, desiring in that might be drowned the distinguished names of French, English, Dutch, Africans, &c.

The first thing they set about was, the raising a fort on each side the harbour, which they made of an octagon figure, and having finished and mounted them with forty guns taken out of the Portuguese, they raised a battery on an angle, of ten guns, and began to raise houses and magazines under the protection of their forts and ships; the Portuguese was unrigged, and all her sails and cordage carefully laid up. While they were very busily employed in the raising a town, a party which had often hunted and rambled four or five leagues off their settlement, resolved to venture farther into the country. They made themselves some huts, at about four leagues distance from their companions, and travelled E. S. E. about five leagues farther into the country, when they came up with a black, who was armed with a bow, arrows, and a javelin: they with a friendly appearance engaged the fellow to lay by his fear, and go with them. They carried him to their companions, and there entertained him three days with a great deal of humanity, and then returned with him near the place they found him, and made him a present of a piece of scarlet baize, and an axe. He appeared overjoyed with the present, and left them with seeming satisfaction.

The hunters imagined that there might be some village not far off, and observing that he looked at the sun, and then took his way directly south, they travelled on the same point of the compass, and from the top of a hill they spied a pretty large village, and went down to it: the men came out with their arms, such as before described, bows, arrows, and javelins; but upon two only of the whites advancing, with presents of axes and baize in their hands, they sent only four to meet them. The misfortune was, that they could not understand one another: but by their pointing to the sun, and holding up one finger, and making one of them go forward, and return again with showing their circumcision, and pointing up to heaven with one finger, they apprehended they gave them to understand there was but one God, who had sent one prophet, and concluded from thence, and their circumcision, they were Mahometans. The presents were carried to their chief, and he seemed to receive them kindly, and by signs invited the whites into their village; but they remembering the late treachery of the Mohilians, made signs for victuals to be brought to them where they were.

Note: *The remainder of Captain Misson's History will be fount I incorporated with that of Captain Tew.*

Captain John Bowen

The exact time of this person's setting out I am not certain of. I find him cruising on the Malabar coast in the year 1700, commanding a ship called the Speaker, whose crew consisted of men of all nations, and their piracies were committed upon ships of all nations likewise. The pirates here met with no manner of inconveniencies in carrying on their designs, for it was made so much a trade, that the merchants of one town never scrupled the buying commodities taken from another, though but ten miles distant, in a public sale, furnishing the robbers at the same time with all necessaries, even of vessels, when they had occasion to go on any expedition, which they themselves would often advise them of.

Among the rest, an English East-Indiaman, Capt. Coneway, from Bengal, fell into the hands of this crew, which they made prize of, near Callequilon. They carried her in, and put her up to sale, dividing the ship and cargo into three shares; one third was sold to a. merchant, native of Callequilon aforesaid, another third to a merchant of Porca, and the other to one Malpa, a Dutch factor.

Loaded with the spoil of this and several country ships they left the coast, and steered for Madagascar; but in their voyage thither, meeting with adverse winds, and, being negligent in their steerage, they ran upon St. Thomas's reef, at the island of Mauritius, where the ship was lost; but Bowmen and the greatest part of the crew got safe ashore.

They met here with all the civility and good treatment imaginable. Bowen was complimented in a particular manner by the governor, and splendidly entertained in his house; the sick men were got, with great care, into the fort, and cured by their doctor, and no supplies of any sort, wanting for the rest. They spent here three months, but yet resolving to set down at Madagascar, they bought a sloop, which they converted into a brigantine, and about the middle of March, 1701, departed, having first taken formal leave of the governor, by making a present of 2500 pieces of eight; leaving him, besides, the wreck of their ship, with the guns, stores, and everything else that was saved. The governor, on his part, supplied them with necessaries for their voyage, which was but short, and gave them a kind invitation to make that island a place of refreshment in the course of their future adventures, promising that nothing should be wanting to them that his government afforded.

Upon their arrival at Madagascar, they put in at a place on the east side, called Maritan, quit their vessel, and settled themselves ashore in a fruitful plain on the side of a river. They built themselves a fort on the river's mouth,

30

towards the sea, and another small one on the other side, towards the country; the first to prevent a surprise from shipping, and the other as a security from the natives, many of whom they employed in the building. They built also a little town for their habitation, which took up the remainder of the year 1701.

When this was done, they soon became dissatisfied with their new situation, having a hankering mind after their old employment, and accordingly resolved to fit up the brigantine they had from the Dutch at Mauritius, which was laid in a cove near their settlement; but an accident, that they improved, provided for them in a better manner, and saved them a great deal of trouble.

It happened that about the beginning of the year 1702, a ship called the Speedy Return, belonging to the Scotch-African and East-India company, Capt. Drummoud, commander, came into the port of Maritan in Madagascar, with a brigantine that belonged to her; they had before taken in negroes at St. Mary's, a little island adjoining to the main land of Madagascar, and carried them to Don Mascarenhas, from whence they sailed to this port on the same trade.

On the ship's arrival, Capt. Drummond, with Andrew Wilky, his surgeon, and several others of the crew, went on shore; in the meantime John Bowen, with four others of his consorts, went off in a little boat, on pretence of buying some of their merchandise brought from Europe: and finding a fair opportunity, the chief mate, boatswain, and a hand or two more only upon deck, and the rest at work in the hold they threw off their mask; each drew out a pistol and hanger, and told them they were all dead men if they did not retire that moment to the cabin. The surprise was sudden, and they thought it necessary to obey: one of the pirates placed himself sentry at the door, with his arms in his hands, and the rest immediately laid the hatches, and then made a signal to their fellows on shore as agreed on; upon which, about forty or fifty came on board, and took quiet possession of the ship, and afterwards the brigantine, without bloodshed, or striking a stroke. Bowen was made, or rather made himself, of course, captain; he detained the old crew, or the greatest part thereof, burnt the Dutch brigantine as being of no use to them, cleaned and fitted the ship, took water, provisions, and what necessaries were wanting, and made ready for new adventures.

Having thus piratically possessed himself of Capt. Drummond's ship and brigantine, and being informed by the crew, that when they left Don Mascarenhas, a ship called the Rook galley, Capt. Honeycomb, commander, was lying in that bay, Bowen resolved, with the other pirates, to sail thither, but it taking up seven or eight days in watering their vessels, and settling their private affairs, they arrived not at the island till after the departure of the said galley, who thereby happily escaped the villainous snare of their unprovoked enemies,

The night after the pirates left Maritan, the brigantine ran on a ledge of rocks off the west side of the island of Madagascar, which not being perceived by the ship, Bowen came into Mascarenhas without her, not knowing what was become of his consort. Here he stayed eight or ten days, in which time he -supplied the ship with provisions, and judging that the Rook galley was gone to some other island, the ship sailed to Mauritius, in search of her; but the pirates seeing four or five ships in the N. W. harbour, they thought themselves too weak to attempt anything there; so they stood immediately for Madagascar again, and arrived safe, first at Port Dauphin and then at Augustin Bay. In a few days the Content brigantine, which they supposed either to have been lost, or revolted that honourable service, came into the same bay, and informed their brethren of the misfortune that happened to them.

The rogues were glad, no doubt, of seeing one another again, and calling a council together, they found the brigantine in no condition for business, being then very leaky; therefore she was condemned, and forthwith hauled ashore and burnt, and the crew united, and all went on board the Speedy Return.

At this place the pirates were made acquainted, by the negroes, of the adventures of another gang that had settled for some time near that harbour, and had one Howard for their captain. It was the misfortune of an India ship called the Prosperous, to come into the bay at the time that these rogues were looking out for employment j who under the pretence of trading (almost in the same manner that Bo wen and his gang had seized the Speedy Return) made themselves master of her, and sailed with her to New Mathelage. Bowen and his gang consulting together on this intelligence, concluded it was more for their interest to join in alliance with this new company , than to act single, they being too weak of themselves to undertake any considerable enterprise, remembering how they were obliged to bear away from the island of Mauritius, when they were in search of the Rook galley, which they might have taken, with several others, had they had, at that time, a consort of equal force to their own ship.

They accordingly set sail from the bay, and came into New Mathelage, but found no ship there, though upon enquiry they understood that the pirate they looked for, had been at the place, but was gone; so after some stay they proceeded to Johanna, but the Prosperous not being there neither, they sailed to Mayotta, where they found her lying at anchor. This was about Christmas, 1702.

Here these two powers struck up an alliance. Howard liking the proposals, came readily into it, and the treaty was ratified by both companies. They stayed about two months at this island, thinking it, perhaps, as likely a place to meet with prey as cruising out for it, and so indeed it happened; for about the beginning of March, the ship Pembroke, belonging to our East-India company, coming in for water, was boarded by their boats, and taken, with the loss of the chief mate and another man that were killed in the skirmish.

The two pirate ships weighed, and went out to sea along with their prize, and that day and the next plundered her of the best part of her cargo, provisions, and stores., and then taking the captain and carpenter away, they let the Pembroke go where the remainder of her crew pleased, and came with their ships into New Mathelage. Here the two captains consulted, and laid a plan for a cruise to India, for which purpose they detained Capt. Wooley, of the Pembroke, lately taken, in order to be their pilot in those seas; but a very hot dispute arose between the two companies which ship he should go aboard of, insomuch that they had gone together by the ears, if an expedient had not been found to satisfy each party, that one might not have the advantage of the other by the captain's skill and knowledge of the Indian coast, and this was to knock the poor man on the head, and murder him: but at last, by the authority of Bo wen, Capt. Woolley escaped the threatened danger, by bringing his company to consent to his remaining on board the Prosperous, where he then was.

The Speedy Return being foul, and wanting a little repair was judged proper for her to go back to Augustin Bay to clean; in the mean while the Prosperous was to have a pair of boot-tops where she lay, and likewise to take in water and provisions, and then to join their consort again at Mayotta, the island appointed for the rendezvous,

The Prosperous put into Mayotta as agreed on, and waiting there some time for Bowen's ship, without seeing or hearing any news of her, went to Johanna, but not meeting with her there, they apprehended some accident had befell her, and therefore left the place, and sailed on the expedition themselves. As to the Speedy Return, she arrived safe at St. Augustin Bay, at Madagascar, and there cleaned and victualled; but tarrying there somewhat too long, the winds hung contrary, and they could not for their lives beat up to Mayotta, and therefore went up to Johanna, where, hearing that their friends had lately left that Island, they steered for the Red Sea, but the wind not proving fair for their design, they bore away for the high land of St, John's near Surat, where they once more fell in company with their brethren of the Prosperous.

They cruised together as was first agreed on, and after some time they had sight of four ships, to which they gave chase j but these separating, two standing to the northward, and two to the southward, the pirates separated likewise, Bowen standing after those that steered southerly, and Howard crowding after the others. Bowen came up with the heaviest of the two, which proved to be a Moorish ship of 700 tons, bound from the Gulf of Mocha to Surat, The pirates brought the prize into Rajapora, on the coast of India, where they plundered her; the merchandise they sold to the natives, but a small sum of current gold they found aboard, amounting to £22,000 English money, they put into their pockets. Two days after, the Prosperous came m, but without any prize; however, they soon made their friends acquainted that they had not succeeded worse than themselves, for at Surat river's mouth, where all the four ships were bound, they came up with their chase, and with a broad side, one of them struck, but the other got into the bay. They stood down the coast with the prize till they had plundered her of the best of her cargo, the most valuable of which was 84,000 sequins, a piece of about ten shillings each, and then they left her adrift, without either anchor or cable,, off Daman.

While they were lying at Rajapora they passed a survey on their shipping, and judging their own to be less serviceable than their prize, they voted them to the flames, and straightway fitted up the Surat ship. They transported both companies aboard of her, and then set fire to the Prosperous and Speedy Return. They mustered at this place 164 fighting men; 43 only were English, the greater number French, the rest Danes, Swedes, and Dutch. They took on board 70 Indians to do the drudgery of the ship, andmounted56 guns, calling her the Defiance, and sailed from Rajapora the latter end of October, in the year 1703 to cruise on the coast of Malabar. But not meeting with prey in this first cruise, they came to an anchor about three leagues to the northward of Cochen, expecting some boats to come off with supplies of refreshments, for which purpose they fired several guns, by way of signal, but none appearing, the quartermaster was sent in the pinnace to confer with the people, which he did with some caution, keeping the boat upon their oars at the shore side. In short, they agreed very well, the pirates were promised whatever necessaries they wanted, and the boat returned aboard.

The next day a boat came off from the town with hogs, goats, wine, &c. with a private intimation from Malpa, the Dutch broker, an old friend of the pirates, that a ship of that country called the Rhimae?, lay then in Mudbay, not many leagues off, and if they would go out and take her, he would purchase the cargo of them, and likewise promised that they should be further supplied with pitch, tar, and all other necessaries, which was made good to them; for people from the factory flocked aboard every hour, and dealt with them as in open market, for all sorts of merchandise, refreshments, jewels, and plate, returning with coffers of money, &c. to a great value.

The advice of the ship was taken very kindly, but the pirates judging their own ship too large to go close into the bay, consulted their friend upon means for taking the said ship, who readily treated with them for the sale of one of less burthen, that then lay in the harbour; but Malpa speaking to one 'Punt, of the factory, to carry her out, b« not only refused to be concerned in such a piece of villany, but reproved Malpa for corresponding with the pirates, and told him, if he should be guilty of so base an action, he must never see the face of any of his countrymen more; which made the honest broker change both his countenance and his purpose.

At this place Capt. Woolley, whom they had taken for their pilot on the Indian coast, being in a very sick and weak condition, was, at his earnest entreaty, discharged from his severe confinement among them, and set ashore, and the next day the pirates sailed, and ranged along the Malabar coast, in quest of more booty. In their way they met a second time with the Pembroke, and plundered her of some sugar, and other small things, and let her go again. From the coast they sailed back for the Island of Mauritius, where they lay some time, and lived after their usual extravagant manner.

Captain Robert Kidd

We are now going to give an account of one whose name is well known in England. The person we mean is Capt. Kidd, whose public trial and execution here, rendered him the subject of all conversation, so that his actions have been chanted about in ballads. However, it is now a considerable time since these things passed, and though the people knew in general that Capt. Kidd was hanged, and that his crime was piracy, yet there were scarce any, even at that time, who were acquainted with his life or actions, or could account for his turning pirate.

In the beginning of king William's war, Capt. Kidd commanded a privateer in the West-Indies, and by several adventurous actions acquired the reputation of a brave man, as well as an experienced seaman. About this time the pirates were very troublesome in those parts: wherefore Capt. Kidd was recommended by the Lord Bellamont, then governor of Bardadoes, as well as by several other persons, to the government here, as a person very fit to be entrusted with the command of a government ship, and to be employed in cruising upon the pirates, as knowing those seas perfectly well, and being acquainted with all their lurking places; but what reasons governed the politics of those times I cannot tell, but this proposal met with no encouragement here, though it is certain it would have been of great consequence to the subject, our merchants suffering incredible damages by those robbers.

Upon this neglect, the lord Bellamont and some others, who knew what great captures had been made by the pirates, and what a prodigious wealth must be in their possessions, were tempted to fit out a ship at their own private charge, and to give the command of her to Capt. Kidd; and to give the thing a greater reputation, as well as to keep their seamen under the better command, they procured the king's commission for the said Capt. Kidd, of which the following is an exact copy:

William Rex,
"William the Third, by the grace of God, King of England, Scotland, France, and Ireland, defender of the faith, &c. To our trusty and well Beloved Capt. Robert Kidd, commander of the ship the Adventure galley, or to any other the commander of the same for the time being, *Greeting:* Whereas we are informed, that Capt. Thomas Too, John Ireland, Capt. Thomas Wake, and Capt. William Maze, or Mace, and other subjects, natives or inhabitants of New York, and elsewhere, in our plantations in America, have associated themselves with divers others, wicked and ill-disposed persons, and do against the law of nations commit many and great piracies, robberies, and depredations on the seas upon the parts of America, and in other parts, to the great hindrance and discouragement of trade and navigation, and to the great danger and hurt of our loving subjects, our allies, and all others, navigating the seas upon their lawful occasions. **Now know ye,** that we being desirous to

35

prevent the aforesaid mischiefs, and as much as in us lies, to bring the said pirates, freebooters and sea-rovers to justice, have thought fit, and do hereby give and grant to the said Robert Kidd (to whom our commissioners for exercising the office of Lord High Admiral of England, have granted a commission as a private man of war, bearing date the 11th day of December, 1695,) and unto the commander of the said ship for the time being, and unto the officers, mariners, and others, which shall be under your command, full power and authority to apprehend, seize, and take into your custody as well the said Capt. Thomas Too, John Ireland, Capt. Thomas Wake, and Capt. William Maze, or Mace, as all such pirates, freebooters, and sea-rovers, being either our subjects, or of other nations associated with them, which you shall meet with upon the seas or coasts of America, or upon any other seas Or coasts, with all their ships and vessels, and all such merchandise, money, goods, and wares as shall be found on board, or with them, in case they shall willingly yield themselves; but if they will not yield without fighting, then you are by force to compel them to yield. And we also require you to bring, or cause to be brought, such pirates, freebooters, or sea-rovers, as you shall seize, to a legal trial, to the end they may be proceeded against according to the law in such cases. And we do hereby command all our officers, ministers, and other our loving subjects whatsoever, to be aiding and assisting to you in the premises. And we do hereby enjoin you to keep an exact journal of your proceedings in the execution of the premises, and set down the names of such pirates, and of their officers and company, and the names of such ships and vessels as you shall by virtue of these presents take and seize, and the quantities of arms, ammunition, provision, and lading of such ships, and the true value of the same, as near as you judge. And we do hereby strictly charge and command you, as you will answer the contrary at your peril, that you do not, in any manner, offend or molest our friends or allies, their ships or subjects, by colour or pretence of these presents, or the authority thereby granted. *In witness whereof,* we have caused our great seal of England to be affixed to these presents. Given at our court at Kensington, the 26th day of January, 1695, in the 7th year of our reign."

Capt. Kidd had also another commission, which was called a commission of reprisals; for it being then war time, this commission was to justify him in the taking of French merchant ships, in case he should meet with any; but as this commission is nothing to our present purpose, we shall not burthen the reader with it.

With these two commissions he sailed out of Plymouth in May, 1696, in the Adventure galley, of 30 guns, and 80 men; the place he first designed for was New York; in his voyage thither he took a French banker, but this was no act of piracy, he having a commission for that purpose, as we have just observed.

When he arrived at New York, he put up articles for engaging more hands, it being necessary to his ship's crew, since he proposed to deal with a desperate enemy. The terms he offered were, that every man should have a share of what Was taken, reserving for himself and owners forty shares. Upon which encouragement he soon increased his company to 155 men.

With this company he sailed first for Madeira, where he took in wine and some other necessaries; from thence he proceeded to Bonavista, one of the Cape-de-Verd Islands, to furnish the ship with salt, and from thence went immediately to St. Jago, another of the Cape-de-Verd Islands, in order to stock himself with provisions. When all this was done, he bent his course to Madagascar, the known rendezvous of pirates. In his way he fell in with Capt. Warren, commodore of three men of war: he acquainted him with his design, kept them company two or three days, and then leaving them, made the best of his way for Madagascar, where he arrived in February, 1696, just nine months from his departure from Plymouth.

It happened that at this time the pirate ships were most of them out in search of prey; so that according to the best intelligence Capt. Kidd could get, there was not one of them at that time about the island: wherefore, having spent some time in watering his ship and taking in more provisions, he thought of trying his fortune on the coast of Malabar, where he arrived in the month of June following, four months from his reaching Madagascar. Hereabouts he made an unsuccessful cruise, touching sometimes at the island of Mohila, and sometimes at that of Johanna, between Malabar and Madagascar. His provisions were every day wasting, and his ship began to want repair: wherefore, when he was at Johanna, he found means of borrowing a sum of money from some Frenchmen who had lost their ship, but saved their effects, and with this he purchased materials for putting his ship in good repair.

It does not appear all this while that he had the least design of turning pirate; for near Mohila and Johanna both, he met with several Indian ships richly laden, to which he did not offer the least violence, though he was strong enough to have done what he pleased with them; and first outrage or depredation I find he committed upon mankind, was after his repairing his ship, and leaving Johanna; he touched at a place called Mabbee, upon the Red Sea, where he took some Guinea corn from the natives, by force. After this, he sailed to Bab's Key, a place upon a little island at the entrance of the Red Sea. Here it was that he first began to open himself to his ship's company, and let them understand that he intended to change his measures; for, happening to talk of the Mocha fleet, which was to sail that way, he said, *We have been unsuccessful hitherto; but courage, my boys, we'll make our fortunes out of this fleet;* and finding that none of them appeared averse to it, he ordered a boat out, well manned, to go upon the coast to make discoveries, commanding them to take a prisoner and bring to him, or get intelligence any way they could. The boat returned in a few days, bringing him word, that they saw fourteen or fifteen ships ready to sail, some with English, some with Dutch, and some with Moorish colours.

We cannot account for this sudden change in his conduct, otherwise than by supposing that he first meant well, while he had hopes of making his fortune by taking of pirates; but now weary of ill success, and fearing lest his owners, out of humour at their great expenses, should dismiss him, and he should want employment, and be marked out for an unlucky man; rather, I say, than run the hazard of poverty, he resolved to do his business one way, since he could not do it another.

He therefore ordered a man continually to watch at the mast head, lest this fleet should go by them; 'and about four days after, towards evening, it appeared in sight, being convoyed by one English and one Dutch man of war, Kidd soon fell in with .them, and getting into the midst of them, fired at a Moorish ship which was next him; but the men of war taking the alarm, bore down upon Kidd, and firing upon him, obliged him to sheer off, he not being strong enough to contend with them. Wow he had begun hostilities, he resolved to go on, and therefore he went and cruised along the coast of Malabar. The first prize he met was a small vessel belonging to Aden: the vessel was Moorish, and the owners were Moorish merchants, but the master was an Englishman; his name was Parker. Kidd forced him and a Portuguese that was called Don Antonio, which were all the Europeans on board, to take on with him; the first he designed as a pilot, and the last as an interpreter. He also used the men very cruelly, causing them to be hoisted up by the arms, and drubbed with a naked ,cutlass, to force them to discover whether they had money on board, and where it lay; but as they had neither gold nor silver on board, he got nothing by his cruelty; however, he took from them a bale of pepper, and a bale of coffee, and so let them go.

A little time after he touched a Carawar, a place upon the same coast, where, before he arrived, the news of what he had done to the Moorish ship had cached them; for some of the English merchants there had received an account of it from the owners who corresponded with them; wherefore, as soon as Kidd came in, he was suspected to be the person who committed this piracy; and one Mr. Harvey and Mr. Mason, two of the English factory, came on board and asked for Parker, and Antonio, the Portuguese; but Kidd denied that he knew any such persons, having secured them both in a private place in the hold, where they were kept for seven or eight days, that is, till Kidd, sailed from thence.

However, the coast was alarmed, and a Portuguese man of war was sent out to cruise. Kidd met with her, and fought her about six hours, gallantly enough; but finding her too strong to be taken he quitted her; for he was able to run away from her when he would. Then he went to a place called Porca, where he watered the ship, and bought a number of hogs of the natives to victual his company.

Soon after this, he came up with a Moorish ship, the master whereof was a Dutchman, called Schipper Mitchell, and chased her under French colours, which they observing, hoisted French colours too; when he came up with her, he hailed her in French, and they having a Frenchman on board, answered him in the same language; upon which he ordered them to send their boat on board; they were obliged to do so, and having examined who they were, and from whence they came, he asked the Frenchman, who was a passenger, if he had a French pass for himself; the Frenchman gave him to understand that he had. Then he told the Frenchman he must pass for captain, and by —, says he, you are the captain: the Frenchman durst not refuse doing as he would have him. The meaning of this was, that he would seize the ship as fair prize, and as if she had belonged to French subjects, according to a commission he had for that purpose; though, one would think, after what he had already done, that he need not have recourse to a quibble to give his actions a colour.

In short, he took the cargo, and sold it sometime after; yet still he seemed to have some fears upon him, lest these proceedings should have a had end; for, coming up with a Dutch ship sometime after, when his men thought of nothing but attacking her, Kidd opposed it; upon which a mutiny arose, and the majority being for taking the said ship, and arming themselves to man the boat to go and seize her, he told them, such as did, never should come on board him again; which put an end to the design, so that he kept company with the said ship some time, without offering her any violence. However, this dispute was the occasion of an accident, upon which an indictment was after wards grounded against Kidd; for Moor, the gunner, being one day upon deck, and talking with Kidd, about the said Dutch ship, some words arose between them, and Moor told Kidd, that he had ruined them all; upon which, Kidd, calling him a dog, took up a bucket and struck him with it, which breaking his skull, he died the next day.

But Kidd's penitential tit did not last long, for coasting along Malabar, he met with a great number of boats, all which he plundered. Upon the same coast he also fell in with a Portuguese ship, which he kept possession of a week, and then having taken out of her some chests of India goods, thirty jars of butter, with some wax, iron, and a hundred bags of rice, he let her go.

Much about the same time he went to one of the Malabar islands for wood and water, and his cooper being ashore, was murdered by the natives; upon which Kidd himself landed, and burnt and pillaged several of their houses, the people running away; but having taken one, lie caused him to be tied to a tree, and commanded one of his men to shoot him; then putting to sea again he took the greatest prize which fell into his hands while he followed this trade: this was a Moorish ship of 400 tons, richly laden, named the Queda Merchant, the master whereof was an Englishman, by the name of Wright; for the Indians often make use of English or Dutchmen to command their ships, their own mariners not being so good artists in navigation. Kidd chased her under French colours, and having come up with her, he ordered her to hoist out her boat, and to send on board of him, which being done, he told Wright he was his prisoner; and informing himself concerning the said ship, he understood there were no Europeans on board, except two Dutch, and one Frenchman, all the rest being Indians or Armenians, and that the Armenians were part owners of the cargo. Kidd gave the Armenians to understand, that if they would offer any thing that was worth his taking for their ransom, he would hearken to it. Upon which, they proposed to pay him

20,000 rupees, not quite £3000 sterling; but Kidd judged this would be making a bad bargain, wherefore he rejected it, and setting the crew on shore, at different places on the coast, they soon sold as much of the cargo as came to ten thousand pounds. With part of it he also trafficked, receiving in exchange provisions, or such other goods as he wanted; by degrees he disposed of the whole cargo, and when the division was made, it came to about £200 a man; and having reserved forty shares to himself, his dividend amounted to about £8000 sterling.

The Indians along. the coast came on board and trafficked with all freedom, and he punctually performed his bargains, till about the time he was. ready to sail; and then thinking he should have no, further occasion for them, he made no scruple of taking their goods and setting them on shore without any payment in money or goods, which they little expected; for as they had been used to deal with pirates, they always found them men of honour in the way of trade; a people, enemies to deceit, and that scorned to rob but in their own way.

Kidd put some of his men on board the Queda Merchant, and with this ship and his own, sailed for Madagascar. As soon as he had arrived and cast anchor, there came on board of him a canoe, in which were several Englishmen, who had formerly been well acquainted with Kidd. As soon as they saw him they saluted him, and told him, they were informed he was come to take them, and hang them, which would be a little unkind in such an old acquaintance. Kidd soon dissipated their doubts, by swearing he had no such design, and that he was now in every respect their brother, and just as bad as they; and calling for a cup of bomboo, drank their captain's health.

These men belonged to a pirate ship, called the Resolution, formerly the Mocha Merchant, whereof one Capt. Culliford was commander, and which lay at anchor not far from them. Kidd went on board with them, promising them his friendship and assistance, and Culliford in his turn came on board of Kidd; and Kidd to testify his sincerity in iniquity, finding Culliford in want of some necessaries, made him a present of an anchor and some guns, to fit him out for sea again.

The Adventure galley was now so old and leaky, that they were forced to keep two pumps continually going; wherefore Kidd shifted all the guns and tackle out of her into the Queda Merchant, intending her for his man of war; and as he had divided the money before, he now made a division of the remainder of the cargo: soon after which, the greatest part of the company left him, some going onboard Capt. Culliford, and others absconding into the country, so that he had not above 40 men left.

He put to sea, and happened to touch at Amboyna, one of the Dutch spice islands, where he was told, that the news of his actions had reached England, and that he was there declared a pirate.

The truth of it is. his piracies so alarmed our merchants, that some motions were made in parliament, to inquire into the commission that was given him, and the persons who fitted him out. These proceedings seemed to lean a little hard upon Lord Bellamont, who thought himself so much touched thereby, that he published a justification of himself in a pamphlet, after Kidd's execution. In a mean time it was thought advisable, in order to stop the course of these piracies, to publish a proclamation, offering the king's free pardon to all such pirates as should voluntarily surrender themselves, whatever piracies they had been guilty of, at any time before the last day of April, 1699— that is to say, for all piracies committed eastward of the Cape of Good Hope, to the longitude and meridian of Socatora, and Cape Cormorin; in which proclamation, Avery and Kidd were excepted by name.

When Kidd left Amboyna he knew nothing of this proclamation, for certainly had he had notice of his being excepted in it, he would not have been so infatuated, as to run himself into the very jaws of danger; but relying upon his interest with the lord Bellamont, and fancying that a French pass or two he found on board some of the ships he took, would serve to countenance the matter, and that part of the booty he got would gain him new friends — I say all these things made him flatter himself that all would be hushed, and that justice would but wink at him. — Wherefore he sailed directly for New York, where he was no sooner arrived, but by the Lord Bellamont's orders, he was secured with all his papers and effects. Many of his fellow-adventurers, who had forsook him at Madagascar, came over from thence passengers, some to New-England and some to Jersey; where hearing of the king's proclamation for pardoning of pirates, they surrendered themselves to the governor of those places A.t first they were admitted to bail, but soon after laid in strict confinement, where. they were kept for some time, till an opportunity happened of sending, them with their captain over to England to be tried.

Accordingly a sessions of admiralty being held at the Old Bailey, in May, 1701, Capt. Kidd, Nicholas Churchill, James How, Robert Lumley, William Jenkins, Gabriel Loff, Hugh Parrot, Richard Barlicorn, Abel Owens, and Darby Mullins, were arraigned for piracy and robbery on the high seas, and all found guilty except three: these were Robert Lumley, William Jenkins, and Richard Barlicorn, who proving themselves to be apprentices to some of the officers of the ship, and producing their indentures in court, where acquitted.

The three above mentioned, though they were proved to be concerned in taking and sharing the ship and goods mentioned in the indictment, yet, as the gentlemen of the long robe rightly distinguished, there was a great difference between their circumstances and the rest; for there must go an intention of the mind and a freedom of the will to the committing an act of felony or piracy. A pirate is not to be understood to be under constraint, but a free agent; for in this case, the bare act will not make a man guilty, unless the will make it so.

Now a servant, it is true, if he go voluntarily, and have his proportion, he must be accounted a pirate, for then he acts upon his own account, and not by compulsion; and these persons, according to the evidence, received their part, but whether they accounted to their masters for their shares afterwards, is the matter in question, and what distinguishes them as free agents,

41

or men that did go under the compulsion of their masters, which being left to the consideration of the jury, they found them *not guilty.*

Kidd was tried upon an indictment of murder also, viz. for killing Moor, the gunner, and found guilty of the same. Nicholas Churchill, and James How pleaded the king's pardon, as having surrendered themselves within the time limited in the proclamation, and Col. Bass, governor of West-Jersey, to whom they surrendered, being in court, and called upon, proved the same. However, this plea was over-ruled by the court, because there being four commissioners named in the proclamation, viz. Capt. Thomas Warren, Israel Hayes, Peter Delannoye, and Christopher Pollard, Esqrs. who were appointed commissioners, and sent over on purpose to receive the submission of such pirates as should surrender, it was adjudged no other person was qualified to receive their surrender, and that they could not be entitled to the benefit of the said proclamation, because they had not in all circumstances complied with the conditions of it.

Darby Mullins urged in his defence, that he served under the king's commission, and therefore could not. disobey his commander without incurring great punishments; that whenever a ship or ships went out upon any expedition under the king's commission, the men were never allowed to call their officers to an account, why they did this, or why they did that, because such a liberty would destroy all discipline: that if anything was done which was unlawful, the officers were to answer it, for the men did no more than their duty in obeying orders. He was told by the court, that acting under the commission justified in what was lawful, but not in what was unlawful. He answered he stood in need of nothing to justify him in what was lawful, hut the case of seamen must he very bard, if they must he brought into such danger for obeying the commands of their officers, and punished for not obeying them, and if they were allowed to dispute the orders, there could be no such thing as command kept up at sea.

This seemed to be the best defence the thing could bear; but his taking a share of the plunder, the seamen's mutinying on board several times, and taking upon them to control the captain, showed there was no obedience paid to the commission; and that they acted in all things according to the custom of pirates and freebooters, which weighing with the jury, they brought him in guilty with the rest.

As to Capt. Kidd's defence, he insisted much on Mis own innocence, and the villany of his men. He said, he went out in a laudable employment and had no occasion, being then in good circumstances, to go a pirating; that the men often mutinied against him, and did as they pleased; that he was threatened to be shot in the cabin, and that ninety-five left him at one time, and set fire to his boat, so that he was disabled from bringing his ship home, or the prizes he took, to have them regularly condemned, which he said were taken by virtue of a commission under the broad seal, they having French passes. The captain called one Col. Hewson to his reputation, who gave him an extraordinary character, and declared to the court, that he had served under his command, and been in two engagements with him against the French, in which he fought as well as any man he ever saw; that there were only Kidd's ship and his own against Monsieur du Cass, who commanded a squadron of six sail, and they got the better of him. But this being several years before the facts mentioned in the indictment were committed, proved of no manner of service to the prisoner on his trial.

As to the friendship shown to Culliford, a notorious pirate, Kidd denied, and said, he intended to have taken him, but his men being a parcel of rogues and villains refused to stand by him, and several of them ran away from his ship to the said pirate.— But the evidence being full and particular against him, he was found guilty as before mentioned.

When Kidd was asked what he had to say why sentence should not pass against him, he answered, that *he had nothing to say, but that he had been sworn against by perjured and wicked people.* And when sentence Was pronounced, he said, *my Lord, it is a very hard sentence. For my part, I am the most innocent person of them all, only I have been sworn against by perjured persons.*

Wherefore about a week after, Capt. Kidd, Nicholas Churchill, James How, Gabriel Loff, Hugh Parrot, Abel Owen, and Darby Mullins, were executed at Execution Dock, and afterwards hung up in chains, at some distance from each other, down the river, where their bodies hung exposed for many years.

Captain Tew

Before I enter on the adventures of this pirate, I must take notice to the reader of the reasons which made me not continue the life of Misson.

In reading the notes, which I have by me, relating to Capt. Tew, I found him joined with Misson; and that I must be either guilty of repetition, or give an account of Tew in Misson's life, which is contrary to the method I proposed, that of giving a distinct relation of every pirate who has made any figure: and surely Tew, in point of gallantry, was inferior to none, and may justly claim a particular account of his actions. However, before I enter on the life of this pirate, I shall continue that of Misson to the time that these two commanders met.

The blacks seeing them so much on their guard, brought out boiled rice and fowls, and after they had satisfied their hunger, the chief made signs that they were the same who had carried a negro to their ships, and sent for the axe and piece of baize they had given him. While this passed, the very negro came from hunting, who seemed overjoyed to see them. The chief made signs that they might return, and ten negroes coming to them, laden with fowls and kids, he gave them to understand, they should accompany them to their ships with these presents. They parted very amicably, and in hopes of settling a good correspondence with these natives. All the houses were neatly framed and jointed, not built from any foundation, but so made, that half a dozen men could lift and transport them from place to place. The hunters, returning to their ships, with these presents and negroes, were joyfully received; and the negroes were not only caressed, but laden with baize, iron kettles, and rum, besides the present of a cutlass for the chief.

While the negroes stayed, which was the space of three days, they examined and admired the forts and growing town, in which all hands were busied, and not even the prisoners excused.

As Misson apprehended no danger from the land, his fort, though of wood, being, he thought, a sufficient defence to his infant colony, he took 160 hands, and went a second time on the coast of Zanguebar, and off Quiloa he gave chase to a large ship which lay by for him. She proved an over-match for the Victoire, which engaged her, with great loss of men, near eight glasses; but finding he was more likely to be taken, than to make a prize, by the advice of his officers and men, endeavoured to leave the Portuguese, which was a 50 gun ship, and had 300 men on board; but he found this attempt vain, for the Portuguese sailed as well as the Victoire, and her commander, who was a resolute and brave man, seeing him endeavour to shake him off, clapped him on, board, but lost most of the men he entered. Mission's crew, not used to be attacked, and expecting no quarter, fought so desperately, that they not only thoroughly cleared their decks, but some of them followed the Portuguese, who leaped into their own ship; which Misson seeing, hoped to make an advantage of their despair, and crying out, *Elle est a nous, a l'abordage — She's our own, board, board her* — so many of his men followed the few, that hardly were there enough left to work the ship. Misson, observing the resolution of his men, grappled the Portuguese ship, and leaped on board himself, crying out, *la mort, ou la victoire — death or victory.* The Portuguese, who thought themselves in a manner conquerors, seeing the enemy not only drive off those who entered them, but board with such resolution, betray to quit the decks in spite of their officers. The captain and Misson met, as he was endeavouring to hinder the flight of his men J they engaged with equal bravery with their cutlasses: but Misson striking him on the neck, he fell down the main hatch, which put an end to the fight, for the Portuguese seeing their captain fall, threw down their arms, and called for quarters, which was granted; and all the prisoners without distinction being ordered between decks, and the powder rooms secured, he put 35 men on board the prize, and made the best of his way to Libertatia. This was the dearest prize he ever made, for he lost 56 men. She was vastly rich in gold, having near £200,000 sterling on board, being her own and the cargo of her companion, which was lost upon the coast, of whose crew she had saved one hundred men out of 120, the rest being lost by endeavouring to swim ashore. This was the reason that the prize was so well-manned, and proved so considerable.

Being within sight of Madagascar, they spied a sloop which stood for them, and when in gun shot, threw out black colours, and fired a gun to windward. Misson brought too, fired another to leeward, and hoisted out his boat, which the sloop perceiving, lay by for. Misson's lieutenant went onboard, and was received very civilly by Capt. Tew, who was the commander, to whom the lieutenant gave a short account of their adventures and new settlement, inviting him very kindly on-board Capt. Misson. Tew told him, he could not consent to go with him till he had the opinion of his men. In the meanwhile, Misson coming along side, hailed the sloop, and invited the captain on board, desiring his lieutenant would stay as a hostage, if they were in 'the least jealous of him, which they had no reason to be, since he was of force so much superior, that he need not employ stratagem. This determined the company on board the sloop, who advised their captain to go with the lieutenant, whom they would not suffer to stay behind, to show the greater confidence in their new friends.

My reader may be surprised that a single sloop should venture to give chase to two ships of such countenance as were the Victoire and her prize; but this wonder will cease, when he is acquainted with the sequel.

Capt. Tew, after being handsomely regaled on board the Victoire, and thoroughly satisfied, returned on board his sloop, gave an account of what he had learned, and his men consenting, he gave orders to steer the same course with Misson, whose settlement it was agreed to visit. I shall here leave them to give an account of Capt. Tew.

Mr. Richier, governor of Bermuda, fitted out two sloops on the privateer account, commanded by Capt. George Drew, and Capt. Thomas Tew, with instructions to make the best of their way to the river Gambia, in Africa, and there, with the advice and assistance of the agent for the royal African company, to attempt the taking the French factory of Goree on that coast

The above commanders having their commissions and instructions from the governor, took their departure from Bermuda, and kept company some time; but Drew springing his mast, and a violent storm coming upon them, they lost each other.

Tew being separated from his consort, thought of providing for his future ease, by making one bold push; and accordingly, calling all hands on deck, he spoke to them to this purpose.

"That they were not ignorant of the design with which the governor fitted them out: the taking and destroying the French factory; that he, indeed, readily agreed to take a commission to this end, though contrary to his judgment, because it was for the sake of being employed; but that he thought it a very injudicious expedition, which, did they succeed in, would be of no use to the public, and only be of advantage to a private company of men, from whom they could expect no reward for their bravery; that he could see nothing but danger in the undertaking, without the least prospect of booty; that he could not suppose any man fond of lighting for fighting's sake; and few ventured their lives, but with some view either of particular interest or public good: but here was not the least appearance of either. Wherefore, he was of opinion, that they should turn their thoughts on what might better their circumstances; and if they were so inclined, he would undertake to shape a course which should lead them to ease and plenty, in which they might pass the rest of their days. That one bold push would do their business, and they might return home, not only without danger, but even with reputation," The crew finding he expected their resolution, cried one, and all, *"A gold chain or a wooden leg — we'll stand by you."*

Hearing this, he desired they would choose a quartermaster, who might consult with him for the common good; which was accordingly done.

I must acquaint the reader, that on board the West-India privateers and freebooters, the quartermaster's opinion is like the Mufti's among the Turks: the captain can undertake nothing which the quartermaster does not approve. We may say the quartermaster is a humble imitation of the Roman tribune of the people; he speaks for, and looks after the interest of the crew.

Tew, now, instead of proceeding on his voyage to Gambia, shaped his course for the Cape of Good Hope, which doubling, he steered for the straits of Babelmandel, entering into the Red Sea, where they came up with a lofty ship bound from, the Indies to Arabia; she was richly laden, and as she was to clear the coasts of rovers, five more, extremely rich (one especially in gold) being to follow her, she had 300 soldiers on board, besides her seamen.

Tew, on making this ship, told his men she carried their fortunes, which they would find no difficulty to take possession of; for though he was satisfied she was full of men, and was mounted with a great number of guns, they wanted the two things necessary, skill and courage: and, indeed, so it proved, ibr he boarded and carried her without loss, every one taking more care to run from danger, than to exert himself in the defence of his goods.

In rummaging this prize, the pirates threw over a great many rich bales, to search for gold, silver, and jewels; and having taken what they thought proper, together with the powder, part of which (as being more than they could handsomely stow) they threw into the sea, they left her, sharing £3000 sterling a man.

Encouraged by this success, Capt. Tew proposed going in quest of the other five ships, of which he had intelligence from the prize; but the quartermaster opposing him, he was obliged to drop the design, and steer for Madagascar.

Here the quartermaster finding this island productive of all the necessaries of life; and the air was wholesome, soil fruitful, and the sea abounding with fish, proposed settling; but only three and twenty of the crew came into the proposal: the rest stayed with Captain Tew, who having given the new settlers their share of plunder, designed to return to America, as they afterwards did; but spying the Victoire and her prize, he thought he might, by their means, return somewhat richer, and resolved to speak with them, as I have already said.

Tew and his company having taken the above resolution of visiting Monsieur Misson's colony, arrived with him, and was not a little surprised to see his fortifications.

When they came under the first fort, they saluted it with nine guns, and were answered by an equal number. All the prisoners, at their coming to an anchor, were suffered to come up, a privilege they had never before granted them, on account of the few hands left them, except two or three at a time.

The joy those ashore expressed at the sight of so considerable a prize as they judged her at first sight, was vastly allayed, when they heard how dear a purchase she had proved to them. However, the reinforcement of the sloop made some amends. Capt. Tew was received by Caraccioli and the rest, with great civility and respect, who did not a little admire his courage, both in attacking the prize he made, and afterwards in giving chase to Misson. He was called to the council of officers, which was immediately held, to consider what methods should be taken with the prisoners, who were, by 190 brought in by this new prize, near as numerous as those of his own party, though Tew joined them with 70 men. It was therefore resolved to keep them separate from the Portuguese and English, who were before taken, to make them believe they were in amity with a prince of the natives, who was very powerful, and to propose to them, at their choice, the assisting the new colony in their works, or being sent prisoners up the country, if they rejected entering in with them. Seventy-three took on, and the rest desired they might be any way employed rather than be sent up the country; 117 then were set to work upon a dock, which was laid out about half a mile above the mouth of the harbour, and the other prisoners were forbid to pass such bounds as were prescribed then on pain of death; lest they, knowing their own strength, should revolt; for I must acquaint the reader, that on the arrival of the Victoire, both their loss and the number of Portuguese they brought in, was known to none but themselves, and the number of those who came over, magnified; besides, the Johanna men were all armed and disciplined, and the Bijoux lay as a guard-ship, where the last prisoners were set to work; but while they provided for their security, both within and without, they did not neglect providing also for their support, for they dug and sowed a large plat of ground with Indian and European corn, and other seeds which they found; or board their prizes. In the meanwhile, Caraccioli, who had the art of persuasion, wrought on many of the Portuguese, who saw no hopes of returning home to join them. Misson, who could not be easy in an inactive life, would have taken another cruise; but fearing the revolt of the prisoners, durst not weaken the colony by the hands he must necessarily take with him. Wherefore, he proposed giving the last prize to, and sending away the prisoners. Caraccioli and Capt. Tew were against it, saying, that it would discover their retreat, and cause their being attacked by the Europeans, who had, settlements along the continent, before they were able to defend themselves. Misson replied, he could not bear to be always diffident of those about him; that it was better to die at once, than live in continual apprehensions of death: that the time was come for sending away the Johanna men, and that they could not go without a ship; neither durst he trust a ship out, not well manned, nor man her while so many prisoners were with him. Wherefore there was a necessity of sending them off, or of putting them all to the sword; a barbarity by which he would not purchase his security. A council was called, and what Capt. Misson had proposed, agreed to. The prisoners were then summoned, and he told them, in few words, that he knew the consequence of giving them liberty; that he expected to be attacked as soon as the place of his retreat was known, and had it in his hands by putting them to death, to avoid the doubtful fate of war; but his humanity would not suffer him to entertain a thought so cruel, and his alliances with the natives, he hoped, would enable him to repel his assailants; but he required an oath of every one, that he should not serve against him. He then inquired into the circumstances of every particular man, and what they had lost, all which he returned, telling the company it should be reckoned as part of his share; and the prisoners, that he did not make war with the oppressed, but the oppressors. .The prisoners were charmed with this mark of generosity, and wished he might never meet a treatment unworthy of that he gave them. The ship victualled for a voyage to the coast of Zanguebar, all her guns and ammunition taken out with the spare sails, and spare rigging, all were ordered to be gone; and 137 departed, highly applauding the behaviour of their enemies. All this while they had heard nothing from the natives, nor had the hunting parties met with any of them, which made Misson suspect they were afraid of his being their neighbour, and had shifted their quarters; but as the Johanna men were upon going away, there came about 50 negroes to them, driving about 100 head of black cattle, 20 negro men bound, and 25 women, for which cattle and prisoners they bartered rum, hatchets, baize, and beads; some hogsheads of which last commodity they had taken on the coast of Angola. Here the negroes belonging to Misson were provided with wives: the natives were caressed, and to the slaves signs made that their liberty was given them; they were immediately clothed and put under the care of as many whites, who, by all possible demonstrations, endeavoured to make them understand that they were enemies to slavery. The natives stayed ten days, which retarded the departure of the Johanna men; but, upon their retiring, the Bijoux sailed with 100 of them on board, under the command of Caraccioli's lieutenant, who excused the keeping them longer than was promised, and not bringing them at once, having no more than two ships. The Portuguese ship, which was unrigged, being made a hulk, the ten men of Misson's company who had settled at Johanna, being desirous to return, were brought to Libertatia with their wives (of which they had two or three a piece) and their children. The Bijoux, at two more voyages? carried over the rest of the Johannians.

Misson hove down the Bijoux, and resolving on a cruise on the coast of Guinea, to strengthen his colony by the capture of some slaving ship, he gave the command of her to Capt. Tew, and he and Caraccioli pressed the work of the dock, lie gave him also 200 hands, of which 40 were Portuguese, 37 negroes, 17 of them expert sailors, 30 English, and the rest French. Tew met with nothing in his way, till he came to the northward of the Cape of Good Hope, when he fell in with a Dutch East India galley of 18 guns, which he took after a small resistance, and with the loss of one man only. On the coast of

Angola he took an English Guineaman with 240 slaves, men, women, and boys. The negroes who had been before taken on this coast, found among these a great many of their acquaintance, and several of their relations, to whom they reported their unexpected change of fortune, the great captain (for so they now called Misson) having humanely knocked off their chains, and of slaves made them free men, and sharers in his fortunes: that the same good fortune had attended them in their falling into his hands, for he abhorred even the name of slavery. Tew, following the orders and acquainted with the policy of Misson, ordered their fetters and handcuffs to be taken off, upon his negro sailors assuring him they would not revolt, and were sensible of their happiness in falling into his hands. Content with these prizes, he made the best of his way home to Libertatia where he arrived without any sinister accident; but I forgot to tell my reader, that he set his Dutch prisoners (nine excepted, who took on with him) ashore, about 30 miles to the northward of the Cape of Saldanha Bay, where had been buried, by Capt. Misson, the English commander. He found a great quantity of English crowns on board his Dutch prize, which were carried into the common treasury; money being of no use where every thing was in common, and no hedge bounded any particular man's property. The slaves he had released in this last cruise were employed in perfecting the dock, and treated on the footing of free people. They were not ignorant of the change of their condition, and were therefore extremely diligent and faithful. A white man, or one of the old standing negroes, wrought with every four, and made them understand the French words (by often repetition, and the help of their country-men's interpreting) used in their works Misson ordered a couple of sloops to be built in a creek, of eighty tons each, which he mounted with eight guns a piece, out of a Dutch prize. These were perfected in a little time, and proved not only shapely vessels, but excellent sailors. The officers of these sloops were chosen by ballotting, and as their first design was only to discover and lay down a chart of the coast, sands, shoals, and depth of water round the island of Madagascar, the schoolmaster being sent with the command of one, Tew desired and had the other. They were manned, each sloop with 50 white and 50 black men; which voyage round the island was of vast advantage in giving the new released Angola negroes a notion of working a vessel; — and they were very industrious both in endeavouring to learn the French language, and to be useful. These sloops, the one of which was called the Childhood, and the other the Liberty, were near four months on this expedition. In the mean while, a few of the natives had come often to the settlement, and began to speak a little French, mixed with the other European languages, which they heard among Misson's people, and six of the native families fixed among them, which was of vast use to the planters of this colony; for they made a very advantageous report to their countrymen of the regularity and harmony they observed in them. The sloops having returned, and an exact chart taken of the coast, Caraccioli had a mind for a cruise. He proposed visiting all the neighbouring islands, and accordingly went out to Mascarenhas, and the other islands near it, taking one half of his crew of negroes, and returned with a Dutch prize, which he took off the above-mentioned island, were they were about fixing a colony. This prize, as it had on board all sorts of European goods, and necessaries for settling, was more valuable than if it had been vastly richer. The negroes growing useful hands, Misson resolved on a cruise to the northward, encouraged by Tew's success; and with all the blacks, which he divided between the two ships, one of which Capt. Tew commanded set out with 500 men. Off the coast of Arabia Felix they fell in with a ship belonging to the Great Mogul, bound for Zidon, with pilgrims to Mecca, who, with Moor mariners, made up the number of 1600 souls. This ship carried 110 guns, but made a very poor defence, being encumbered with the goods and number of passengers they carried. The two adventurers did not think it their business to cannonade: they therefore boarded as soon as they came up with her, and the Moors no sooner saw them entered, but they discharged one volley of small arms at random, we may suppose, because no execution was done, and fled the decks. Being masters of this ship, which did not cost them a single man, they consulted what they should do with her, and the prisoners, and it was resolved to set them ashore between Ain and Aden.

They now made the best of their way for Madagascar, putting 200 hands on board the prize, which proved a very heavy sailer, and retarded them very much. Off the Cape Guarde Fin they were overtaken with a cruel storm, which was near wrecking them on the island called Irmanos; but the wind coming about due north, they had the good luck to escape this danger. Though the fury of the wind abated, yet it blew so hard for twelve days together, that they could only carry their coursers reefed. They spied a sail in their passage, but the weather would not permit their endeavouring to speak with her. In a word, they returned to Libertatia with their prize, without any other accident; but the captors could make no estimate of her value, she having on board a vast quantity of diamonds, besides rich silks, raw silks, spices, carpets, wrought and bar gold. The prize was taken to pieces, as she was of no use; her cordage and knee timber preserved, with all the bolts, eyes, chains, and other iron work, and her guns planted on two points of the harbour, where they raised batteries, so that they were now so strongly fortified they apprehended no danger from any number of shipping which could be brought into those seas to attack them. They had, by this time, cleared, sown, and enclosed a good parcel of ground, and taken in a quantity of pasturage, where they had above 300 head of black cattle, bought of the natives. The dock was now finished, and the Victoire growing old and unfit for a long voyage, and the last storm having shook, and loosened her very much, she was pulled to pieces and rebuilt, keeping the same name. She was rigged, victualled, and fit to go to sea, and was! to sail to the coast of Guinea for more negroes, when one of the sloops came in, which had been sent out rather to exercise the negroes, than with any view of making a prize, and brought word that five lofty ships chased her into the bay, and stood for their harbour; that she judged them to be Portuguese by their built, and 50 gun ships, full of men. This proved the real truth. The alarm was given, the forts and batteries manned, and every man stood to his arms. Misson took upon him the command of 100 negroes, who were well disciplined, (for every morning they had been used to perform their exercise, which was taught them by a French Serjeant, one of their company, who belonged to the Victoire) to be ready where his assistance should be required, Tew commanded all the English. They had hardly ordered their affairs when these ships hove in sight, and stood directly for the harbour with Portuguese colours. They were warmly received by the two forts, which did not stop them, though it brought one of them on the careen. They entered the harbour, and thought they had done their business, but were saluted so warmly from the forts, batteries, sloops, and ships, that two of them sunk downright, and a great many men were drowned, though some got on board the other ships. The Portuguese, who did not imagine they had been so well fortified, and thought in passing the two forts they should without difficulty land their men, and easily root out this nest of pirates, found now their mistake, for they durst not venture to hoist out a boat. They had wisely, however, contrived to enter just before the turn of the tide. Finding the attempt vain, and that they had lost a great many men, they clapped upon a wind, and with the help of the tide of ebb, made more haste out than they did to get in, leaving two of their ships sunk in the harbour; but they did not. get off so cheaply, for no sooner were they clear of the forts, but Misson, manning with the utmost expedition both the ships and sloops, gave them chase, and engaged them at the mouth of the bay, The Portuguese defended themselves with a great deal of gallantry, and one of them beat off the Libertarians twice, who boarded them from the two sloops; two of them, finding themselves hard pressed made a running fight, and got off, and left the third to shift as well as she could. The Bijoux and Victoire finding the Portuguese endeavoured to clear themselves and knowing there was little to be got by the captures, gave over the chase, and fell upon the third, who defended himself till his decks swam with blood, and the greater number of his men killed; but finding all resistance vain, and that he was left to an unequal fight by his companions, he called for quarter, and good quarter was given, both to himself and men. This prize yielded them a great quantity of powder and shot, and, indeed, they expected nothing of value out of her. None of the prisoners were stripped, and the officers, Misson, Caraccioli, and Tew invited to their tables, treating them very civilly, and extolling the courage they had shown in their defence. Unhappily two prisoners were found on board, who had been released, and had sworn never to serve against them; these were clapped in irons, and publicly tried for their perjury. The Portuguese officers being present, the witnesses proved them the very discharged men, and they were condemned to be hanged at the point of each fort; which execution was performed the next morning after their condemnation, with the assistance of the Portuguese chaplain, who attended, confessed, and absolved them. This was the engagement with the pirates, which made so much noise in the Lisbon Gazette, and these the men whom the English ignorantly took for Avery; who, we had a notion here in London, had 32 sail of men of war, and had taken upon himself the state and title of king.

This execution seeming to impugn the maxims of the chiefs, Caraccioli made an harangue, in which he told them, "that there was no rule could be laid down which did not allow exceptions: that they were all sensible how tender the Commodore Monsieur Misson was in shedding blood; and that it was a tenet of his faith, that none had power over the life of another, but God alone who gave it; but notwithstanding, self-preservation sometimes made it absolutely necessary to take away the life of another, especially an avowed and obliged enemy, even in cold blood. As to the bloodshed in a lawful war, in defence of that liberty they had generously asserted, it was needless to say anything, but he thought it proper to lay before them reasons for the execution of the criminals, and the heinousness of their crimes. They had not only received their lives from the bounty of the Libertatians, but their liberty, and had everything restored them which they laid claim to; consequently their ingratitude rose in proportion to the generous treatment they had met with: that indeed, both he and Capt. Misson would have passed by the perjury and ingratitude which they had been guilty of, with a corporeal punishment, which had not extended to the deprivation of life, but their gallant friend and companion, the English commander, Capt. Tew, used such cogent reasons for an exemplary punishment deter others from the like crimes, that they must have been enemies to their own preservation in not following his advice: that the lives of their whole body ought to be preferred to those of declared and perjured enemies, who would not cease to endeavour their ruin; and, as they were well acquainted with their settlement, might be fatal instruments of ft, if they were again restored to that liberty which they had already abused: that he was obliged to do Capt. Tew the justice, to acknowledge he was inclined to the side of mercy, till he was thoroughly informed of the blackness of their ingratitude, and then he thought it would be cruelty to themselves to let those miscreants experience a second time their clemency. Thus an absolute necessity had obliged them to act contrary to their declared principles; though, to state the case rightly, these men, not the Libertarians, were the authors of their own deaths." Here the assembly crying out, *"their blood is on their own heads, they sought their deaths, and hanging is too good for them;"* Caraccioli gave over, and every one returned satisfied to his private or the public affairs.

Some difference arising between Misson's and Tew's men, on a national quarrel, which the latter began, Capt. Tew proposed their deciding the quarrel by the sword; but Caraccioli was entirely against it, alleging, that such decision must necessarily be a damage to the public, since the brave men who fell, would be weakening of their colony. He therefore desired Capt. Tew to interpose the authority he had over his crew, and he and Misson would endeavour to bring their men to an amicable agreement; and for the future, as this accident proved the necessity, wholesome laws should be made, and a form of government entered upon. Both parties were therefore called, and Caraccioli showed them the necessity of their living in unity among themselves, who had the whole world for enemies; and as he had a persuasive and insinuating way of argument with the assistance of Capt. Tew, this. affair was ended to the satisfaction of both parties.

The next day the whole colony was assembled, and the three commanders proposed a form of government, as necessary to their conservation; for where there was no coercive laws, the weakest would always be the sufferers, and everything must tend to confusion: that men's passions, blinding them to justice, and making them ever partial to themselves, they ought to submit the differences which might rise to calm and disinterested persons who could examine with temper, and determine according to reason and equity: that they looked upon a democratical form, where the people were themselves the makers and judges of their own laws, the most agreeable; and therefore, desired they would divide themselves into companies of ten men, and every such company choose one to assist in settling a form of government, and in making wholesome laws for the good of the whole: that the treasure and cattle they were masters of should be equally divided, and such lands as any particular man would enclose, should, for the future, be deemed his property, which no other should lay any claim to, if not alienated by a sale.

This proposal was received with applause, and they decimated themselves that very day, but put off the meeting of the states till a house was built, which they set about very cheerfully, and finished it in about a fortnight; it being of framed timber, and they having among them a great number who understood the handling of an axe.

When this body of politicians met, Caraccioli opened the sessions with a handsome speech, showing the advantage flowing from order; and then spoke to the necessity of lodging a supreme power in the hands of one who should have that of rewarding brave and virtuous actions, and of punishing the vicious, according to the laws which the state should make: by which he Was to be guided: that such a power, however, should not be for life, nor be hereditary, but determine at the end of three years, when a new choice should be made by the state, or the old confirmed for three years longer f by which means, the ablest men would always be at the head of affairs, and their power being of short duration, none Would dare to abuse it: that such a chief should have the title of *Lord Conservator,* and all the ensigns of royalty to attend him.

This was approved *nem. con.* and Misson was chosen conservator, with power to create great officers, &c. and with the title of *Supreme Excellence.*

A law was then made for the meeting of the State once every year at least, but oftener, if the conservator and his council thought it necessary for the common good to convene them; and that nothing of moment should be undertaken without the approbation of the State.

In a word their first session lasted ten days; and a great many wholesome laws were enacted, registered in the state book, and dispersed among the crews.

Capt. Tew, the conservator honoured with the title of Admiral, and Caraccioli was made Secretary of State. He chose a council of the ablest among them, without distinction of nation or colour; and the different languages began to be incorporated, and one made out of the many. An equal division was made of their treasure and cattle, and every one began either to enclose land for himself, or his neighbour who would hire his assistance.

Admiral Tew proposed building an arsenal, and augmenting their naval force. The first was agreed to be proposed to the State at the next convention; but the latter was thought unnecessary, till the number of inhabitants was augmented; for, should they all be employed in the sea service, the husbandry would be neglected, which would be of fatal consequence to the growing colony.

The Admiral then proposed the fetching in those Englishmen who had followed the quartermaster; but the council rejected this, alleging, that as they deserted their captain, it was a mark of a mutinous temper, and they might infect others with a spirit of disorder; that, however, they might have notice given them of the settlement, and if they made it their earnest entreaty to be admitted, and would desert the quartermaster, it should be granted as a particular favour done them, at the instance of the Admiral, and upon his engaging his parole of honour for their quiet behaviour.

The Admiral then desired he might take a cruise; that he hoped to meet with some East-India ships, and bring in some volunteers, for the number of subjects being the riches of a nation, he thought the colony stood more in need of men, than of anything else; that he would lie in the way of the Cape, and did not question doing good service; and as he went to the northward, would call upon his own men.

The Victoire was according to the Admiral's desire fitted out, and in a few days he sailed with 300 men onboard. He came to an anchor at the settlement his men had made, hoisted an English, ensign in his fore shrouds, and fired a gun; but after he had waited some time, perceiving no signal from the shore, he landed and sent back his boat. Soon after the boat returned towards the ship, two of his men came up to him, to whom he gave an account of Misson's settlement. They invited him into the wood to see that of theirs, and to advise with their companions, about the proposed migration. The governor, alias quartermaster, received him mighty civilly, but told him, that he could see no advantage to themselves in changing their present situation, though they might prove a great one to the new colony, by adding to their force so many brave fellows: that they there enjoyed all the necessaries of life; were free and independent of all the world; and it would be madness again to subject themselves to any government, which, however mild, still exerted some power. That he was governor for three months, by the choice of his companions; but his power extended no farther than to the judging in matters of small difference which might arise, which he hoped to do impartially while his authority continued; that they had agreed among themselves, and confirmed that, agreement by oath to support the decrees of the governor for the time, that their tranquility might not be disturbed by the humour of any one man: and that this power of determining, was to devolve at the expiration of three months, to him on whom the lot should fall by balloting, provided he had not before enjoyed the honour, for such a one was not to draw; by which agreement, every one would be raised, in time, to the supreme command, which prevented all canvassing and making interest for votes, as when determined by suffrage; left no. opening for making divisions and parties, and was a means to continue to them that repose inseparable from an unity among themselves. However, continued he, "if you will go to America or Europe, and show the advantage which may accrue to the English, by fixing a colony here, out of that love we bear our country, and to wipe away the odious appellation of pirates, with pleasure we will submit to any who shall come with a commission from a lawful government; but it is ridiculous to think we will become subjects to greater rogues than ourselves."

Capt. Tew finding the quartermaster spoke the sentiments of his companions, took leave, and returned to his ship: but went on shore again in the evening, the wind not serving to weigh, it blowing due west. He asked the governor how he got acquainted with the natives? He answered, by meeting them a hunting, and using them well: that he wheedled one of them down to their huts, the fellow being alone, and they three in company, he supposed, thought it best to go with seeming willingness. After him several came, and they lived very friendly with them. The captain, had brought ashore with him some rum and brandy, and they were drinking a bowl of punch, when on a sudden, a violent storm arose. Capt. Tew ran to the shore, and made a signal for his boat to carry him off, but the sea ran too high to venture out of the ship. The storm all the while increased, and the Victoire, in less than two hours, parting her cables, was driven ashore where it was very steep, and perished, with all her men, in Capt. Tew's sight.

The captain stayed with his old companions, without knowing which way to return to his friends he had left with Misson, not one of whom was (luckily for them,) on board the ship. At the end of three months they saw a large ship, which Tew believed was the Bijoux; but she took no notice of the fires they made. As he expected she would return after a short cruise, he, and his companions, made large fires every night on the shore, and visited the coast very often. About a month after this, as they came early to the sea-side, they were surprised at the sight of two sloops which lay at anchor, about a cannon shot from the shore. They had not been long looking upon them, when a canoe was hoisted out of one, and made to them, with six men who rowed, and one sitter.

Tew soon knew him to be Capt. Misson. He came ashore, and embracing the former, told him, all their proposed happiness was vanished; for without the least provocation given, in the dead of the night, the natives came down upon them in two great bodies, and made a great slaughter, without distinction of age or sex, before they could put themselves in a posture of defence; that Caraccioli (who died in the action) and he, got what men together they could, to make a stand; but finding all resistance vain against such numbers, he made a shift to secure a considerable quantity of rough diamonds and bar gold, and to get on board the two sloops with 45 men: that the Bijoux being gone to cruise, and the number of men he had carried with him in the Victoire, had weakened the colony, and given the natives the boldness to attack them, but for what reason he could not imagine.

Tew gave him an account of the disaster which had happened, and after having mutually condoled their misfortunes, Tew proposed their going to America, where Misson might, with the riches he had, pass his life unknown, and in a comfortable manner. Misson answered he could not yet take any resolution, though he had thoughts of returning to Europe, and privately visiting his family, if any were alive, and then retire from the world. They dined with the quartermaster, who pressed their return to America, to procure a commission for the settling a colony. Misson told Tew, he should have one of the sloops, and what volunteers would keep him company, for his misfortunes had erased all thoughts of future settlements; that what riches they had saved, he would distribute equally, nay, he would be content, if he had only a bare support left him. On this answer, four of the quartermaster's company offered to join Capt. Tew,

In the afternoon they visited both sloops, and Misson putting the question to the men, 30 went on board of one sloop, though they parted with great reluctance from their old commander; and 15 stayed with Misson. The four men who joined Tew made the number of his crew 34: they stayed about a week, in hopes of the Bijoux's return upon the coast; but she not appearing, they set sail, Captain Misson having first shared the treasure, with Tew and his other friends and companions, hoping to meet the Bijoux on the Guinea coast, for which they shaped their course. Off Cape Infantes, they were overtaken with a storm, in which the unhappy Misson's sloop went down, within musket shot of Capt. Tew, who could give him no assistance.

Tew continued his course for America, and arrived at Rhode-Island without any accident. His men dispersed themselves, as they thought fit, and Tew sent to Bermuda for his owner's account, fourteen times the value of their sloop; and not being questioned by any, lived in great tranquillity. The French belonging to Misson, took different routes, one of whom dying at Rochelle, the French manuscript of Misson's life was found among his papers, and transmitted to me by a friend and correspondent.

Capt. Tew lived unquestioned. He had an easy fortune, and designed to live quietly at home; but those of his men,, who lived near him, having squandered their shares, were continually soliciting him to take another trip. He withstood their request a considerable time; but they having got together (by the report they made of the vast riches to be acquired) a number of resolute fellows, they, in a body, begged him to head them but for one voyage. They

56

were so earnest in their desire, that he could not refuse complying. They prepared a small sloop, and made the best of their way to the straits entering the Red Sea, where they met with, and attacked a ship belonging to the Great Mogul in the engagement, a shot carried away the rim of Tew's belly, who held his bowels with his hands some small space. When he dropped, it struck such a terror in his men, that they suffered themselves to be taken, without further resistance.

Captain John Halsey

John Halsey was a Boston man, of New-England, commanded the Charles, brigantine, and went out with a commission from the governor, to cruise on the banks of Newfoundland, where he took a French banker, which he appointed to meet him at Fayal; but missing his prize here, he went among the Canary Islands, where he took a Spanish barcalonga, which he plundered and sunk: from thence he went to the island of Bravo, one of the Cape-de-Verds, where he wooded and watered, turned ashore his lieutenant, and several of his men here running away from him, the governor sent them on board again, his commission being as yet in force. From hence he stood away to the southward, and doubling the Cape of Good Hope, made for Madagascar and the bay of Augustin, where he took in wood and water, with some straggling seamen, who were cast away in the Degrave Indiamen, Capt. Young, commander. After this, he shaped his course for the Red Sea, and met with a Dutchman of 60 guns, coming from Mocha, whom he kept company with si Week. Though he was resolved upon turning pirate, he intended to rob only the Moor ships, which occasioned a dispute between him and his men; they insisting on the ship's being a Moor, and he asserting she was Dutch, was positive in his resolve of meddling with no European ships. The men were for boarding, but his obstinacy not being to be conquered, they broke Halsey and his gunner, confined both, and were ready to board the Dutchman, when one of the crew perceiving he was about to run out his lower tier, knocked down the quartermaster (whose business it is to be at the helm, in time of chase or engagement, according to the rules of pirates) clapped the helm hard a-wether, and wore the brigantine. The Dutchman stayed, and fired a shot, which taking a swivel gun, carried it aft, narrowly missed the man at helm, and shattered the taffarel. The men, perceiving they had caught a Tartar, made the best of their way to shake her off, and some were running down between decks, whom the surgeon pricked up again with his sword, though he was no way consenting to their designed piracy. The captain and gunner were again reinstated after they had seen their mistake, and then they steered for the Nicobar Islands, where they met with a country ship, called the Buffalo, commanded by Capt. Buckley, an Englishman, coming from Bengal, which they took after a short engagement there being only three Europeans on board, the captain and two mates; the rest were Moors. This ship fell seasonably in their way, she being bound for Achen, with butter, rice, and cloth, and the pirates, at that time, were in great straits both for provision and clothing. They took the two mates to sea with them, but left the captain and the Moors at Cara Nicobar, at an anchor, and then took a cruise. Capt. Buckley, who was sick, died before their return. In the cruise they met Captain Collins, in a country sloop, bound also to Achen, He had also two English mates with him, but the rest of his company consisted of Moors. Him they carried to the same harbour where they left the Buffalo.

Here a dispute arose among the pirates. Some were for returning to the West-Indies, others were against it, for they had got no money, and that was what engaged their search. They parted upon this; one part went on board the Buffalo, made one Rowe captain, and Myers, a Frenchman, master, whom they had picked up at Madagascar. The sloop's deck they ripped up, and mended with it the bottom of the brigantine which Halsey still commanded. The ship shaped her course for Madagascar, and the brigantine made for the straits of Malacca, to lie in the track of the Manilla ships. I must observe, that Capt. Buckley's two mates, whom they intended to force with them, were by strength of entreaty, permitted to go away with a canoe. In these straits, they met an European built ships, of 26 guns, which they had not the courage to attack, being soured by the Dutchman. They afterwards stood in shore, and came to an anchor. A few days after they made a vessel, which they supposed a China junk, and gave chase, but when they came pretty nigh, notwithstanding the pilot assured them she was what they supposed, they swore it was a Dutchman, and would not venture upon him; so leaving off their chase they stood in shore, and came again to an anchor under the peninsula. They lay here some days, and then spied a tall vessel, which they chased, and which proved to be the Albemarle East-Indiamen, Capt. Bews, commander, coming from China. They came up with him, but thinking it too warm a ship after exchanging a few shot, the brigantine made off, and the Albemarle chased in her turn. They however got clear, having a better share of heels, and came again to an anchor. Having not above 40 hands, the water growing scarce, and not daring to venture ashore for fear of the Dutch, a council was called, and it was resolved to make the best of their way to Madagascar, to pick up more hands, refresh, and set out on new adventures. Pursuant to this resolution, they steered for that island, but fell in their way on Mascarenhas, where, making a small present to the governor, they were supplied with what they wanted. From hence they went to a place on Madagascar, called by the pirates Hopeful Point; by the natives, Harangby, near the island of St. Mary's in the lat. of 17, 40, S. where they met with the Buffalo, and the Dorothy, a prize, made by Capt. Thomas White and his company, being about 90 or 100 men, settled near the same place, in petty governments of their own, having some of them 5 or 600, some 1000 negro subjects, who acknowledged their sovereignty. Here they again repaired their brigantine, took in provisions and all necessaries, augmented their company to about 100 men, and set out for the

Red Sea. They touched at Johanna, and there took in a quantity of goats and cocoa nuts for fresh provisions, and thence in eleven days reached the Straits of Babelmandel. They had not cruised here many days, when they spied the Moorish fleet from Mocha and Jufa, consisting of 25 sail, which they fell in with, and had been taken, if their oars had not helped them off, it falling a dead calm. They had not apprehended the danger so great, if they had not judged these ships convoyed by some Portuguese men of war. Some days after this, they met a one mast vessel, called a grab, coming from Mocha, which they spied within gun-shot in a thick fog: they fired a shot which cut her halliards, and then took possession of her with their boats. She was laden with drugs, but they took only some necessaries and 2000 dollars; and having learned that four English vessels lay at Mocha, of which one was from Jufa, they let her go.

Three days after they spied the four ships, which they at first took to be the trees of Babelmandel. At night they fell in with r and kept them company till morning, the trumpets sounding on both sides all the time, for the pirate had two on board as well as the English. When it was clear day, the four ships drew into a line, for they had hailed the pirate, who made no ceremony of owning who he was, by an answering according to their manner, *From the seas*. The brigantine bore up till she had slung her gaff. One of the ships perceiving this, advised Capt. Jago, who led the van, in a ship of 24 guns and 70 men, to give chase, for the pirate was on the run; but a mate, who was acquainted with the way of working among pirates, answered he would find his mistake, and said he had seen many a warm day, but feared this would be the hottest. The brigantine turned up again, and coming astern, clapped the Rising Eagle aboard, a ship of 16 guns, and the sternmost. Though they entered their men, the Rising Eagle held them a warm dispute for three quarters of an hour, in which Capt. Chamberlain's chief mate and several others were killed, the purser was bounded, jumped overboard and drowned. In the mean while the other ships called to Capt. Jago to board the pirate; who bearing away to clap him aboard, the pirate gave him a shot, which raked him fore and aft, and determined Capt. Jago to get out of danger; for he run away with all the sail he could pack, though he was fitted out to protect the coast against pirates. His example was followed by the rest, every one steering a different coast. Thus they became masters of the Rising Eagle. I cannot but take notice, that the second mate of the Rising Eagle, after quarters were called for, fired from out the forecastle, and killed two of the pirates, one of whom was the gunner's consort, who would have revenged his death by shooting the mate, but several Irish and Scots, together with one Captain Thomas White, once a commander among the pirates, but then a private man, interposed and saved him, in regard that he was an Irishman. They examined the prisoners to know which was the ship from Jufa, that had money onboard; and having learned it was the Essex, they gave chase, came up with her, hoisted the bloody flag at the main-mast-head, fired one single gun, and she struck, though she was fitted for close quarters, and there was not on board the brigantine above 20 hands, and the prize was astern so far, that her top-mast scarce appeared out of the water. In chasing this ship, they passed the other two, who held the fly of their ensigns in their hands ready to strike. When the ship had struck, the captain of her asked, who commanded the brigantine? He was answered, Capt. Halsey. Asking again, who was quartermaster? He was told Nathaniel North, to whom he called, as he knew him very well. North, learning his name was Punt, said, *Capt. Punt, I am sorry you are fallen into our hands.* He was civilly treated, and nothing belonging to himself or the English gentlemen, who were passengers, touched, though they made bold to lay hands on £40,000 in money, belonging to the ship. They had about £10,000 in money out of the Rising Eagle. They discharged the Essex, and with the other prize and the brigantine, steered for Madagascar, where they arrived and shared their booty. Some of the passengers, who had been so well treated, came afterwards with a small ship from India (with license from the governor of Madras) called the Greyhound, laden with necessaries, in hopes to barter with the pirates for the dry goods they had taken, and recover them at an easy rate. They were received very kindly, an invoice of their goods was asked, the goods agreed for, shared and paid in money and bale goods. In the mean while came in a ship from Scotland, called the Neptune, 26 guns, 54 men, commanded by Capt. Miller, with a design to slave, and to go thence to Batavia to dispose of her negroes (having a supercargo on board, brought up among the Dutch) and thence to Malacca, to take on hoard the cargo of a ship, called the Speedwell, lost on her return from China; but finding here another ship trading with the pirates, and having many necessaries, French brandy, Madiera wine, and English stout on board, Capt. Millar thought it better to trade for money than slaves. The merchants of the Greyhound, nettled to see any but themselves take money, for the pirates never haggled about a price, told them, *They could not do the governor of Madras a more grateful piece of service than to make prize of the Neptune, which was a ship fit for that purpose.* To which some of the Scotch and Irish answered, *They had not best put such a design on foot, for if the company once got it into their heads to take one, they would go nigh to take both ships.* In a short time after came on a hurricane, which obliged the Neptune to cut away all her masts, and lost the three ships belonging to the pirates, which was their whole fleet. They having now no ship, and several of them no money, having been stripped at play, their thoughts were bent on the Neptune. The chief mate of her, Daniel Burgess, who had a spleen to the captain, joining privately with the pirates (among whom he died) got all the small masts and yards ashore; and the pirates being requested to find him proper trees for masting, told Capt. Miller they had found such as would serve his turn, desiring he would take a number of hands ashore to get them down to the water, which (he suspecting no harm) accordingly did, and he and his men were seized, and the long boat detained ashore. The captain was forced to send for the second mate, and afterwards for the gunner; the mate, who was the captain's brother, went, but the gunner, suspecting foul play, refused. In the evening, Burgess came on board, and advised the surrender of the ship, which, though but sixteen were left on board, they scrupled, and proposed going under the cover of their own guns to fetch their top-mast and yards, and with them put to sea; but the chief mate, Burgess, whose villany was not then known, persuaded them to give up a ship they could neither defend nor sail; which was no small satisfaction to the Greyhound, little thinking how soon they would meet with the same treatment; for two days after, the pirates manned the Neptune's pinnace, seized the Greyhound, took away all the money they had paid, and shifting out of the Neptune ten pipes of Madeira, with two hogsheads of brandy, into the Greyhound, and putting on board the captain, second mate, boatswain and gunner of the Neptune, and about fourteen of her hands, ordered her to sea. The rest of the Neptune's company being young men fit for their purpose, they detained, most of whom, by hard drinking, fell into distempers and died. As to Capt. Halsey, while the Scotch ship was fitting, he fell ill of a fever, died and was buried with great solemnity and ceremony; the prayers of the church of England was read over him, colours were flying, and his sword and pistol laid on his coffin, which was covered with a ship's jack; as many minute guns fired as he was years old, viz. 46, and three English vollies, and one French volley of small arms. He was brave in his person, courteous to all his prisoners, lived beloved, and died regretted by his own people. His grave was made in a garden of watermelons, and fenced in with pallisades to prevent his being rooted up by the wild hogs, of which there are plenty in those parts.

P. S. The Neptune seized as above, was the year after Capt. Halsey's death, ready to go to sea; but a hurricane happening, she was lost, and proved the last ship that gang of pirates ever got possession of.

Captain Thomas White

He was born at Plymouth, where his mother kept a public house. She took great care of his education, and when he was grownup, as he had an inclination to the sea, procured him the king's letter. After he had served some years onboard a man of war, he went to Barbadoes, where he married, got into the merchant service, and designed to settle in the island. He had the command of the Marygold brigantine given him, in which he made two successful voyages to Guinea and back to Barbadoes. In his third, he had the misfortune to be taken by a French pirate, as were several other English ships, the masters and inferior officers of which they detained, being in want of good artists. The brigantine belonging to White, they kept for their own use. and sunk the vessel they before sailed in; but meeting with a ship on the Guinea coast more fit for their purpose, they went on board her, and burnt the brigantine.

It is not my business here to give an account of this French pirate, any father than Capt. White's story obliges me, though I beg leave to take notice of their barbarity to the English prisoners, for they would set them up as a butt or mark to shoot at; several of whom were thus murdered in cool blood, by way of diversion.

White was marked out for a sacrifice by one of these villains, who, for I know not what reason, had sworn his death which he escaped thus. One of the crew, who had a friendship for White, knew this fellows design to kill him in the night, and therefore advised him to lie between him and the ship's side, with intention to save him; which indeed he did, but was himself shot dead by the murderous villain, who mistook him for White.

After some time cruising along the coast, the pirates doubled the Cape of Good Hope, and shaped their course for Madagascar, where, being drunk and mad, they knocked their ship on the head, at the south end of the island, at a place called by the natives Elexa. The country thereabouts was governed by a king, named Mafaly.

When the ship struck, Capt. White, Capt. Boreman, (born in the' Isle of Wight, formerly a lieutenant of a man of war, but in the merchant's service when he fell into the hands of the pirates) Capt. Bowen and some other prisoners, got into the long-boat, and with broken oars and barrel staves, which they found in the bottom of the boat, paddled to Augustin Bay, which is about 14 or 15 leagues from the wreck, where they landed, and were kindly received by the king of Bavaw (the name of that part of the island) who spoke good English.

They stayed here a year and a half at the king's expense, who gave them a plentiful allowance of provision, as was his custom to all white men, who met with any misfortune on his coast. His humanity not only provided for such, but the first European vessel that came in, he always obliged to take in the unfortunate people, let the vessel be what it would; for he had no notion of any difference between pirates and merchants.

At the expiration of the above term, a pirate brigantine came in, on board which the king obliged them to enter, or travel by land to some other place, which they durst not do; and of two evils chose the least, that of going on board the pirate vessel which was commanded by one William Read, who received them very civilly.

This commander went along the coast, and picked up what Europeans he could meet with. His crew, however, did not exceed forty men. He would have been glad of taking on board some of the wrecked Frenchmen, but for the barbarity they had used towards the English prisoners. However, it was impracticable, for the French pretending to lord it over the natives, whom they began to treat inhumanly, were set upon by them, one half of their number cut off, and the other half made slaves.

Read, with this gang, and a brigantine of 60 tons, steered his course for the gulf of Persia, where they met a grab (a one-masted vessel) of about 200 tons, which was made prize. They found nothing on board but bale goods, most of which they threw overboard to search for gold, and to make room in the vessel; but as they learned afterwards, they threw over, in their search, what they so greedily hunted after, for there was a considerable quantity of sold concealed in one of the bales they tossed into the sea.

In this cruise Capt. Read fell ill and died, and was succeeded by one James. The brigantine being small, crazy, and worm-eaten, they shaped their course for the island of Mayotta, where they took out the masts of the brigantine, fitted up the grab, and made a ship of her. Here they took in a quantity of fresh provisions, which is in this island very plentiful, and very cheap; and found a twelve oared boat, which formerly belonged to the Ruby Eastindiamen, which had been lost there.

They stayed here all the monsoon time, which is about six months; after which they resolved for Madagascar. As they came in with the land, they spied a sail coming round from the East side of the island. They gave chase on both sides, so that they soon met. They hailed each other, and receiving the same answer from each vessel, *viz. from the seas,* they joined company.

This vessel was a small French ship, laden with liquors from Martinico, first commanded by one Fourgette, to trade with the pirates for slaves, at Ambonawoula, on the East side of the island, in the lat. of 17 degrees 30 minutes and was by them taken after the following manner.

The pirates, who were headed by George Booth, now commander of the ship, went on board (as they had often done) to the number of ten, and carried money with them, under pretence of purchasing what they wanted.. This Booth had formerly been gunner of a pirate ship, called the Dolphin. Capt Fourgette was pretty much upon his guard, and searched every man as he came over the side, and a pair of pocket pistols were found upon a Dutchman, who was the first entered. The captain told him, *he was a rogue, and had a design upon his ship,* and the pirates pretended to be so angry with this fellow's offering to come on board with arms, that they threatened to knock him on the head, and tossingly him rough into the boat, ordered him ashore, though they had before taken an oath on the bible, either to carry the ship or die in the undertaking.

They were all searched, but they however contrived to get on board four pistols, which were all the arms they had for the enterprise, though Fourgette had 20 hands on board, and his small arms on the awning, to be in readiness.

The captain invited them into the cabin to dinner, but Booth chose to dine with the petty officer though one Johnson, Isaac and another, went down.

Booth was to give the watch-word, which was *hurrah.* Standing near the awning, and being a nimble fellow, at one spring threw himself upon it, drew the arms to him, fired his pistol forward among the men, one of whom he wounded, (who jumping overboard was lost) and gave the signal.

Three, I said, were in the cabin, and seven upon deck, who with handspikes and the arms seized, secured the ship's crew. The captain and his two mates, who were at dinner in the cabin, hearing the pistol, fell upon Johnson, and stabbed him in several places with their forks, but they being silver did him no great damage. Fourgette snatched his piece, which he snapped at Isaac's breast several times, but it would not go off. At last, finding his resistance vain, he submitted, and the pirates set him, and those of his men, who would not join them, on shore, allowing him to take his books, papers, and whatever else he claimed as belonging to himself; and besides treating him very humanely, gave him several casks of liquor, with arms and powder, to purchase provisions in the country.

I hope this digression, as it was in a manner needful, will be excused. I shall now proceed.

After they had taken in the Dolphin's company, which were on the island, and increased their crew, by that means, to the number of 80 hands, they sailed to St. Mary's, where Capt. Mosson's ship Jay at anchor, between the island and the main. This gentleman and his whole ship's company had been cut off, at the instigation of Ort-Vantyle, a Dutchman of NewYork.

Out of her they took water casks and other necessaries; which having done, they designed for the river Methelage. On the west side of Madagascar, in the lat. of 16 degrees or thereabouts, to salt up provisions and to proceed to the East Indies, cruise off the islands of St. John, and lie in wait for the Moor ships from Mocha.

In their way to Methelage they fell in (as I have said) with the pirate, on board of which was Capt. White. They joined company, came to an anchor together in the above-named river, where they had cleaned, salted, and taken in their provisions, and were ready to go to sea, when a large ship appeared in sight, and stood into the same river.

The pirates knew not whether she was a merchantman or man of war. She had been the latter, belonging to the French king, and could mount 50 guns; but being taken by the English, she was bought by some London merchants, and fitted out from that port to slave at Madagascar, and go to Jamaica. The captain was a young, inexperienced man, who was put in with a nurse.

The pirates sent their boats to speak with them, but the ship firing at them, they concluded it a man of war, and rowed ashore; the grab standing in, and not keeping her wind so well as the French built ship, run among a parcel of mangroves, and a stump piercing her bottom, she sunk: the other run aground, let go her anchor, and came to no damage, for the tide of flood fetched her off.

The captain of the Speaker, for that was the name of the ship which frightened the pirates, was not a little vain of having forced these two vessels ashore, though he did not know whether they were pirates or merchantmen, and could not help undressing himself in these words: "How will my name ring on the exchange, when it is known I have run two pirates aground;" which gave handle td a satirical return from one of his men after he was taken, who said, "Lord I how our captain's name will ring on the exchange, when it is heard, he frightened two pirate ships ashore, and was taken by their two boats afterwards.

When the Speaker came within shot, she fired several times at the two vessels; and when she came to an anchor, several more into the country, which alarmed the negroes, who, acquainting their king, he would allow him no trade, till the pirates living ashore, and who had a design on his ship, interceded for them, telling the king, they were their countrymen, and what had happened was through a mistake, it being a custom among them to fire their guns by way of respect, and it was owing to the gunner of the ship's negligence that they fired shot.

The captain of the Speaker sent his purser ashore, to go up the country to the king, who lived about 24 miles from the coast, to carry a couple of small arms inlaid with gold, a couple of brass blunderbusses, and a pair of pistols, as presents, and to require trade. As soon as the purser was ashore, he was taken prisoner, by one Tom Collins, a Welshman, born in Pembroke, who lived on shore, and had belonged to the Charming Mary, of Barbadoes, which went out with a commission but was converted to a pirate. He told the purser he was his prisoner, and must answer the damage done two merchants who were slaving. The purser answered, that he was not commander; that the captain was a hot rash youth, put into business by his friends, which he did not understand: but however, satisfaction should be made. He was carried by Collins on board Booth's ship, where, at first, he was talked to in pretty strong terms; but after a while very civilly used, and the next morning sent up to the king with a guide, and peace made for him.

The king allowed them trade, and sent down the usual presents, a couple of oxen between twenty and thirty people laden with rice, and as many more with the country liquor, called *toke*.

The captain then settled the factory on the shore side, and began to buy slaves and provisions. The pirates were -among them, and had opportunities of sounding the men, and knowing in what posture the ship lay. They found by one Hugh Man, belonging to the Speaker, that there were not above 40 men on board, and that they had lost the second mate and 20 hands in the long-boat, on the coast, before they came into this harbour, but that they kept a good look put, and had their guns ready primed. However, he, for a hundred pounds, undertook to wet all the priming, and assist in taking the ship.

After some days the captain of the Speaker came on shore, and was received with a great deal of civility by the heads of the pirates, having agreed before to make satisfaction. In a day or two after, he was invited by them to eat a barbecued shoat, which invitation he accepted. After dinner, Capt. Bowen, who was, I have already said, a prisoner on board the French pirate, but now become one of the fraternity, and master of the grab, went out, and returned with a ease of pistols in his hand, and told the captain of the Speaker, whose name I won't mention, that he was his prisoner. He asked, upon what account? Bowen answered, "they wanted a ship, his was a good one, and they were resolved to have her, to make amends for the damage he had done them."

Tn the mean while his boat's crew, and the rest of his men ashore, were told by others of the pirates, who were drinking with them, that they were also prisoners: softie of them answered, *Zound's we don't trouble our heads what we are, let's have t'other bowl of punch.*

A watch word was given, and no boat to be admitted on board the ship. This word, which was for that night, *Coventry,* was known to them. At 8 o'clock they manned the twelve-oared boat, and the one they found at Mayotta, with 24 men, and set out for the ship. When they were put off, the captain of the Speaker desired them to come back, as he wanted to speak with them. Capt. Booth asked what he wanted! He said "they could never take his ship." "Then," said Booth, "we'll die in or along side of her."— "But," replied the captain, "if you will go with safety, don't board on the larboard side for there is a gun out of the steerage loaded with partridge, which will clear the decks." They thanked him, and proceeded.

When they were near the ship they were hailed, and the answer was, *the Coventry.* "All well," said the mate, "get the lights over the side;" but spying the second boat, he asked what boat that was? One answered, it was a raft of water; another that it was a boat of beef; this disagreement in the answers made the mate suspicious, who cried out— *Pirates, take to your arms my lads,* and immediately clapped a match to a gun, which, as the priming was before wet by the treachery of Hugh Man. only fizzed. They boarded in the instant, and made themselves masters of her, without the loss of a man on either side.

The next day they put necessary provisions on board the French built ship, and gave her to the captain of the Speaker, and those men who would go off with him, among whom was Man, who had betrayed his ship; for the pirates had both paid him the £100 agreed, and kept his secret. The captain having thus lost his ship, sailed in that which the pirates gave him, for Johanna, where he fell ill and died with grief.

The pirates having here victualled, they sailed for the Bay of St. Augustine where they took in between 70 and 80 men, who had belonged to the ship Alexander commanded by Capt. James, a pirate. They also took up her guns, and mounted the Speaker with 54, which made up their number 240 men, besides slaves, of which they had about 20.

From hence they sailed for the East-Indies, but stopped at Zanguebar for fresh provisions, where the Portuguese had once a settlement, but now inhabited by Arabians. Some of them went ashore with the captain to buy provisions. The captain was sent for by the governor, who went with about 14 in company. They passed through the guard, and when they had entered the governor's house, they were all cut off; and, at the same time, others who where in different houses of the town were set upon, which made them fly to the shore. The longboat, which lay off a grappling, was immediately put in by those who looked after her. There were not above half a dozen of the pirates who brought their arms ashore, but they plied them so well, for they were in the boat, that most of the men got; into her. The quartermaster ran down sword in hand, and though he was attacked by many, he behaved himself so well, that he got into a little canoe, put off, and reached the long-boat.

In the interim, the little fort the Arabians had, played upon the ship, which returned the salute very warmly. Thus they got on board, with the loss of Capt. Booth and 20 men, and set sail for the East-Indies. When they were under sail, they went to voting for a new captain, and the quartermaster, who had behaved so well in the last affair with the Arabians, was chosen; but he declining all command, the crew made choice of Bowen for captain. Pickering to succeed him as master, Samuel Herault, a henchman, for quartermaster, and Nathaniel North for captain quartermaster.

Things being thus settled, they came to the mouth of the Red Sea, and fell in with 13 sail of Moor ships, which they kept company with the greater part of the day, but afraid to venture on them, as they took them for Portuguese men of war. At length part were for boarding, and advised it. The captain though he said little, did not seem inclined. for he was but a young pirate, though an old commander of a merchantman. Those who pushed for boarding, then desired Capt. Boremen, already mentioned, to take the command; but he said he would not be an usurper; that nobody was more fit for it than he who had it; that for his part he would stand by his fuzil, arid went forward to the forecastle with such as would have him take the command, to be ready to board; on which, the captain's quartermaster said, if they were resolved to engage, their captain, (whose representative he was) did not want resolution: therefore ordered them to get their tacks on board (for they had already made a clear ship) and get ready for boarding; which they accordingly did, and coming up with the sternmost ship, they fired a broadside into her, which killed two Moors, clapped her on board and carried her; but night coming on, they made only this prize, which yielded them £500 per man. From hence they sailed to the coast of Malabar. The adventures of these pirates on this coast are already set down in Captain Bowen's life, to which I refer the reader, and shall only observe, that Capt. White was all this time before the mast, being a forced man from the beginning.

Bowen's crew dispersing, Capt. White went to Methelage, where he lived ashore with the King, toot-having an opportunity of getting off the island, till another pirateship, called the Prosperous, commanded hy one Howard, who had been bred a lighterman on the river Thames, came in. This ship was taken at Augustin, by some pirates from shore, and the crew of their own longboat, which joined them, at the instigation of one Ranten, boatswain's mate, who sent for water. They came on board in the night and surprised her, though not without resistance, in which the captain and chief mate were killed, and several others wounded.

Those who were ashore with Capt. White, resolving to enter in this ship, determined him to go also, rather than be left alone with the natives, hoping, by some accident or other, to have an opportunity of returning home. He continued on board this ship, in which he was made quartermaster, till they met with, and all went on board of Bowen, as is set down in his life, in which ship he continued after Bowen left them. At Port Dolphin he went off in the boats to fetch some of the crew left ashore, the ship being blown to sea the night before. The ship not being able to get in, and he supposing her gone to the west side of the island, as they had formerly proposed, he steered that course in his boat with 26 men. They touched at Augustin, expect the ship, but she not appearing in a week, the time they waited, the king ordered them to be gone, telling them they imposed on him with lies, for he did not believe they had any ship: however he gave them fresh provision: they took in water, and made for Methelage. Here as Capt. White was known to the king, they were kindly received, and stayed about a fortnight in expectation of the ship, but she not appearing, they raised their boat a streak, salted the provision the king gave them, put water aboard, and stood for the north end of the island, designing to go round, believing their ship might be at the island of St. Mary. When they came to the north end, the current, which sets to the N. W. for eight months in the year, was so strong they found it impossible to get round. Wherefore they got into a harbour, of which there are many for small vessels. Here they stayed about three weeks or a month, when part of the crew were for burning the boat, and travelling over land to a black king of their acquaintance, who name was Reberimbo, who lived at a place called Manangaromasigh, in lat. 15 deg. or thereabouts.; As this king had been several times assisted by the whites in his wars, he was a great friend to them. Capt. White dissuaded them from this undertaking, and with much ado, saved the boat; but one half of the men. being resolved to go by land, they took what provisions they thought necessary, and set out. Capt. White, and; those who stayed with him, convoyed them a day's journey, and then returning, he got into the boat with his companions, and went back to Methelage, fearing these men might return, prevail with the rest, and burn the boat.

Here he built a deck on his boat, and layby three months, in which time there came in three pirates with a boat, who had formerly been trepanned on board the Severn and Scarborough men of war, which had been looking for pirates on the east side; from which ships they made their escape at Mohila, in a small canoe to Johanna, and from Johanna to Mayotta, where the king built them the boat which brought them to Methelege. The time of the current's setting with violence to the N.W. being over, they proceeded together in White's boat (burning that of Mayotta) to the north end, where the current running yet too strong to get round, they went into a harbour and stayed there a month, maintaining themselves with fish and wild hogs, of which there was a great plenty. At length, having fine weather, and the strength of the current abating they got round; and after sailing about 40 miles on the east side, they went into a harbour, where they found a piece of a jacket, which they knew belonged to one of those men who had left them to go over land. He had been a forced man, and a ship carpenter. This they supposed he had torn to wrap round his feet: that part of the country being barren and rocky. As they sailed along this coast, they came to an anchor in convenient harbours every night, till they got as far as Manangaromaisigh, where king Reberimbo resided, where they went in to inquire for their men, who left them at the north end, and to recruit with provisions. The latter was given them, but they could get no information of their companions.

From hence they went to the island of St. Mary, where a canoe came off to them with a letter directed to any white man. They knew it to be the hand of one of their former shipmates. The contents of this letter was to advise them to be on their guard, and not trust too much to the blacks of this place, they having been formerly treacherous. They inquired after their ship, and were informed, that the company had given her to the Moors, who were gone away with her, and that they themselves were settled at Amboynavoula, about 20 leagues to the southward of St. Mary, where they lived among the negroes as so many sovereign princes.

One of the blacks, who brought off the letter went onboard their boat, carried them to the place called Olumbah, a point of land made by a river on one side, and the sea on the other, where twelve of them lived together in a large house they had built, and fortified with about twenty pieces of cannon.

The rest of them were settled in small companies of about 12 or 14 together, more or less, up the said river, and along the coast, every nation by itself, as the English, French, Dutch &c. They made inquiry of their consorts after the different prizes which belonged to them, and they found ail very justly laid by to be given them, if ever they returned, as were what belonged to the men who went over land. Capt. White, hankering after home, proposed going out again in the boat; for lie was averse to settling with them; and many others agreed to go under his command; and if they could meet with a ship to carry them to Europe, to follow their old vocation. But the others did not think it reasonable he should have the boat, but that it should be set to sale for the benefit of the company. Accordingly it was set up, and Capt. White bought it for 400 pieces of eight, and with some of his old consorts, whose number was increased by others of the ship's crew, he went back the way he had come to Methelage. Here he met with a French ship of about 50 tons, and 6 guns, which had been taken by some pirates who lived at Maratan, on the east side of the island, and some of the De-grave East-Indiaman's crew, to whom the master of her refused a passage to Europe; for as he had himself been a pirate, and quartermaster to Bowen, in the Speaker, he apprehended their taking away his ship. War then subsisting between England and France, he thought they might do it without being called in question as pirates. The pirates who had been concerned in taking Herault's ship, for that was his name, had gone up the country, and left her to the men belonging to the Degrave who had fitted her up, cleaned and tallowed her, and got in some provision, with a design to go to the East-Indies, that they might light on some ship to return to their own country.

Capt. White, finding these men proposed joining him, and going round to Ambonavoula, to make up a company, it was agreed upon, and they unanimously chose him commander. They accordingly put to sea. and stood away round the south end of the island, and touched at Don Mascarenhas, where he took in a surgeon, and stretching over again to Madagascar, fell in with

Ambonavoula, and made up his complement of 60 men. From hence he shaped his course for the island of Mayotta, where lie cleaned his ship, and waited for the season to go into the Red Sea. His provisions being taken in, the time proper, and the ship well fitted, he steered for Babelmandel, and running into a harbour, waited for the Mocha ships.

He here took two grabs laden with provisions, and having some small money and drugs aboard. These he plundered of what was for his turn, kept them a fortnight by him, and let them go. Soon after they spied a lofty ship, upon which they put to sea; but finding her European built, and too strong to attempt, for it was a Dutchman, they gave over the chase, and were glad to shake him off, and return to their station. Fancying they were here discovered, from the coast of Arabia, or that the grabs had given information of them they stood over for the Ethiopian shore, keeping a good look out for the Mocha ships. A few days after, they met with a large ship of about 1000 tons and 600 men, called the Malabar, which they chased, kept company with all night, and took in the morning, with the loss of only their boatswain, and two or three men wounded. In the taking this ship, they damaged their own so much, by springing their foremast, carrying away their bowsprit, and beating in part of their upper works, that they did not think her longer fit for their use. They therefore filled her with prisoners, gave them provision and sent them away.

Some days after this they spied a Portuguese man of war of 44 guns, which they chased, but gave it over, by carrying away their main-top-mast, so that they did not speak with her, for the Portuguese took no notice of them. Four days after they had left this man of war, they fell in with a Portuguese merchantman, which they chased with English colours flying. The chase, taking White for an English man of war or East-Indiaman, made no sail to get from him, but on his coming up, brought to, and sent his boat on board with a present of sweet-meats for the English captain. His boat's crew was detained, and the pirates getting into his boat with their arms, went on board, and fired on the Portuguese, who being surprised, asked if war was broke out between England and Portugal? They answered in the affirmative, but the captain could not believe them. However they took what they liked, and kept him with them.

After two days they met with the Dorothy, an English ship, Capt. Penruddock, commander, coming from Mocha. They exchanged several shot in the chase, but when they came along side of her, they entered their men, and found no resistance, she being navigated by Moors, no Europeans, except the officers being on board. On a vote, they gave Capt. Penruddock (from whom they took a considerable quantity of money) the Portuguese ship and cargo, with what bale he pleased to take out of his own, bid him go about his business, and make what he could of her. As to the English ship, they kept her for their own use.

Soon after, they plundered the Malabar ship, out of which they took as much money as came to £200 sterling a man, but missed 50,000 sequins, which were hid in a jar under a cow's stall, kept for the giving milk to the Moor supercargo, an ancient man. They then put the Portuguese and Moor prisoners on board the Malabar, and sent them about their business. The day after they had sent them away, one Capt. Benjamin Stacy, in a ketch of 6 guns fell into their hands. They took what money he had and what goods and provisions they wanted Among the money were 500 dollars, a silver mug and two spoons belonging to a couple of children on board, who were under the care of Stacy. The children took on for their loss, and the captain asking the reason of their tears, was answered by Stacy, that the above sum and plate was all the children had to bring them up. Capt. White made a speech to his men, and told them it was cruel to rob the innocent children; upon which, by unanimous consent, all was restored them again. Besides, they made a gathering among themselves, and made a present to Stacy's mate, and other of his inferior officers, and about 120 dollars to the children. They then discharged Stacy and his crew, and made the best of their way out of the Red Sea.

They came into the bay of Defarr, where they found a ketch at anchor, which the people had made prize of, by seizing the master and boat's crew ashore. They found a French gentleman, one Monsieur Berger, on board, whom they carried with them, took out about 2000 dollars, and sold the ketch to the chief ashore for provision.

Hence they sailed for Madagascar, but touched at Mascarenhas, where several of them went ashore with their booty, about £1200 a man. Here taking in fresh provisions, White steered for Madagascar, and fell in with Hopeful Point where they shared their goods, and took up settlements ashore, where White built a house, bought cattle, took off the upper deck of his ship, and was fitting her up for the next season. When she was neat ready for sea, Capt. John Halsey, who had made a. broken voyage, came in with a brigantine, which being a more proper vessel for their turn, they desisted from working on the ship, and those who had a mind for fresh adventures, went on board Halsey among whom Capt. White entered before the mast.

At his return to Madagascar, White was taken ill of a flux, which in about five or six months ended his days. Finding his time was drawing nigh, he made his will, left several legacies, and named three men of different nations, guardian to a son be had by a woman of the country, requiring he might be gent to England with the money he left him, by the first English ship, to be brought up in the Christian religion, in hopes he might live a better man than his father. He was buried with the same ceremony they used at the funerals of their companions, which is mentioned in the account of Halsey. Some years after, an English ship touching there, the guardians faithfully discharged their trust, and put him on board with the captain, who brought up the hoy with care, acting by him as became a man of probity and honour.

Captain Condent

Captain Condent was a Plymouth man born, but we are as yet ignorant of the motives and time of his first turning pirate. He was one of those who thought fit to retire from Providence, on Governor Rogers' arrival at that island, in a sloop belonging to Mr. Simpson of New York, a Jew merchant of which sloop he was then quartermaster. Soon after they left the island, an accident happened on board, which put the whole crew into consternation. They had among them an Indian man, whom some of them had heat: in revenge, he got most of the arms forward into the hold, and designed to blow up the sloop; upon which, some advised scuttling the deck and throwing grenade shells down; hut Condent said, that was too tedious and dangerous since the fellow might fire through the deck and kill several of them. He, therefore, taking a pistol in one hand, and his cutlass in the other, leaped into the hold. The Indian discharged a piece at him, which broke his arm; but, however, he ran up and shot the Indian. When he was dead, the crew hacked him to pieces, and the gunner, ripping up his belly, tore out his heart, broiled and ate it.

After this, they took a merchantman called the Duke of York; and some disputes arising among the pirates, the captain, and one half of the company, went on board the prize; the other half, who continued in the sloop, chose Condent captain. He shaped his course for the Cape-de-Verd Islands, and in his way took a merchant ship from Madeira, laden with wine, hound for the West-Indies, which he plundered and let go; then coming to the Isle of May, one of the said islands, he took the whole salt fleet, consisting of about 20 sail. Wanting a boom, betook out the mainmast of one of these ships to supply the want. Here he took upon himself the administration of justice, inquiring into the manner of the commanders behaviour to their men, and those against whom complaint was made he whipped and pickled. He took what provision and other necessaries he wanted, and having augmented! his company by volunteers and forced men, he left the ships and sailed to St. Jago, where he took a Dutch ship, which had formerly been a privateer. This proved also an easy prize, for he fired but one broadside, and clapping her on board, carried her without resistance, for the captain and several men were killed, and some wounded by his great shot.

The ship proving for his purpose, he gave her the name of the Flying Dragon, went on board with his crew, and made a present of his sloop to a mate of an English prize, whom he had forced with him. From hence he stood away for the coast of Brazil, and in his cruise took several Portuguese ships, which he plundered and let go.

After these, he fell in with the Wright galley, Capt. John Spelt, commander, hired by the South Sea company, to go to the coast of Angola for slaves, and thence to Buenos Ay res. This ship he detained a considerable time, and the captain being his townsman, treated him very civilly. A few days after he took Spelt, he made prize of a Portuguese, laden with bale goods and stores. He new rigged the Wright galley, and put on board of her some of the goods. Soon after he had discharged the Portuguese, lie met with a Dutch East Indiaman of 28 guns, whose captain was killed the first broadside, and took her with little resistance, for he had hoisted the pirate's colours on board Spelt's ship.

He now, with three sail, steered for the island of Ferdinando, where he hove down and cleaned the Flying Dragon. Having careened, he put 11 Dutchmen on board Capt. Spelt, to make amends for the hands he had forced from him, and sent him away, making him a present of the goods he took from the Portuguese ship. When he sailed himself, he ordered the Dutch to stay at Ferdinando 24 hours after his departure; threatening, if he did not comply, to sink his ship, if he fell a second time into his hands, and to put all the company to the sword. He then stood for the coast of Brazil, where he met a Portuguese man of war of 70 guns, which he came up with. The Portuguese hailed him, and he answered, *from London, bound to Buenos Ayres.* The Portuguese manned his shrouds and cheered him, when Condent fired a broadside and a volley of small arms, which began a smart engagement for the space of' three glasses; but Condent finding himself over-matched, made the best of his way, and being the best sailer, got off.

A few days after, he took a vessel of the same nation, who gave an account, that he had killed above 40 men in the guarda del Costa, beside a number wounded. He kept along the coast to the southward, and took a French ship of 18 guns, laden with wine and brandy, bound for the South Sea, which he carried with him into the River of Plate. He sent some of his men ashore to kill some wild cattle, but they were taken by the crew of a Spanish man of war. On their examination before the captain, they said they were two Guinea ships, with slaves belonging to the South Sea company, and on this story were allowed to return to their boats. Here five of his forced men ran away, with his canoe; he plundered the French ship, cut her adrift and she was stranded. He proceeded along the Brazil coast, and hearing a pirate ship was lost upon it, and the pirates imprisoned, he used all the Portuguese who fell into his hands, who were many, very barbarously, cutting off their ears and noses; and as his master was a papist, when they took a priest, they made him say mass at the mainmast, and would afterwards get on his back and ride him about the decks, or else load and drive him like a beast. He from this went to the Guinea coast, and took Capt. Hill, in the Indian Queen.

In Luengo Bay he saw two ships at anchor, one a Dutchman of 44 guns, the other an English ship, called the Fame, Capt. Bowen, commander. They both cut and ran ashore; the Fame was lost, hut the Dutch ship the pirate got off and took with him. When he was at sea again, he discharged Captain Hill, and stood away for the East-Indies. Near the Cape he took an Osterid East-Indiaman, of which Mr. Nash a noted merchant in London, was supercargo. Soon after he took a Dutch East-Indiaman, discharged the Ostender, and made for Madagascar. At the Isle of St. Mary, he met with some ofCa.pt.

Hatsey's crew, whom he took on hoard with other stragglers, and shaped his course for the East-Indies, and in the way, at the island of Johanna, took, in company with two other pirates he met at St. Mary's, the Cassandra East-Indiaman, commanded by Capt. James Macraigh. He continued his course for the East-Indies, where he made a very great booty; and returning, touched at the isle of Mascarenhas, where he met with a Portuguese ship of 70 guns, with the viceroy of Goa on board. This ship he made prize of, and hearing she had money on board, they would allow of no ransom, but carried her to the coast of Zanguebar, where was a Dutch fortification, which they took and plundered, razed the fort, and carried off several men voluntarily. From hence they stood for St. Mary's, where they shared their booty, broke up their company, and settled among the natives. Here a snow came from Bristol, which they obliged to carry a petition to the governor of Mascarenhas for a pardon, though they paid the master very generously. The governor returned answer ne would take them into protection if they would destroy their ships, which they agreed to, and accordingly sunk the Flying Dragon, Sec. Condent and some others went to Mascarenhas, where Condent married the governor's sisterin-law, and remained some time; but, as I have been credibly informed, he is since come to France, settled at St. Maloes, and drives a considerable trade as a merchant.

Captain Bellamy

As we cannot, with any certainty, deduce this man from his origin, we shall begin where we find him first a declared enemy to mankind. Capt. Bellamy and Paul Williams, in two sloops, had been upon a Spanish wreck, and not finding their expectation answered, they resolved not. to lose their labour, and agreed to *go upon the account,* a term among the pirates, which speaks their profession. The first who had the misfortune to fall in their way, was Capt. Prince, bound from Jamaica to London, in a galley built at that port, whose cargo consisted of elephant's teeth, gold dust, and other rich merchandise. This prize not only enriched but strengthened them. They immediately mounted this galley with 28 guns, and put on board 150 hands, pf different nations; Bellamy was declared captain and the vessel had her own name continued, which was Whidaw. This happened about the latter end of February, 1717. They, now thus-fitted for continuing their desperate resolution, shaped their course for Virginia, which coast they very much infested, taking several vessels. They were upon shifting this station, when they were very near, as the psalmist expresses it, *going quick down into hell;* for the heavens beginning to lower, prognosticated a storm. At the first appearance of the sky being likely to be overcast, Bellamy took in all his small sails, and Williams doubled-reefed his mainsail, which was hardly done when a thunder shower overtook them with such violence, that the Whidaw was very near oversetting. They immediately put before the wind, for they had no other way of working, having only the goose wings of the foresail to scud with. Happy for them the wind was at W. by N. for had it been easterly, they must have infallibly perished upon the coast. The storm increased towards night, and not only put them by all sail, hut obliged the Whidaw to bring her yards aportland, and all they could do with tackles to the goose neck of the tiller, four men in the gunroom, and two at the wheel, was to keep her head to the sea, for had she once broached to, they must infallibly have foundered. The heavens, in the mean while, were covered with sheets of lightning, which the sea, by the agitation of the saline particles, seemed to imitate. The darkness of the night was such, as the scripture says, *as might be felt;* the terrible hollow roaring of the winds, could be only equalled by the repeated, I may say, incessant claps of thunder, sufficient to strike a dread of the Supreme Being, who commands the sea and the winds, one would imagine in every heart; but among these wretches, the effect was different, for they endeavoured by their blasphemies, oaths, and horrid imprecations, to drown the uproar of jarring elements. Bellamy swore he was sorry he could not run out his guns to return the salute, meaning the thunder, that he fancied the gods had got drunk over their tipple, and were gone together by the ears. They continued scudding all that night under their bare poles: the next morning the mainmast being sprung in the step, they were forced to cut it away, and at the same time, the mizen came by the board. These misfortunes made the ship ring with blasphemy, which was increased, when, by trying the pumps, they found the ship made a great deal of water; though by continually plying them, they kept it from gaining. The sloop, as well as the ship, was left to the mercy of the winds. though the former, not having a tant mast, did not lose it. The wind shifting round the compass, made so outrageous find short a sea, that they had little hopes cl safety; it broke upon the poop, drove in the taffarei, and washed the two men away from the wheel, who were saved in the netting. The wind after four days and three nights, hated its fury, and fixed in the N.N.E. point, hourly decreasing, and the weather clearing up they spoke to the sloop, and resolved for the coast of Carolina. They continued this course hut a day and a night, when the wind coming about to the southward, they changed their resolution to that of going to Rhode Island. All this while the Whidaw's leak continued, and it was as much as the lee pump could do to keep the water from gaining, though it was kept continually going. Jury-masts were set up, and the carpenter finding the leak to be in the bows, occasioned by the oakum working out of a seam, the crew became very jovial again. The sloop received no other damage than the loss of the mainsail, which the first flurry tore away from the boom. In their cruise off Rhode-Island, the beginning of April, they took a sloop commanded by Capt. Beer, belonging to Boston, in the lat. of South Carolina, 40 leagues from land. They put the said captain on board the Whidaw, while they rifled and plundered his vessel, which Williams and Bellamy proposed returning to him, but the crews being averse to it, they sunk her, and put the captain ashore upon Block Island.

I cannot pass by in silence, Capt. Bellamy's speech to Capt. Beer. *I am sorry they won't let you have your sloop again, for I scorn to do any one a mischief, when it is not for my advantage; — the sloop, we must sink her, and she might be of use to you. Though you are a sneaking puppy, and so are all those who will submit to be governed by laws which rich men have made for their own security? for the cowardly whelps have not the courage otherwise to defend what they get by their knavery; but ye altogether: them for a pack of crafty rascals, and you, who serve them, for a parcel of hen-hearted numskulls. They vilify us, the scoundrels do, when there is only this difference, they rob the poor under the cover of law, forsooth, and we plunder the rich under the protection of our own courage. Had you not belter make one of us, than sneak after these villains for employment?* Captain Beer told him, that his conscience would not allow him to break through the laws of God and man. *You are a devilish conscience rascal,* replied Bellamy; *I am a free prince, and I have as much authority to make war on the whole world, as he who has a hundred sail of ships at sea, and an army of 100,000 men in the field; and this my conscience tells me: but there is no arguing with such sniveling puppies, who allow superiors to kirk them about deck at pleasure.*

The pirates, wanting neither provisions nor water, and the Widaw's damage being repaired, passed the time very jovially.

A fortnight after setting Capt. Beer ashore, Williams boarded and took a vessel off Cape Cod, laden with wine; the crew of which increased the number of their prisoners. They put seven men on board the prize, with orders to keep company with the ship and sloop, and left on board her the master.

As they had been long off the careen, they stood away to the northward, and made the best of their way to Penobscot river. When they were at the mouth of it, it was thought more eligible to careen in the river Mechisses. They entered it as agreed, and run up about two miles and a half, where they came to an anchor with their prizes. The next morning all the prisoners were set ashore with drivers, and orders to assist in building huts; the guns were also set ashore, and a breast work raised, with embrasures for the cannon on each side of the river. This took up four days. A magazine was dug deep in the earth, and a roof raised over it by the poor slaves, the prisoners, whom they treated after the same manner as the negroes are used by the West-India planters. The powder being secured, and everything out, they hove down the sloop, cleaned her, and when she had all in again, they careened the Whidaw by the largest prize.

They now thought of cruising again, and accordingly steered for Fortune's Bay in Newfoundland. They made some prizes on the Banks, forced all the men, and sunk the vessels.

They had not been long on this coast before they were separated by a storm, which held some days. Off the island of St. Paul the Whidaw spied a sail, which she immediately gave chase to. The ship brought to and lay by for her, and proved a Frenchman of 36 guns, carrying soldiers to Quebec. The Whidaw engaged with great resolution, and the French did not show less, for he boarded the Whidaw and was twice put off, with the loss of men on both sides. Bellamy, after two hour's engagement, thought the Frenchman too hard a match, and was for shaking him off; but his enemy was not as willing to part with him, for he gave chase, and as he sailed altogether as well as Bellamy, the latter had certainly been taken, and had received the due punishment of his crimes, had not the night coming on favoured his escape. He lost in this engagement 36 hands, besides several wounded.

The Whidaw returned to the coast of Newfoundland, and off Placentia Bay met with his consort and the prize. They resolved to visit again the coast of New-England, the Whidaw being much shattered in the late engagement, having received a great many shot in her hull. They ran down this coast, and between St. George's Banks and Nantucket Shools, took the Mary Anne.

The master of the vessel, taken formerly off Cape Cod, was left on board her, and as he was very well acquainted with the coast, they ordered him to carry the light and go ahead; and the pirates commonly kept him at the helm. He upon a night of public rejoicing, seeing all the pirates drunk, laid hold of the opportunity, and run his vessel ashore about midnight, near the land of Eastham, out of which he alone escaped with life. The Whidaw, steering after the light, met with the same fate. The small vessel ran into a sandy bay, and the men got ashore without difficulty.

When the Whidaw struck, the pirates murdered all their prisoners, that is, all their forced men; as it is concluded, from the mangled carcasses which were washed ashore; but not a soul escaped out of her or Williams, who was also lost.

The pirates, to the number of seven, who escaped, were seized by the inhabitants, and on the information of the master who escaped, and on their own confession were imprisoned, condemned, and executed. They were all foreigners, very ignorant and obstinate; but by the indefatigable pains of a pious and learned divine, who constantly attended them; they were at length, by the special grace of God, made sensible of, and truly penitent, for the enormous crimes they had been guilty of.

Captain William Fly

As to the birth of this pirate, we can discover nothing by the inquiries we have hitherto made; and indeed had we succeeded in our search, it would have been of no great consequence; for it is certain by the behaviour of the man, he must have been of very obscure parents; and by his education, (as he was no artist) very unfit in all respects, except that of cruelty, for the villainous business he was in. We have been informed, that he had been in a pirate in a private capacity, and having escaped justice, had an opportunity of re-

77

penting his former crimes, and as a foremast man, or petty officer, of getting his bread in a warrantable way. But no — ignorant as he was of letters, he was ambitious of power, and capable of the most barbarous actions to acquire it.

Capt. Green, of Bristol, in April, 1726, shipped this Fly as boatswain, at Jamaica, being bound, in the Elizabeth snow, of Bristol, for the coast of Guinea. Fly, who had insinuated himself with some of the men, whom he found ripe for any villany, resolved to seize the said snow, and murder the captain and mate, and taking the command on himself, turn pirate. He proposed this design to his brothers in iniquity, who approving it, he, having the watch at one o'clock in the morning, on the 27th day of May, went up to one Morrice Cundon, then at the helm, accompanied by Alexander Mitchel, Henry Hill, Samuel Cole, Thomas Winthrop, and other conspirators, and swore if he spoke one word, or stirred either hand or foot, he would blows his brains out; and tucking up his shirt above the elbows with a cutlass in his hand, he, with Mitchel, went into the captain's cabin, and told him he must turn out. The captain, asking what was the matter, was answered by Mitchel, they had no time to answer impertinent questions; that if he would turn out and go upon deck quietly, it would save them the trouble of scraping the cabin; if he would not, a few buckets of water and a scraper would take his blood out of the deck: that they had chosen Capt. Fly for commander, and would allow of no other, and would not waste their provisions to feed useless men.

The Captain replied, that since they had so resolved, he should make no resistance; but begged they would not murder him, since his living could be no obstacle to their designs; that he had never been harsh to either of them, and therefore they could not kill him out of revenge; and if it w 7 as only for their security, he desired, if they would not take his word to do nothing to obstruct the measures they had resolved on, they would secure him in irons, till he might be put somewhere on shore, *Ah,* says Fly, *to live and hang us, if we are ever taken: no, no, walk up, that, bite won't take; it has hanged many an honest fellow already.* Mitchel and Fly then laying hold of him, pulled him out of his bed. The poor captain entreating them to spare his life for his soul's sake, told them he would bind himself down by the most solemn oaths, never to appear against them; that he was unfit to appear before the judgment seat of a just and pure God; that he was loaded with sins, and to take him off before he had washed those stains, which sullied his soul, by the tears of repentance, would be a cruelty beyond comparison greater than that of depriving him of life, were he prepared for death, since it would be, without any offence committed against them, dooming him to eternal misery. However, if they would not be persuaded that his life was consistent with their safety, he begged they would allow some time to prepare himself for the great change: that he begged no other mercy than what the justice and compassion of the laws would allow them, should they hereafter be taken. -- *your blood*, said Mitchel, *no preaching. Be -- a' you will, what's that to us? Let him look out who has the watch. Upon deck you dog, for ice shall lose no more time about you.*

They hauled him into the steerage, and forced him upon deck, where one of the hell-hounds asked if he had rather take a leap like a brave fellow, or be tossed over like a sneaking rascal? The captain addressing himself to Fly, said, B*oatswain, for God's sake don't throw me overboard; if you do I am for ever lost; Hell's the portion of my crimes — him*, answered Fly, s*ince he's so Godly, we'll give him time to say his prayers, and I'll be parson. Say after me.* Lord have mercy on me. S*hort prayers are best, so no more words and over with him, my lads.* The captain still cried for mercy, and begged an hour's respite only, but all in vain; he was seized by the villains and thrown overboard. Me caught, however, and hung by the main sheet, which Winthrop seeing, fetched the cooper's broad axe, and chopping off the unhappy master's hand,' he was swallowed up by the sea.

The captain being thus dispatched, Thomas Jenkins, the mate, was secured and brought upon deck, to share the same cruel fate. His entreaties were as useless as the captain's; the sentence they had passed upon him was not to be reversed; they were deaf to his prayers and remonstrances, strangers to humanity and compassion. He was of the captain's mess, they said, and they should e'en drink together; it was a pity to part good company.

Thus they jested with his agonies. He, however, made some struggle, which irritating his murderers one of them snatched up the axe, with which Winthrop had lopped off the captain's hand, and gave him a great cut on the shoulder, by missing his head, where the blow was aimed, and he was thrown into the sea. He swam notwithstanding, and called out to the doctor to throw him a rope, who, poor man, could not hear him, being secured, and laid in irons in his own cabin; and had he heard, and been able to have thrown the rope required, could it be expected that these hardened wretches would have relented, and shown him mercy. But the sinking man will catch at a straw, and hope, they say, is the last that deserts us. While we have life we are apt to flatter ourselves some lucky accident may favour us.

It was next debated what should be done with the doctor. Some were for sending him to look after the captain and mate; but the majority, as he was a useful man, thought it better to keep him. All obstacles being removed, Mitchel saluted Fly captain, and with the rest of the crew who had been in the conspiracy, with some ceremony, gave him possession of the great cabin.

Here a bowl of punch being made, Morice Cundon was called down, and one John Fitzherbert, set to the helm in his place. At the same time the carpenter and Thomas Streaton were brought before the captain, who told them they were three rascals, and richly deserved to be sent after the captain and mate, but that they were willing to show them mercy, and not put them to death in cold blood and he would therefore only put them in irons, for the security of the ship's crew. They were accordingly ordered out, and ironed. Fly then told his comrades it was convenient to resolve on some course, when word was brought them, that a ship was very near them. The council broke up, and made a clear ship, when in a very little while after, they found it was the Pompey, which had left Jamaica in company with the snow. The

Pompey, standing for the snow which did not make from her, soon hailed and asked how Capt. Green did, and was answered by Fly, that he was very well. They did not think fit to attack this ship, but returned to hold their consultation, it was resolved to steer for North Carolina.

Upon their arrival on that coast they spied a sloop at anchor within the bar. She was called the John and Hannah, and commanded by Capt. Fulker who thinking the snow might want a pilot, stepped into his boat with his mate, Mr. Atkinson, and Mr. Roan, two passengers, and a young lad, in order to bring her in. When they came on board, they were told, that the snow was from Jamaica, with a cargo. Capt. Fulker and Mr Roan were desired to walk down to the captain, who was in the cabin. Fly received them very civilly, ordered a bowl of punch, and hearing Capt. Fulker had brought another passenger on board Mr. Atkinson was also invited down.

The punch being brought in, Capt. Fly told his guest, *that he was no man to mince matters; that he and his comrades were gentlemen of fortune, and should make hold to try if Capt. Fulker's sloop was a better sailer than the snow. If she was, she would prove much jitter for their business, and they must have her.* The snow came to an anchor about a league off the sloop, and Fly ordered Fulker, with six of his own hands, into the boat to bring her along side of the snow; but the wind proving contrary, their endeavours proved also vain, and they returned again in the boat, bringing Capt. Fulker back with them. As soon as they got on board the snow, Fly fell into a violent passion, cursing and abusing Fulker for not bringing off the sloop. He gave him his reason, and said it was impossible. *You lie you dog,* replied the pirate, *but your hide shall pay for your roguery, and if I can't bring her off, I'll burn her where she lies.* He then ordered Cupt. Fulker to the geers; no reason, no arguments could prevail; he was stripped and lashed after a very inhuman manner; and the boat's crew being sent again, with much ado carried her off as far as the bar, where she bilged and sunk. The pirates then endeavoured to set what remained of her out of water on fire, but they could not burn her.

The snow getting under sail to look out for some booty, Fulker and the others desired they might be set at liberty, but it was denied them for the present, though not without a promise that they should be released the first vessel they took. On the 5th of June they left Carolina, and the next day spied a sail, which proved the John and Betty, commanded by Capt. Gale, bound from Barbadoes to Guinea. Fly gave chase, but finding the ship wronged him, lie made a signal of distress, hoisting his jack at the main-top-mast head; but this decoy did not hinder the ship making the best of her way. Fly continued the chase all night, and the wind slackening, he came within shot of the ship, and fired several guns at her under his black ensign. The ship being of no force, and the pirates ready to board, the captain struck; and Fly, manning his long-boat, the crew being well armed with pistols and cutlasses, went on board the prize, and sent Capt. Gale, after having secured his men, prisoner on board the snow This prize was of little value to the pirates, who took nothing but some sail-cloth and small arms, and after two days let her go, but took away six of his men, setting on board Capt. Fulker, a passenger, and Capt. Green's surgeon. They kept Mr. Atkinson, knowing he was a good artist, and lately master of the Boneta brigantine, as a pilot for the coast of New-England, which they were satisfied he was well acquainted with.

Upon Mr. Atkinson's desiring to have his liberty with the others, Capt. Fly refused it with the most horrid oaths and imprecations, and insisted upon it that he should act as their pilot; assuring him at the same time, if he pilotted them wrongs his life should be the forfeit.

Mr. Atkinson answered, it was very hard he should be forced to take upon himself the pilotage, when he did not pretend to know the coast, and that his life should answer for any mistake his ignorance of it might make him guilty of, and therefore begged he might be set on board Capt. Gale; and that they would trust their own knowledge, since he did not doubt their being better artist on board. *No no* replied Fly, *that won't do — your palavering won't save your bacon,; so either discharge your trust like an honest man, (for go you shan't) or Til send you with my service to the d—l: so no more words about the matter.*

There was no reply made, and they stood for the coast of New-England. Off Delaware Bay they made a sloop, commanded by one Harris, bound from NewYork to Pennsylvania. She had on board about fifty passengers. Fly gave chase, and coming up with her, hoisted his black ensign, and ordered her to strike, which she immediately did; and Fly sent Capt. Atkinson on board, to sail her, though he would not allow him (Atkinson) any arms, The pirates ransacked this prize, but not finding her of any use to them, after a detention of 24 hours, they let her go, with her men, excepting only a well made young fellow, whose name was James Benbrooke, whom they kept.

Fly, after having released the prize, ordered Capt. Atkinson to carry the snow into Martha's Vineyard, but he wilfully missed this place. Fly, finding himself beyond Nantucket, and that has design was balked, called to Atkinson, and told him *he was a rascally scoundrel, and that it was a piece of cruelty to let such a villain live, who designed the death of so many honest fellows.* Atkinson, in his defence, said, he never pretended to know the coast, and that it was very hard he should die for being thought an abler man than he really was. Had he pretended to be their pilot, and did not know his business, he deserved punishment; but when he was forced upon a business which he before declared he did not understand, it would be certainly cruel to make him suffer for their mistake. *You are an obstinate villain* replied Fly, *and your design is to hang us; but blood and wounds, you dog, you shall live to see it —* and saying this, he ran into his cabin and brought a pistol, with design to shoot Atkinson; but by the interposition of Mitchel, who thought him innocent of any design, he escaped.

Atkinson, who perceived his life every minute in danger, began to ingratiate himself with the pirates and gave them hopes, that with good and gentle usage, he might be brought to join them. This he did not say in express terms, but by words he now and then let drop, as by accident. They were not a little rejoiced at the idea of having so good artist to join them; nay some of them hinted to him, that if he would take upon him the command, they were ready to dispossess Capt. Fly, who carried his command too high, and was known to all the crew to be no artist, and to understand nothing beyond the business of a boatswain. Atkinson thought it his interest to keep them in the opinion that he would join; but always declined hearing any thing as to the command.

This made him less severely used, and protected him from the insults of Fly, who imagined he would betray them the first opportunity, therefore, more than once proposed his being thrown overboard, which was never approved by the snow's company.

From Nantucket they stood to the eastward, and off Brown's Bank made a fishing schooner. Fly, coming up with her, fired a gun, and hoisting his black ensign, swore, *if they did not instantly bring to, and send their boat on board, he would sink her.* The schooner obeyed, and sent away her boat on board the snow. He examined the captain as to what vessels were to be met with, and promised, if he could put him in the way of meeting with a good sailor, to let him go, and give him his vessel, or he should otherwise keep her. The poor man told him he had a companion which would soon be in sight, and was a much better vessel. Accordingly about 12 at noon, the same day, which was the 23d of June, the other schooner hove in sight; upon which Fly manned this prize with six pirates and a prisoner named George Tasker, and sent her in chase, having himself on board the snow, no more than three pirates, Capt. Atkinson, (who had worked himself into some favour with him) and fifteen forced men; but he took care to have his arms upon deck by him.

The men who had not taken on with Fly, were, Atkinson, Capt. Fulker's mate, and two youths belonging to him; the carpenter and gunner belonging to Capt. Green; six of Capt. Gale's men, and the aforesaid Benbrooke, who belonged to Capt. Harris, with three of the men out of the schooner. Atkinson, seeing the prisoners and forced men were five to one of the pirates, thought of delivering himself from the bondage he was in: and as by good luck several other fishing vessels hove in sight, right ahead of the snow, he called to Capt. Fly, and told him he spied several other vessels ahead, desiring he would come forward and bring his glass. Fly did so, and leaving his arms on the quarter deck, set on the windlass to see if he could make out what they were. Atkinson, who had concerted his measures with one Walker and the above mentioned Benbrooke, secured the arms on the quarter deck, and gave them a signal to seize Fly; which they did, with very little trouble, and afterwards made themselves masters of the other three pirates and the snow, the rest of the prisoners, not knowing any thing of, or what the design might be, remaining altogether inactive, and brought the snow and pirates to Great Brewster, where a guard was put on board, June 28, 1726.

Soon after, the said pirates were brought to their trial, that is, on the 4th of July following, before the Honourable William Dumnier, Esq. Lieutenant Governor and commander in chief of the province of Massachusetts Bay, President of the Special Court of Admiralty, at the court-house of Boston, assisted by 18 gentlemen of the council; before whom they were found guilty of murder and piracy condemned to be executed, and accordingly were executed the 12th of July. Fly was ordered to be hanged in chains at the entrance of the harbour of Boston. Thus ended the short reign of an obdurate wretch, who only wanted skill and power to be as infamous as any who scoured the seas. The names of the three pirates, executed with him, were, Samuel Cole, George Condick, and Henry Greenvil.

Captain Thomas Howard

We have said, in another life, viz. White's that he was a lighterman on the river Thames. His father was of that business, and had the character of a very honest man. After his father's decease, he grew very extravagant, and squandered away not only what he had left his son, but what he had allotted for his widow, whose indulgence, putting every thing into her son's hands, was followed by being herself turned out of doors, for he sold the house over her head. After having ruined himself and mother, his friends fearing the wickedness of his inclination would bring scandal upon them, persuaded him to go to sea, and procured him a voyage to Jamaica, on board a merchant ship. At this island he ran away from his ship, and associating himself with some desperate fellows, they stole a canoe, and went away to the Grand Camanas, to join some others of their own stamp, who lurked thereabouts, with design *to go on the account,* the term for pirating. They met those they looked for, made up a company of 20 men, surprised and made themselves masters of a turtling sloop, and set out in search of booty.

The first prizes they made were only turtlers, which, however, increased the number of their crew, some being willing to join them, others being forced, with threats of being set on shore, on some desolate key. After some time cruising, they met with an Irish brigantine, which had provisions and servants on board. They made an exchange with the master, gave him provision to carry him to Jamaica, and allowed five hands to go with him. The rest (except the servants, who readily took on with the pirates) were all forced. Not long after, they surprised a sloop which had been trading on the Spanish coast. As she had 6 guns, and was a fit vessel for their turn, they changed her against the brigantine. Several hands belonging to this sloop entered volunteers, and several more were obliged to join them by compulsion. After this capture, they steered for the coast of Virginia, and in their way, met with a large New England brigantine, laden with provisions bound for Barbadoes. This they made prize of, and shifting their own guns on board her, sent the master away with the sloop, after forcing some of his men with them. They had now a vessel of ten guns, and a crew of 80 men, of whom one James was captain, and Howard quartermaster.

While they lay on the coast of Virginia, they made prize of several ships from England, out of which they took men, liquors, provisions, clothes and whatever else they liked or thought necessary. As these ships had several felons on board, who were transports, they had out of them a number of volunteers, besides forced men; so that they had a large complement. Among other Virginia ships which fell into their hands, they made prize, with little trouble, of a fine galley, mounted with 24 guns, which afforded them a great many volunteers, as she had a number of transported malefactors and servants on board. They changed their brigantine for this ship, and soon after, the man of war, which waited on this coast, heaving in sight, they thought proper to take their departure.

From the coast of Virginia, they shaped their course for that of Guinea, where they took a great many ships of different nations, all which they rifled of what they thought fit. Out of these ships they forced on board a number of men, equal to the number of those formerly compelled, who desired, and whom they permitted, to be discharged, after much entreaty.

After they had been some months on the coast, they spied a large three decked Portuguese ship, from Brazil, mounted with 36 guns. They gave chase and came up with her. The captain would make no resistance; but his mate, who was an Englishman, named Rutland, thinking it a shame to give up such a ship, resolved to defend her; which the Portuguese captain consented to, but went himself out of harm's way. Rutland, who had been master of an English brigantine, taken from him on the same coast by another gang of pirates, fought them the better part of a forenoon; but the Portuguese flying the decks, and only 30 men, who were English, Dutch, and French, standing by him, he was obliged to ask quarters, which were given. When the pirates came on board, they asked Rutland if he was commander? He answered, no. They inquired after him, and being told he was some where in the hold, they searched, and found him hid in the powder room; whence they hauled him up, and whipped him round the deck for his cowardice. Rutland, and those who fought the ship, were forced on board, and their complement being now 180 men, they exchanged their galley for the Portuguese ship, carried her in shore, and ripping off her upper deck, made her deep waisted, by cutting down some of her gunnel. This prize they named the Alexander.

They went down the coast in this ship, and made several prizes, some of which they discharged, and put on board such of their forced men as begged their discharge; others they sunk, and burnt others.; but forced on board carpenters, caulkers, armourers, surgeons, and musicians. In their way to Cape Lopez, where they designed, and afterwards did clean, they found a large Bristol ship at an anchor, which had lost a great many men by sickness, and had then but few healthy on board, who got into the boat, and endeavoured to get on shore, but were prevented by the pirates. Here they changed some more of their forced men, and did intend to change their ship; but on a survey, found the Bristol ship too old for their purpose, and therefore left her at an anchor, after they had taken what they thought of use to them. This ship belonged to one Mr. Godly, of Bristol.

They met with nothing else in their way to Cape Lopez, where they cleaned their ship, took in wood and water, and then stood away to sea again. At their leaving Cape Lopez, they spied an English ship, which they came up with and engaged. The merchantman made an obstinate defence, and finding the design to board, made to close quarters. Howard, and seven or eight more, entered; but the pirate's boatswain not having secured his lashing, they fell astern, and left these men on board the merchant ship, who seeing themselves in danger, hauled up the boat, which the chase had astern, and cutting the rope, got on board the Alexander, which being considerably the larger ship, and drawing a great deal more water, struck on an unknown bank, which the merchantman went over, and by this lucky accident escaped.

This obliged the pirates to start their water, and throw over the wood to get the ship off, which put them under a necessity of going back to Cape Lopez to take in those necessaries. After having a second time wooded and watered, they put again to sea, fell in with and took two Portuguese brigantines, which they burnt, and setting the men on shore, they made for, and doubled the Cape of Good Hope, and shaped their course for Madagascar, where to the northward of, and near a small island, they run the ship on a reef, where she stuck fast The captain being then sick in his bed, the men went ashore on the small adjacent island, and carried off a great deal of provisions and water to lighten the ship, on board of which none but the captain, the quartermaster, and about eleven more were left.

The quartermaster, who was Howard, with the others, took all the treasure, put it on board the boats, and made off for the main of Madagascar. The captain, hearing nobody stir upon deck, made shift to crawl out of his cabin, and seeing them put off, fired the two fore chase guns at them, which alarmed (to no purpose) the men ashore. As the sea ebbed, the ship Jay dry, and they could walk to her from the island. She might have been saved had they the boats to carry out an anchor; but for want of them they brought everything ashore, at tide of flood, upon rafts. As the ship lay in a quiet place, they had opportunity to rip her up, and build a vessel out of her wreck. The major part of the crew being English and Dutch who sided together, they forced about 36 Portuguese and French (thinking their crew two numerous for their provisions in the present circumstances) to get upon a raft, and take their chance with the sea-breeze to get to the island of Madagascar, about three leagues from them. They finished a vessel of 60 tons, but the day they designed to have launched her, a pirate brigantine hove in sight, who took them on board.

Howard and his consorts stood along the W. side of the island, with design to round the N. end, and to go to St. Mary's but finding the current too strong to stem, they lay there about a fortnight. In the interim they spied three sail of tall ships, which were men of war under Commodore Littleton, viz. the Anglesa, Hastings, and Lizard, who had carried a pardon to the island of St.

Mary's, accepted of by many of the pirates. Thinking these might be also pirates, they made a smoke, which brought the boats ashore; but finding they were men of war's boats, the pirates thought fit to abscond; wherefore, finding nothing nor anybody, the said men of war's boats returned, and the ships kept their cruise.

They had here plenty of fish and wild hogs which they found in the woods. One day, when Howard was hunting, his comrades took the opportunity, went off, rounded the north end, and left Mr. Howard to provide for himself.

About four or five-and-twenty leagues from the Cape, they went into a fine harbour on the east side, not frequented, nay, hardly known to the European ships. They were here received handsomely, treated and provided with fresh meat, and what necessaries they wanted, by the king of this district, whose name was Mushmango, who had formerly been driven from Augustin by war, and travelling through the heart of the country, had here fixed his settlement. When the boats were victualled, and while Johnson, who took on him the command after they had deserted Howard, was ashore with three more, the rest went off with the boats and booty, and stood away to the southward, along the coast, designing for St. Mary's, going every night into some harbour, or coming to an anchor under some point when the winds proved contrary.

Johnson addressed himself to the king, and told him the boat and goods were his property; upon which he went along shore with a number of men, and found the boat at an anchor, and all asleep, except one to look out, at whom the king fired his blunderbuss, and killed him. The report of the piece awakened the others, who cut and stood on the coast. The king returned, gave Johnson an account of his expedition, and furnished him a canoe, some calabashes of fresh water, provisions and lances, that he might pursue after his people, Johnson kept the shore on board till he came to the island of St. Mary's, where he heard his comrade fugitives were gone to, and settled at Ambonavoula, in a village belonging to the natives on the river of Manansallang. Leaving his canoe, he went into one belonging to an inhabitant, who carried him to his companions.

After he had been here some few months, Fourgette, already mentioned in White's life, came in with his ship from Martinico. With this vessel they sailed to the west side, and came to an anchor at an island called Anquawla, 30 leagues from the place where they left Howard.

Some of the subjects of the king of Anquawla had before met with, and brought hither, Capt. Howard, who seeing the ship at anchor near shore, hailed her, and desired the boat might be sent to fetch him. off, which was accordingly done, and he joined the rest of the crew. Here two boys ran away from them, whom they demanded of the king; but he not delivering them, they went ashore by day-break, surprised his town, and brought off twelve of his concubines, whom they detained on board, till their boys, who were blacks, were returned, and then delivered them back. From this ship he went on board the Speaker, where he continued till she was lost on Mauritius, when he came back to Madagascar, and settled at Augustin. Here he tarried till the Prosperous, a ship of 36 guns, commanded by Capt. Hilliard, came in, which Howard and some other pirates (with the assistance of the boatswain and some of the crew belonging to the ship,) seized. In taking this ship, the captain and his chief mate were killed and several others wounded, Howard was by the company declared captain. Several of the ships crew took on with them, and they went round the south end to the east side, till they came the length of Maritan, where they found some of the Speaker's company, whom they took on board, and made up their complement about 70 men.

From hence they steered for the island of St. Mary's, where they heeled their ship, watered, wooded, and shipped some more hands. Here they had an invitation from one Ort Van Tyle, who lived on the main of Madagascar, to come to the ceremony of christening two of his children. They were kindly received and treated by him, but it having been reported that this Ort Van Tyle had murdered some pirates, they in revenge, though they had no certainty of the fact, took him prisoner, plundered his house, and what goods they could not take off in a great canoe belonging to him, they threw into the river or burnt. Ort Van Tyle they designed to carry on board, and hang at the yard-arm; but one of the pirates helped him to escape, and he took into the woods, where meeting some of his blacks, he waylaid his canoe and Howard's pinnace by the river side. Besides what goods they had on board of this Dutchman's they had several women and children belonging to him and some white men, who had left them under his care. The pirates set the women to the paddles, and the canoe was overset on the bar; Ort Van Tyle fired on the men, and shot one through the arm and through the thigh, whom with his comrade, he took prisoner, and kept with him. The rest of the men got ashore on the south side of the river and escaped him; the women on the north side, and returned home. When the pinnace came down, he fired and shot the captain through the arm, but he got on board, where his arm was set. After this, the Prosperous sailed for Metheiage, where they victualled, with a design to go to the East-Indies. While they lay here, came in a large Dutch ship, well manned, and of 40 guns. The Prosperous was not strong enough to attack her, and the Dutch, fearing he should spoil his trade, would not meddle with Howard, though hard words passed, and the Dutchman threatened to fall foul on him if he did not leave the place, which Howard thought fit to do, and sailed to Mayotta.

A few days after the departure of the Prosperous, Capt. Bowen, in the Scotch ship, came in, anchored within small arm shot, and right a head of the Dutchman, whom he saluted with 11 guns, shot and all, which the other returned with 15, after the same manner; drums heating and trumpets sounding on both sides. The Dutchman, however, was surprised, and under apprehensions. He hailed the pirate, and answer was returned, *From the seas.* He then bid them send their boat on board, which accordingly went with the quartermaster, who told the captain, that they had no design on him, but were going against the Moors, and came in for provision. He replied, they could get none there, and the best way was to be gone; however, the quartermaster went ashore, (where the Dutch had made his factory, and had some goods) and shot down three oxen, which he ordered the natives to help to cut in pieces. The Dutchman, perceiving a friendship between the natives and pirates, seeing Bowen full of men, and hearing two more pirates were expected, thought fit to go off in the night, and leave the goods he had put on shore.

A few days after, Bowen, seizing the goods left, went for Mayotta, where he joined the Prosperous, and lay for the season to go to the East-Indies. After some stay here, their salt provision perishing, they returned to Madagascar to revictual, Bowen to St. Augustin, and Howard (onboard of whose ship was Capt. Whatey, taken as related in Bowen's life) to Methelage, agreeing to meet at the island of St. Johns, to lie for the Moors fleet; whereafter some disappointments, they met, and got sight of the Moors fleet, one of which fell a prize to Bowen; but the Prosperous being a heavy sailer, did not come up with them till they were at an anchor at the bar of Surat, where they waited to lighten. The Moors seeing few hands on board, for Howard concealed his men, and not imagining a pirate would venture up, concluded him an English East Indiaman Howard clapped the largest on board, which stood him a smart engagement and killed him about 30 men. At length the pirates forced Capt. Whaley who spoke the Moors language to go on board and offer quarter, which they excepted. There was on board this prize a nobleman belonging to the Great Mogul, who had been at Jaffa to buy horses for his master. The prize yielded them a great booty, though they found but part of the money which was on board. They intended to carry her to Madagascar, but her bowsprit being wounded in the boarding, she lost all her masts; wherefore they sent her adrift, and she ran ashore at Deman, belonging to the Portuguese.

From hence he steered to the Malabar coast, where he met Bo wen and his prize, which mounted 58 guns. Both crews went on board Bowen, sunk the Prosperous, and burnt the Scotch ship, called the Speedy Return. Hence they stood along the coast of India; and Howard, with about 20 more, landed with what they had, and retired among the natives, where Howard married a women of the country, and being a morose, ill-natured fellow and using her ill, he was murdered by her relations.

Captain Lewis

This worthy gentleman was an early pirate. We first find him a boy on board the pirate Banister, who was hanged at the yard arm of a man of war in sight of Port Royal, Jamaica. This Lewis and another boy were taken with him. and brought into the island hanging by the middle at the mizen peak. He had a great aptitude for languages, and spoke perfectly well that of the Mosquil Indians, French, Spanish, and English. I mention, our own, because it is doubted whether he was French or English, for we cannot trace him back to his origin, He sailed out of Jamaica till he was a lusty lad, and was then taken by the Spaniards at the Havana, where he tarried some time; but at length he and six more ran away with a small canoe, and surprised a Spanish periagua, out of which two men joined them, so that they were now nine in company. With this periagua they surprised a turtling sloop, and forced some of the hands to take on with them; the others they sent away in the periagua.

He played at this small game, surprising and taking coasters and turtlers, till with forced men and volunteers he made up a company of 40 men. With these he took a large pink built ship, bound from Jamaica to the bay of Campeachy, and after her, several others bound to the same place; and having intelligence that there lay in the bay a fine Bermuda built brigantine of 10 guns, commanded by Capt. Tucker, he sent the captain of the pink to him with a letter, the purport of which was, that he wanted such a brigantine, and if he would part with her, he would pay him 10,000 pieces of eight; if he refused this, he would take care to lie in his way, for he was resolved, either by fair or foul means to have the vessel. Capt. Tucker, having read the letter sent for the masters of vessels then lying in the bay, and told them, after he had shown the letter, that if they would make him up 54 men, (for there were about 10 Bermuda sloops) he would go out and fight the pirates. They said no, they would not hazard their men, they depended on their sailing, and every one must take care of himself as well as he could.

However, they all put to sea together, and spied a sail under the land, which had a breeze while they lay becalmed. Some said he was a turtler; others, the pirate, and so it proved; for it was honest Capt. Lewis, who putting out his oars, got in among them. Some of the sloops had four guns, some two, some none. Joseph Dill had two, which he brought on one side, and fired smartly at the pirate, but unfortunately one of them split, and killed three men. Tucker called to all the sloops to send him men, and he would fight Lewis, but to no purpose; nobody came on board him. In the mean while a breeze sprung up, and Tucker, trimming his sails, left them, who all fell a prey to the pirate; into whom, however,' he fired a broadside at going off. One sloop, whose master I will not name, was a very good sailor, and was going off; but Lewis firing a shot, brought her to, and he lay by till all the sloops were visited and secured. Then Lewis sent on board him, and ordered the master into his sloop. As soon as he was on board, he asked the reason of his lying by, and betraying the trust his owners had reposed in him, which was doing like a knave and coward, and he would punish him accordingly; *for,* said he, *you might have got off, being so much a, better sailor than my vessel.* After this speech, he fell upon him with a rope's end, and then snatching up his cane, drove him about the decks without mercy. The master, thinking to pacify him, told him he had been out trading in that sloop several months, and had on hoard a good quantity of money, which was hid, and which, if he would send on board a black belonging to the owners, he would discover to him. This had not the desired effect, but one quite contrary; for Lewis told him he was a rascal and villain for this discovery, and he would pay him for betraying his owners, and redoubled his strokes. However, he sent and took the money and negro, who was an able sailor. He took out of his prizes what he had occasion for, 40 able negro sailors, and a white carpenter. The largest sloop, which was about 90 tons, he took for his own use, and mounted her with 12 guns. His crew was now about 80 men, whites and blacks.

After these captures, he cruised in the Gulf of Florida, laying in wait for the West-India homeward bound ships that took the leeward passage, several of which, falling into his hands, were plundered by him, and released. From hence he went to the coast of Carolina, where he cleaned his sloop, and a great many men whom he had forced, ran away from him. However, the natives traded with him for rum and sugar, and brought him all he wanted, without the government's having any knowledge of him, for he had got into a very private creek; though he was very much on his guard, that he might not be surprised from the shore.

From Carolina he cruised on the coast of Virginia, where he took and plundered several merchantmen, and forced several men, and then returned to the coast of Carolina, where he did abundance of mischief. As he had now an abundance of French on board, who had entered with him, and Lewis, hearing the English had a design to maroon them, he secured the men he suspected, and put them in a boat, with all the other English, ten leagues from shore, with only ten pieces of beef, and sent them away, keeping none but French and negroes. These men, it is supposed all perished in the sea.

From the coast of Carolina he shaped his course for the banks of Newfoundland, where he overhauled several fishing vessels, and then went into Trinity Harbour in Conception Bay, where there lay several merchantmen, and seized a 24 gun galley, called the Herman. The commander, Capt. Beal, told Lewis, if he would send his quartermaster ashore he would furnish him with necessaries. He being sent ashore, a council was held among the masters, the consequence of which was, the seizing the quartermaster, whom they carried to Capt. Woodes Rogers. He chained him to a sheet anchor which was ashore, and planted guns at the point, to prevent the pirate getting out, but to little purpose; for the people atone of these points firing too soon, Lewis quitted the ship, and, by the help of oars and the favour of the night, got out in his sloop, though she received many shot in her hull. The last shot that was fired at the pirate did him considerable damage.

He lay off and on the harbour, swearing he would have his quartermaster, and intercepted two fishing shallops, on board of one of which was the captain of the galley's brother. He detained them, and sent word, if his quartermaster did not immediately come off, he would put all his prisoners to death. He was sent on board without hesitation. Lewis and the crew inquired how he had been used, and he answered, very civilly. "It's well," said the pirate, "for had you been ill-treated, I would have put all these rascals to the sword." They were dismissed, and the captain's brother going over the quartermaster stopped him, saying, he must drink the gentlemen's health ashore, particularly Capt. Rogers', and, whispering him in the ear, told him, if the crew had known of his being chained all night, he would have been cut in pieces, with all his men. After this poor man and his shallop's company were gone, the quartermaster told the usage he had met with, which enraged Lewis, and made him reproach his quartermaster, whose answer was, that he did not think it just the innocent should suffer for the guilty.

The masters of the merchantmen sent to Capt. Tudor Trevor, who lay at St. John's in the Sheerness man of war. He immediately got under sail, and missed the pirate but four hours. She kept along the coast and made several prizes, French and English, and put into a harbour where a French ship lay making fish. She was built at the latter end of the war, for a privateer, was an excellent sailor, and mounted 24 guns. The commander hailed him: the pirate answered, from Jamaica with mm and sugar, The Frenchman bid him go about his business; that a pirate sloop was on the coast, and he might be the rogue: if he did not immediately sheer off, he would fire a broadside into him. He went oft' and lay a fortnight out at sea, so far as not to be descried from shore, with resolution to have the ship. The Frenchman being on his guard, in the mean while raised a battery on the shore, which commanded the harbour. After a fortnight, when he was thought to be gone off, he returned, and took two of the fishing shallops belonging to the Frenchman, and manning them with pirates, they went in. One shallop attacked the battery; the other surprised, boarded, and carried the ship, just as the morning star appeared, for which reason he gave her that name. In the engagement the owner's son was killed, who made the voyage out of curiosity only. The ship being taken, seven guns were fired, which was the signal, and the sloop came down and lay alongside the ship. The captain told him lie supposed he only wanted his liquor; but Lewis made answer, he wanted his ship, and accordingly hoisted all his ammunition and provision into her. When the Frenchman saw they would have his ship, he told her trim, and Lewis gave him the sloop; and excepting what he took for provision, all the fish he had made. Several of the French took on with him, who, with others, English and French, had by force or voluntarily, made him up 200 men.

From Newfoundland he steered for the coast of Guinea, where he took a great many ships, English, Dutch, and Portuguese. Among these ships was one belonging to Carolina, commanded by Capt. Smith. While he was in chase of this vessel an accident happened, which made his men believe he dealt with the devil; for he carried away his fore and main-top-mast; he, Lewis, running up the shrouds to the main-top, tore off a handful of hair, and throwing it into the air, used this expression, good devil, take this till I come. And it was observed, that he came afterwards faster up with the chase than before the loss of his top-masts.

Smith being taken, Lewis used him very civilly, and gave him as much, or more in value than he took from him, and let him go, saying, he would come to Carolina when he had made money on the coast, and would rely on his friendship.

They kept some time on the coast, When they quarrelled among themselves, the French and English, of which the former was more numerous, and they resolved to part. The French therefore chose a large sloop newly taken, thinking the ship's bottom, which was not sheathed, damaged by the Worms. According to this agreement they took on board what ammunition and provision they thought fit out of the ship, and put off, choosing one Le Barre captain. As it blew hard, and the -decks were encumbered, they came to an anchor under the coast, to stow away their ammunition, goods, &c. Lewis told his men they were a parcel of rogues, and he would make them refund; accordingly run alongside, his guns being all loaded and new primed, and ordered him to cut away his mast, or he would sink him. Le Barre was obliged to obey. Then he ordered them all ashore. They begged the liberty of carrying their arms, goods, &c. with them, but he allowed them only their small arms and cartridge-boxes. Then he brought the sloop along side, put every thing on board the ship, and sunk the sloop.

Le Barre and the rest begged to be taken on board. However, though he denied them, he suffered Le Barre and some few to come, with whom lie and his men drank plentifully. The negroes on board Lewis told him the French had a plot against him. He answered, he could not withstand his destiny; for the devil told him in the great cabin, he should be murdered that night.

In the dead of the night, the rest of the French came on board in canoes, got into the cabin and killed Lewis. They fell on the crew; but, after an hour and a half's dispute, the French were beat off, and the quartermaster, John Cornelius an Irishman, succeeded Lewis.

Captain John Cornelius

Having now the command of the Morning Star, Cornelius kept on the coast, and made several prizes, both English and Portuguese. The former fie always discharged, after he had taken what he thought fit, but the latter he commonly burnt.

While he was thus ravaging the coast, two English ships, which had slaved at Whidaw, one of 56 guns, and the other 12, which fought close, were ready to sail; and having notice of a pirate, who had done great mischief, resolved to keep company together for their defence. The captain of the small ship lay sick in his cabin, and she was left to the care of the mates. When they had got under sail, 200 negroes jumped overboard from the larger ship, which obliged her to bring to and get out her boats. The mate of the other went into the cabin, told the accident, and advised lying by and sending their boats to assist their consort '; but the captain being ill, and willing to get off the coast, bid him keep on his way, for it would be dangerous; having 400 slaves on board; and being but weakly manned, when the boats were gone they might rise upon him. The mate urged the danger of the pirates, should they leave their consort. The captain answered, the seas were wide, and he would not bring to; accordingly they kept on their way with a fresh gale.

Two days after, the mate, about 8 in the morning, ordered a man to the mast-head, who spied a sail, which made them prepare for an engagement. There was on board one Robert Williams, who had served the African company three years on the Guinea coast, who spoke the negro tongue very well. He told the slaves he had picked out, to the number of 50, that the ship in sight he believed would fight them, and if they got the better, would certainly, as they were cannibals, kill and eat them all; and therefore it behooved them to fight for their lives. They had lances and small arms given them.

About 10, Cornelius came up with them, and being hailed, answered he was a man of war, in search of pirates, and bid them send their boat on board; but they refusing to trust him, though he had English colours and pendant flying, the pirate fired a broadside, and they began a running fight of about 10 hours, in which time the negroes discharged their arms so smartly, that Cornelius never durst attempt to board. About 8 at night the ship blew up abaft. They immediately cut the lashings of the long-boat, but the ship going down, they had not time to get her out, and barely enough to launch the yawl, which lay on the forecastle. The ship went down on one side, and Robert Williams running on the other, was hooked by the mizen-truss,, and was carried down with her; but having his knife in his hand, and a, great presence of mind, he cut the waistband of his trowsers, where he was caught, got clear, and swam after the boat, into which about 16 had gotten, and either knocked those on the head, or cut off their hands, who laid hold on it; however, with much entreaty, he was permitted to lay one hand on to ease him. They madeJo the pirate, who refused to receive them,, without they would enter with him: which, to save their lives, they all agreed to, and were then civilly received, and dry clothes given them. These and one negro were all the souls saved.

In a little time after this he took two Portuguese ships, which he plundered and kept with him: and one foggy morning, hearing the firing of guns, which by the distance of time, he judged to be minute guns, as they really were, for the death of an English commander, he called his men on board from the prizes, sent them about their business, and directed his course by the report of the cannon he had heard. In about two hours he spied the ship that had fired, came up with her very soon, and took her without resistance. The officers of the ship which blew up, finding this prize English, and that the pirate did not intend to detain her begged to be discharged, as they had all large families, which must perish without their support. Cornelius, taking them into considerations, discharged Mr. Powis of Limehouse, who has since been a commander, and raised a fortune. The then chief mate, Mr. George Forelong, the boatswain, carpenter, and other married men, he set on board the prize, and was very generous to them out of the plunder of the Portuguese ships, because they had made a broken voyage; but Robert Williams and the other bachelors he detained, and forced some out of the prize, which he let go.

After this he took three Portuguese ships at an anchor, which he plundered and burnt, after he had hove down -by one of them. He continued some time longer on the coast, did a great deal of mischief to the trade, and forced a great many men; these he put to do all the slavery of the ship, and they were beat about the decks, without daring to resent it. I shall take notice of an instance of this kind, to show how far revenge will carry a man. One Robert Bland was at the helm, and called Robert Williams to take whip staff, till he went to play. Williams refused it; upon which Bland drubbed him with the lanyard of the whipstaff very severely. Williams, that he might revenge himself, and have liberty to fight Bland, went that instant and entered himself a volunteer in the ship's books, and asked leave to fight Bland, which was allowed him, but with no other weapons than his fists. He, however, challenged his antagonist, who was too hard for him; so he turned pirate to be heartily thrashed.

Cornelius, thinking they had been long enough on the Guinea coast, doubled the Cape, off which he spied the Lizard, and two more men of war, under the command of Commodore Littleton. Cornelius was for giving chase, but finding his men unwilling there being, as they gave for reason, 70 forced men on board, and these ships being, as they suspected, men of war, he made the best of his way for Madagascar, went up the river Methelage, on the west side, and anchored against Pombotoque, a small village of blacks.

The quartermaster went ashore, and the black governor examined him, for several of these blacks speak English. He told the governor they were come for provision and to trade; upon which he sent a couple of oxen on board, and then ordered some of the inhabitants to go up with the quartermaster to the king. The boat's crew seeing a number of blacks come down to the strand without the quartermaster, apprehended some mischief had befallen him; but were eased of their fears, when they saw two oxen given them, and were told the 'white man, who was gone to the king, would be back next day, it not being above 20 miles from the shore.

When the quartermaster, who carried up a blunderbuss, a fine gun, and a pair of pistols, for a present to the king, told him they wanted provisions, heasked where they were bound? To which he answered, to seek their fortunes, for at present they were very poor. *Look ye,* replied the king, *I require nothing of you; all white men I look upon as my children; they helped me to conquer this country, and all the cattle in it are at their service. I will send down provisions' enough, and when that is spent, you shall have more.* He accordingly sent 1000 head of cattle, out of which he bid them choose what they would, and they salted 100 fat oxen.

Besides the present of oxen, the king sent 100 blacks laden with rice. Cornelius sent him a present of two barrels of powder, and would have given him more, with small arms in return, but he sent them word he would have no more, nor any of their arms, not being in want of either. On the contrary, if they wanted, he would send them ten barrels of powder, as they were his children; bade them proceed on their voyage, and if they were richer when they came back, and would send him any present, he would accept it, but not now, they were so poor.

Here Cornelius lost 70 men by their excesses. Having been long without fresh provisions. the eating immoderately, and drinking *toke* (a liquor made of honey) to excess, threw them into violent fevers, which carried them off.

The blacks, having given Cornelius an account of the Speaker's having sailed from Methelage about three months before for the East-Indies, he, having taken in his provisions, steered the same course, in hopes to join in consort with her; hat the Speaker lying off the Red Sea, and the Morning Star going into the Gulf of Persia, they never met. They run up a pretty way in the gulf, and lay under Antelope Island, where they kept a look out, and whence they made their excursions, and took a number of prizes.

Here they designed to heave down and clean, and they had got a good part of their goods and water casks ashore, when the look-out discovered two lofty ships, one of them wearing a flag at the foretop-mast head. This put them into great confusion: they got what casks and necessaries they could on board, and lay till the ships came abreast of them, when they got under sail at once, their sails being furled with rope yarns, and came close alongside the larger ship, which was a Portuguese of 70 guns, as the other was of 26. They exchanged a broadside with her, and the smaller ship engaged so close, that they threw hand grenades into each other; but Cornelius' business was to run, and the great ship put in stays twice to follow him, but missing, was obliged to ware, which gave the pirate a great advantage. The small ship, in staying tailed aground: she, however, gave chase till she had run a good way ahead of her consort, which the pirate seeing, brought to, and stayed for her, as did the Portuguese for her consort, not caring to engage him singly. When it was quite dark, Cornelius ran up the other shore, passed the Portuguese ships (which kept down the gulf) and came again to anchor at his old station, where he found his enemies had been ashore in their boats and stayed his casks. He here cleaned, and finding no money to be got out of any prizes made, and bale goods being of little value to them, they from hence went away to the island of Johanna, where it was designed to maroon the blacks, who were the greater number and all bred among the English. Robert Williams, fearing they would next maroon the English, who were not above a third of the whites, gave the negroes notice of the design, who secured all the arms of the ship, and gave Williams the command till they should get to Madagascar, keeping a good guard on the French and Dutch. When they came to Methelage they gave the ship to the king, her bottom being eaten so much with the worms that she was no longer fit for service; and they all went and lived with the king. About five months after they broke up, Cornelius died, and was buried with the usual ceremony.

Captain David Williams

This man was born in Wales, of very poor parents, who bred him up to the plough and the following of sheep, the only things he had any notion of till he went to sea. He was never esteemed among the pirates as a man of good natural parts, perhaps on account of his ignorance of letters; for as he had no education, he knew as little of the sailing a ship, set aside the business of a foremast man, as he did of history, in which, and natural philosophy, he was equally versed. He was of a morose, sour, unsociable temper, very choleric, and easily resented as an affront, what as brave and "a more knowing man would not think worth notice; but he was not cruel, neither did he turn pirate from a wicked or avaricious inclination, but by necessity; and we may say, though he was no forced man, he could not well avoid the life he fell into.

When he was grown a lusty lad he would see the world, and go seek his fortune, as the term is among the country youths, who think fit to withdraw themselves from the subjection of their parents. With this whim in his head, he got to Chester, where he was received, and sailed on board a coaster, till he had made himself acquainted with the rigging, learned to knot, splice, and do the other parts of a common sailor's duty; then coming to London, he shipped himself on board the Mary Indiaman, bound for Bengal and Madras, which voyage he performed outward, and it was not his fault that he did not come home in the same ship; for, in her return, falling short of water, they steered for the island of Madagascar, and fell in with the east side, in lat. 20 deg. or thereabouts. The captain manned and sent ashore the long-boat to seek for water, but a large surf running, she came to an anchor, at some little distance from shore, and David Williams, with another, being good swimmers, stripped and swam off in search of water. While they were ashore, the wind, which blew full upon the island, and freshening, caused the surf to run too high for them to get off; and the long-boat, after waiting some time, seeing no possibility of getting these men on board, weighed and stood for the ship, which filled her sails and stood for St, Augustin's Bay, where she watered, and proceeded on her voyage.

Thus our poor Welshman and his companion were left destitute on an island altogether unknown to them, without clothes or subsistence but what the fruits of the trees offered. They rambled some little time along the coast, and were met by the natives, and by them carried up into the country, where they were humanely treated, and provided with all the necessaries of life, though this was not sufficient to expel his consort's melancholy, who took his being left behind so much to heart, that he sickened and died in a very little time.

Some time after, the prince of the country, who entertained Williams, had a quarrel with a neighbouring king, which broke into a war. Williams took the field with his patron, but the enemy being superior in number, got the victory, and took a great many prisoners, among whom was the unfortunate Welshman. The king whose prisoner he was, treated him very kindly; and being master of an old musket, gave it him, saying *such arms were better in the hands of a white man than those of any of his subjects, who were not so much used to them; that he should be his friend and companion, and should fare as well as himself if he would assist him in his wars.*

It will not be amiss here to take notice, that this island, on the east side is divided into a great number of principalities or kingdoms, which are almost in continual war one with another; the grounds of which are very trivial, for they will pick a quarrel with a neighbour, especially if he has a number of cattle, (in which, and slaves, consist their riches) on the slightest occasion, that they may have an opportunity of plunder; and when a battle or two is lost, the conquered makes his peace, by delivering up such a certain number of bullocks and slaves as shall be demanded by the victorious prince. On the west side the island, the principalities are mostly reduced under one prince, who resides near Methelage, and who is, as we have said in the lives of other pirates, a great friend to white men; for his father, who founded his empire by the assistance of the Europeans, left it in charge with his son, to assist them with what necessaries they should require, and do them all friendly offices; but if he disobeyed this command, and should ever fall out with the white men, or spill any of their blood, he threatened to come again, turn him out of his kingdom, and give it to his younger brother. These menaces had a very great effect on him, for he firmly believed his father would, on his diso-bedience, put them in execution; for there is not on earth, a race of men equally superstitious.

But to return to Williams, he lived with this prince in great tranquility, and was very much esteemed by him, (for necessity taught him complaisance.) After some time, his new patron was informed that his vanquished enemy had formed a grand alliance, in order to make war upon him; wherefore, he resolved to begin, and march into the countries of the allies, and ravage the nearest before they could join forces. He raised an army, and accordingly marched southward. At the news of his approach, the inhabitants abandoned all the small towns, and sending messengers to their friends, raised a consid-erable body to oppose him, suffering him to overrun a great deal of ground without molestation. At length being reinforced, they took their opportunity, and setting upon him when his men were fatigued, and his army encumbered with booty, they gained a signal victory. The king had the good luck to get off, but Williams was a second time taken prisoner.

He was carried before the conqueror, who, (having been an eye witness of his bravery, for Williams killed a number of his enemies with his shot, and behaved very well, defending himself with the butt end of his musket for some time, when he was surrounded) reached him his hand, and told him, he made war with his enemies only, that he did not esteem the white men such, but should be glad of their friendship. Here Williams was used with more respect than he had been even by his last patron, and lived with this prince some years; but a war breaking out, he was routed in a set battle, in which Williams was his companion. In the pursuit, the poor Welchman, finding he could not get off, clapped his musket at the foot of a tree, and climbing up, he capitulated. He was now terribly afraid of being cut to pieces, for he had shot and wounded a great number of the enemy. They, however, promised him good quarter, and kept their word.

The king of Maratan, who took him, used him as well as any of the former had done, and carried him always with him to the wars, in which fortune was more propitious, for the parties Williams commanded had constantly the better of their enemies, and never returned without great booties of cattle and slaves, for all the prisoners they take are so, until redeemed; though these prisoners are, for the most part, women and children, they seldom giving quarter to any other. The fame of his bravery and success, spread itself round the country; and his name alone was so terrible, that the giving out he was at the head of any party, was giving the enemy an overthrow without a battle.

This reaching the ears of Dempaino, a mighty prince who lived 200 miles from him, and who had several petty princes tributaries, he sent an ambassador to demand the white man; but his patron, who had no mind to part with him, denied that he had any white man with him; that he who was called so was a native of the country. For the reader's better understanding this passage, I must inform him, that there is a race of what they call white men, who have been settled on Madagascar, time out of mind, and are descended from the Arabs; but mixing with the negroes, have propagated a race of mulattoes, who differ in nothing from the manner of living of the black natives.

To proceed, the ambassador desired to see this man, and Williams coming to him, being extremely tanned, he had passed for what he was reported, had he been before apprized of what had been said, to have answered accordingly, for he spoke the language perfectly; or had the ambassador not examined him; who, after he had some time viewed him, asked him of what country he was, and whether it was true that he was one of Madagascar. Williams answered, he was an Englishman, and was left in the country, relating the particulars, as I have already set them down, adding, he had been five years in the island.

The ambassador then told the king, that he must send the white man with him, for such were the orders of his master, the great Dempaino, who was lord over most of the kings on the side of the country where he resided; and that it would be dangerous for him to disobey the commands of so great a monarch.

The king answered, those who were subject to Dempaino ought to obey his commands; but for him, he knew no man greater than himself, therefore should receive laws from none; and with this answer dismissed the ambassador; who, at his return, reported to his master the very words, adding, they were delivered in a very haughty strain. Dempaino, who was not used to have his commands disputed, ordered one of his generals to march with 6000 men, and demand the white man, and in case of refusal, to denounce war; that he should send him back an express of it, and he would follow in person with an army to enforce a compliance.

These orders were put in execution with the greatest despatch and secrecy; so that the town was invested, before any advice was given of the approach of an enemy. The general told the king, it was in his choice to have peace or war with his master, since it depended on the delivery of the white man. The king, thus surprised, was obliged, however contrary to his inclinations, to give Williams up to the general, who returned with him to Dempaino, without committing any hostilities; though he threatened to besiege the town, and put all but the women and children to the sword, if the king of Maratan did not pay the expense of sending for the white man, which he rated at 100 slaves, and 500 head of cattle. The king objected to this as a hard condition, and an unjust imposition, but was obliged to acquiesce in it.

He was received by Dempaino with a great many caresses, was handsomely clothed according to the country manner, had slaves allotted to wait on him, and everything that was necessary and convenient; so that king Dempaino was at the trouble of sending 6000 men, one would think, for no other end than to show the great value and esteem he had for the Europeans. He continued with this prince till the arrival of a ship, which was some years after his leaving Maratan, when the Bedford galley, a pirate, commanded by Achen Jones, a Welchman, came on the coast, on board of which ship Williams was permitted to enter. They went to Augustin, where, laying the ship on shore, they broke her back by carelessness, and lost her. The crew lived here till the arrival of the Pelican, another pirate, mentioned in North's life; some of them went on board this ship, and steered for the East-Indies. Williams shifted out of this on board the Mocha frigate, a pirate, commanded by Capt. Culiiford, and made a voyage; then, returning to St. Mary's they shared the booty they had got in the Red Sea.

Some of the crew, being West-Indians, having an opportunity, returned home; but Williams remained here till the arrival and taking of Captain Fourgette, which has been already mentioned. He was one of those who took the Speaker, went a voyage in her, and returned to Maratan. Here the king seeing him asked him, what present he intended to make him for former kindness Williams answered, he had been overpaid by the prince whom he took him from, and by his services; which answer so irritated his Maratanian Majesty, that he ordered him to quit his country; and he could hardly after that see him with patience.

From hence he went on board the Prosperous, Capt, Howard, commander, who went to St. Mary's, and thence to the main, as is said in that pirate's life, and was one of the men left behind when they had a design to carry off Ort Van Tyle. This Dutchman kept him to hard labour, as planting potatoes, &c. in revenge for the destruction and havoc made in his plantations by the crew of the Prosperous. He was here in the condition of a slave six months at the expiration of which time, he had an opportunity to run away, leaving his consort, Thomas Collins, behind him, who had his arm broke when he was taken by the Dutchman.

Having made his escape from a rigid, revengeful master, he got to a black prince, named Rebaiharang, with whom he lived half a year. He from hence went and kept company with one John Pro, another Dutchman, who had a small settlement on shore, till the arrival of the men of war, commanded by Commodore Richards, who took both Pro and his guest Williams, put them in irons on board the Severn, till they came to Johanna, where the captain of the Severn undertook for $2000 to go against the Mohilians, in which expedition several of the man of war's crew were killed, and the two pirates made their escape in a small canoe to Mohila, where they sheltered themselves awhile in the woods, out of which they got provisions, and made over for Johanna. Here they recruited themselves and went away for Mayotta. The king of tins island built them a boat, and giving them provisions and what necessaries they required, they made for and arrived at Madagascar, where, at Methelage, m lat. 16 de o40 m. or thereabouts, they joined Captain White. Here they lay about three months; then setting fire to their boat, they went into White's, and rounding; the nortfc end, came to Ambonavoula. Here Williams remained till Capt. White bought the ship Hopewell, on board of which he entered before the mast, and made a voyage to the Red Sea, towards the end of which he was chosen quartermaster. At their return they touched at Mascarenhas for provisions, where almost half the company went ashore and took up their habitations.

From Mascarenhas they steered for Hopewell (by some called Hopeful) Point, on Madagascar, where dividing their plunder, they settled themselves. Twelve months after, the Charles brigantine, Capt. Halsey, came in, as is mentioned in his life. Williams went on board him and made a voyage, At their return they came to Maratan, lived ashore, and assisted the king in his war against his brother, which being ended in the destruction of the latter, and a pirate lying at Ambonavoula, sending his longboat to Manangcaro, within ten leagues of Maratan, Williams and the rest went on board, and in three months after he had been at Ambonavoula, he was chosen captain of the Scotch ship, mentioned in Halsey's life. This ship he worked upon with great earnestness, and made the Scotch prisoners labour hard at the fitting her up for a voyage; and she was nearly ready for sea, when a hurricane forced her ashore, and she was wrecked.

Some time after this he set up and finished a sloop, in which he and ten of his men designed for Mascarenhas; but missing the island, they went round Madagascar, to Methelage, where he laid his vessel ashore and tarried a year; but the king being tired with his morose temper, and he disagreeing with every body, was ordered to be gone, and accordingly fitting up his vessel, he put to sea, intending to go round the north end of the island; but the wind being at E. S. E. ano. the current setting to N. W. he put back to a port called the Boyn, within ten leagues of Methelage, in the same king's dominions whom he had left. The governor of this place was descended from the Arabs, and it was here that the Arabians traded,.

When he came to an anchor, he and three of his men (he had but five with him) went on shore paddled by two negroes, David Eaton and William Dawson, two of the men, required a guide, to shotr them the way to the king's town; the governor ordered them one, and at the same time laid an ambush for them in the road, and caused them to be murdered. When they had left the Boyn, Williams and Meyeurs, a Frenchman, who also came ashore in the canoe, went to buy some samsams, which are agate beads. As they were looking over these goods, a number of the governor's men came about them, seized them both, and immediately despatched Meyeurs. Williams they bound, and tortured almost a whole day, by throwing hot ashes on his head and in his face, and putting little boys to beat him with sticks. He offered the governor 2000 dollars for his life, but he answered, he would have that and the money too; and accordingly, when he was near expiring, they made an end of him with their lances.

After this barbarous murder, the governor thought of seizing the sloop, on board of which were no more than two white men, six negro boys, and some women slaves of the same colour. However, he thought it best to proceed by stratagem, and therefore putting a goat and some calabashes of toke on board Williams' canoe, with twelve negroes armed, and the sloop negroes to paddle, he sent to surprise her. When the canoe came pretty near the vessel, they hailed, and asked if they would let them come on board? One of the men asked Williams' negroes where the captain was? He answered, drinking toke with the governor, and sent them provision and toke. A negro wench advised the white man, whose name was William Noakes, not to let them come on board, for as four white men went ashore, and none of them appeared, she suspected some treachery. However, on the answer made him from the canoe, he resolved to admit them, and called them on board. No sooner were they come on deck, than one of them, snatching Noakes' pistol, shot him through the head, and seizing the other white man, threw him overboard and drowned him; after which, being masters of the vessel, they carried her in and rifled her.

The king was at this time hunting, as is his custom to hunt boars three months in the year; but an account of these murders soon reached him. However, he continued the accustomed time of his diversion; but when he returned home, and the whites who were about him demanded justice, he bade them be quiet, they might depend upon his doing it. He sent to the governor of Boyn, and told him, he was glad that he had cut off Williams and his crew, an example he was resolved to follow, and clear the country of them all; that he had some affairs to communicate to him, and desired he would come to court as soon as possible, but take care he was not seen by any of the whites, for fear they should revenge the death of their companions.

The governor, on these orders, came away immediately, and stopped at a little town, two miles distant from the king's, and sent word he there waited his commands.

The king ordered him to be with him early next morning, before the white men were out of their beds. He set forward accordingly the next day betimes, but was seized on the road by negroes placed for that purpose, and brought bound to the king, who, after having reproached him with the barbarity of the action he had been guilty of, sent him to the white men, bidding them put him to what death they pleased; but they sent word back, he might dispose of the lives of his subjects as he thought fit, but for their part, they would never draw a drop of blood of any who belonged to him. Upon: which answer the king's uncle ordered him to be speared, and he was accordingly thrust through the body with lances. The king, after this execution, sent to Boyn, and had everything brought which had belonged to Williams and his men, and divided it among the whites, saying, he was sorry the villain had but one life, to make atonement for the barbarity he had been guilty of.

Captain Samuel Burgess

Captain Samuel Burgess was born in New York, and had a good education. He sailed some time as a privateer in the West-Indies, and very often, the gang he was with, when the time of their cruising was expired, would make no ceremony of prolonging the commission by their own authority.

By his privateering he got together some little money, and returned home, where the government having no notice, or at least taking none, of his piratical practice, in staying beyond the date of his commission, he went out mate of a ship, in the service of Frederick Phillips, bound to the island of Madagascar, to trade with the pirates, where they had the misfortune to lose their ship, and lived 18 months at Augustin, when an English pirate coming in, the king of the country obliged him to go on board her, though much against his inclination, for he was tired of a roving life: but their choice was to go or starve, for the king would keep them no longer.

He went with this free-booter to the East-Indies, where they made several rich prizes, and returned to St. Mary's, where they took in provisions, wood, and water. Several of their gang knocked off here; but the captain, Burgess, and the remainder, went away for the West-Indies, disposed of their plunder on the Spanish coast, and then returning to NewYork, purposely knocked the ship on the head at Sandy Hook, after they had secured their money ashore.

The government not being informed of their piracy, they lived here without molestation, and, in a short time, Burgess married a relation of Mr. Phillips, who built a ship, called the Pembroke, and sent him a second time to Madagascar. In his way to this island, he went into the river of Dilagou on the

African coast, where he took in a quantity of elephant's teeth; and thence to Augustin, where he met with several of his old ship-mates, with whom he traded for money and slaves. Leaving this place, he went to Methelage, where he also took some money and negroes; and from thence he shaped his course for St. Mary's, on the east side, where he also drove a considerable trade with his old comrades, took several of them passengers, who paid very generously for their passage; and taking with, him an account of what was proper to bring in another trip, he returned to NewYork, without any sinister accident. This voyage cleared =£5000, ship and charges paid.

His owner, encouraged by this success, bade him choose what cargo he pleased, and set out again. Accordingly he laded with wine, beer, &c. and returning to Madagascar, arrived at Maratan, on the east side, where he disposed of a great part of his cargo at his own rates. At Methelage he disposed of the rest, and returned, clearing for himself and owner, £10,000, besides 300 slaves he brought to New-York.

After a short stay at home, he set out again on the old voyage, fell in first with Methelage, where he victualled and traded, and from thence went round the south end, and sold part of his cargo at a large profit, to his old acquaintance. He made a trading voyage round the island, and at St. Mary's met another ship belonging to his owner, which had orders to follow his directions. He remained at this port till he had disposed of the cargoes of both ships. He then shaped his course homewards, with about twenty pirate passengers, who had accepted the pardon brought by Commodore Littleton.

In his way he touched at the Cape of Good Hope for wood, water, and fresh provision. While he was here, the Loyal Cook, an East-Indiaman, came in, who made prize of Burgess, and carried him to the East-Indies. He there would have delivered Burgess' ship to the governor of Madras, but the governor would have no hand in the affair, and told the captain, he must answer to the East India company and Burgess' owner for what he had done.

Most of the pirate passengers thought themselves cleared by the act of grace; but some, not willing to trust to it, got off with what gold they could, in a Dutch boat. They who trusted to the pardon, were clapped in gaol, and died in their irons. I cannot omit the simplicity of one of them, who had, however, the wit to get off. When he designed to go away, he looked for his comrade for the key of his chest, to take his gold with him, which amounted to seventeen hundred pounds; but this comrade being ashore, he would not break open the chest, for it was a pity, he said, to spoil a good new lock; so left his money for the captain of the East-Indiaman.

The news of this capture came to the owner before the ship returned, and he sued the Company; but at their request, waited for the arrival of the Loyal Cook, which brought Burgess prisoner to England soon after. The Captain finding himself in an error, and that what he had done could not be justified, absconded; and the Company made good the ship and cargo to the owner. Burgess was set at liberty, continued some time in London, was impeached, and piracy sworn against him by Culliford, who, notwithstanding he came home on the act ol grace, was. committed to Newgate, tried, and acquitted, though he was beggared.

Burgess' owner laboured very hard, and expended great sums of money to save him. However, though he pleaded the necessity of his going on board the pipate, he was tried and condemned; but by the intercession of the bishops of London and Canterbury, was pardoned by the queen.

After this, he made a broken voyage to the South Sea, lieutenant of a privateer, and returning to London, was out of business a whole year. He then shipped himself as mate on board the Hannah, afterwards called the Neptune, and went to Scotland to take in her cargo, the owner being of that country; but before she got thither, he broke, the ship was stopped, and lay eighteen months before she was disposed of. At length, being set to sale, six Scotch gentlemen bought her, the old officers were continued, and she proceeded on her first designed voyage to Madagascar, in which the captain and Burgess quarrelling, caused the loss of the ship; for the latter, who was acquainted with the pirates, when they arrived at Madagascar, instigated them to surprise her. The manner how, being already set down in Halsey's life, I need not repeat.

I shall only take notice, that Capt. Miller being decoyed ashore, under pretence of being shown some trees, fit for masting, Halsey invited him to a surloin of beef, and a bowl of arrack punch; he accepted the invitation, with about twenty pirates. One Emmy, who had been a waterman on the Thames, did not come to table, but sat by, muffled side, up in a great coat, pretending he was attacked by the ague, though he had put it on to conceal his pistols only. After dinner, when Halsey went out, as for something to entertain his guests, (Miller and his supercargo,) Emmy clapped a pistol to the captain's breast, and told him he was his prisoner. At the same instant, two other pirates entered room, with each a blunderbuss in his hand, told the captain and his supercargo, that no harm should come to either, if they did not bring it upon themselves by an useless resistance. While this passed within doors, the wood being lined with pirates, all Miller's men, whom he had brought ashore to fall timber, were secured, but none hurl and all civilly treated. When they had afterwards got possession of the ship, in the manner mentioned before, they set all their prisoners at liberty.

Miller with eleven of his men, was sent off, a said in Halsey's life. The company chose Burgess quartermaster, and shared the booty they had made out of the Scotch ship, and the Greyhound.

Soon after happened Halsey's death, who left Burgess executor in trust for his widow and children, with a considerable legacy for himself; and other pirates grumbling at a new comer's being preferred to all of them, took from Burgess, £3000 of Halsey's money, and £1200 of his own, which was his share of the two prizes. Though he had been treated in this manner, they were idle enough to give him the command of the Scotch ship, and ordered him to fit her out with all expedition, and to take on board some men and goods left in the brigantine. He set to work on the ship, with full design to run away with her; but some pirates, who were in another part of the island, being informed of these proceedings, thought it not prudent to trust him, so he left the ship, and getting among his old comrades, by their interposition had all his money returned.

After this he lived five months on the island of St. Mary's, where his house was, by accident, burnt down, out of which he saved nothing but his money. He then went on board David Williams, when he missed the island of Mascarenhas, and returned to Methelage, where he tarried with the king, and was one of the men among whom he divided Williams' effects.

From Methelage he went with a parcel of sam-sams to Augustin, with which he bought fifty slaves, whom he sold to the Arabians. In his return to Methelage, he met Capt. North, in a sloop, with 30 of Miller's men on board. These men proposed taking Burgess, who had, as they said, betrayed, ruined, and banished them their country, by forcing them to turn pirates; but North would not consent: upon which they confined him, took Burgess and stripped him of all the money, and then releasing their captain, gave him £300 as his share, which he returned to Burgess on his arrival at Methelage.

Burgess lived here two or three years, till he was carried off by some Dutchmen. They belonged to an East-Indiaman, and were taken by two French ships, which being bound for Mocha, and short of provisions, came into Methelage to victual, where they set 80 of their prisoners ashore. When they parted from this port, they sailed for Johanna, where they left the Dutch officers, who built a ship, and came back for their men. Burgess being of great use to them, they took him on board, and steered for a port, where some Dutch, taken in another ship, were marooned; but they were wrecked at Youngoul, where Burgess continued 18 months. After this time was expired, he was desirous of leaving the place, and addressed himself to the king who was uncle to the king of Methelage, he requested his black majesty to send him back to that port which he readily complied with, where Burgess continued almost five years, afflicted with sickness, in which he lost one eye. While he was here, the Drake pink, of London, came in for slaves. He took Burgess, with design to carry him home; but Capt. Harvey, in the Henry, which belonged to the same owners, arriving, and being a stranger to the trade, at the request of Capt. Maggot, commander of the Drake, and on promise of a ship when the West Indies, he entered as third mate, and continued with him. Captain Harvey carrying it pretty high, and disagreeing with the king, lay here nine months before he could slave. Burgess was sent up to tell the king he had not fulfilled his agreement with Capt. Harvey. The king resented being reproached bv a man whom he had entertained so many years, and reviled him. He was, however, carried to dinner with some of the principal blacks, and drank very plentifully with them of toke, in which it is supposed he was poisoned, for he fell ill and died soon after, leaving what he had to the care of the chief mate, for the use of his wife and children.

Captain Nathaniel North

Captain North was born at Bermuda, and was the son of a sawyer, which business he himself was bred up to, but took at last to the seas, at the age of 17 or 18, shipping himself cook on board a sloop, built at Bermuda, for some gentlemen of Barbadoes, with design to fit her out for a privateer. She was bound to her owners, but the master took Santa Udas in the way, and loaded with salt. When they came to Barbadoes, all the crew was pressed, and North with his companions were put on board the Reserve.

The master applied himself to the governor, and got all his men cleared, North excepted, who, as he was a lad, was neglected, and left on board the man of war, which soon after sailed for Jamaica. Sometime before the Reserve was relieved from this station, he laid hold of an opportunity to run away, and shipped himself on board a sugar drover, in which way of life he continued about two years, and being an able sailor, though no artist, he was offered to go master of one of these coasters, which he refused, and went on board a privateer.

The first cruise he made, they took a couple of good prizes, which made every man's share very considerable; but North, as he got his money lightly, so he spent it, making the companions of his dangers the companions of his diversions, or rather joining himself with them, and following their example; which all (who are acquainted with the way of life of a successful Jamaica privateer) know is not an example of the greatest sobriety and economy. His money being all spent, he took the same method for a recruit, that is, he went a second time privateering, and met with such success, that he engaged very heartily in this course of life, and made several lucky cruises. Some time after, he grew tired, thought of trading, and shipped himself on board a brigantine, bound for the Spanish coast, commanded by one Capt. Reesby. This vessel went both on the trading and privateering account, so that the men shipped for half wages, and equal shares of what prizes they should make, in the same manner as to the shares, as on board a privateer. Their trading answered very poorly, and their privateering business still worse, for they returned without making any prize. They were forced to leave the Spanish coast on account of a Spanish guarda-la-costa, of 40 guns and 350 Frenchmen, commanded by a captain of the same nation. When they made the island of Jamaica, they fell in with Bluefields, off which place two French privateer sloops were cruising, one of which was formerly a privateer of Jamaica, called the Paradox. They immediately clapped Captain Reesby on board, taking him for a trader from the Spanish coast, and weakly manned. However, they were soon sensible of the mistake, for Reesby took one of them, and the other was obliged to a good pair of heels for his safety. Reesby lost 10 men killed outright in the engagement, and had 7 wounded. The latter, though he had made but a broken voyage, he put ashore at Bluefields, and ordered great care to be taken of them, at the owners' expense. Here he took in fresh provision, and then beat up to Port Royal, where Reesby paid his men very honourably, gave them a handsome entertainment, and begged they would not leave him, as he had a very great value for them all; but for North particularly, who was a good swimmer, managed a canoe with great dexterity, and feared nothing.

Upon this desire of the captain's North and the greater part tarried ashore till Capt. Reesby was refitted, and went a second voyage with him to the coast, at seventeen dollars a month, and no share. They carried 300 negroes, besides bale goods, and disposed of all the slaves and goods to -great advantage. Upon their return to Jamaica, after some stay on the island, Capt. Reesby not going out again, North went once more a privateering, and made considerable booty. While North was ashore after a cruise, he was pressed on board the Mary man of war, made a cruise in her to the Spanish coast, and returned to Jamaica; but hearing the Mary was to go to England, he, and three more, resolved to swim ashore from the keys, where the men of war lie, but he was taken as he was going off the head, and whipped. He, however, found means to make his escape, before the ship left the island, and went on board the Neptune sloop, a privateer, commanded by Capt. Lycence, then lieutenant of the Reserve, who, while the ship was in the carpenters' hands, got a commission of the governor to take a cruise. Capt. Moses, who commanded the Reserve, went on board their sloop, under the command of his lieutenant, for diversion only. They cruised off Hispaniola, where they met with a French letter-of-marque, of 18 guns, and 118 men, who had the day before engaged the Swan man of war, and shook her off. The Neptune attacked her, and Capt. Moses was one of the first wounded, and carried down. Lycence ordered to board, but the quartermaster, who steered, mistook the helm, the sloop off, and the French pouring in a volley of small shot, Capt. Lycence was killed, which being told to Moses, as the surgeon dressed him, he ordered North to the helm, bid them not to be discouraged, and he would be upon deck immediately. Accordingly, he came up as soon as dressed, laid the ship on board, where they made a very obstinate resistance; but the French captain being killed, who received eleven shot before he dropped, they, at length, became masters.

The privateer lost 10 men, and 20 Were wounded. The French had 50 killed and wounded, among whom was the captain, who had received two shot, as he was going down to the surgeon to get his blood stanched, and came upon deck just as he was boarded, where, encouraging his men, he was distinguished and aimed at. When they had Drought the prize into Jamaica, as she was an English bottom, built at Bristol, and called the Crown, the former owners sued to have half the ship and cargo, and recovered one third.

Capt. Moses' ship not being fitted, he would take a second cruise in a privateer, and North went with, him. Some time after their return, Capt. Moses being cruising in the Reserve, North, who was ashore, was pressed on board the Assistance man of war; and on the Reserve's coming in, being recommended by Capt. Moses to his own captain, he was handsomely treated, and made one of the barge's crew. He was very easy till the Assistance was ordered to England, and then, as he was apprehensive of going into a cold climate, he took his leave and said nothing. He then went on board a privateer again, and made several prizes, two of which were English bottoms, and sued for by former owners. North thinking -it hard to venture his life, and have part of his prize money taken away, and the press being hot in Jamaica, he resolved to sail no more with the English; but went to Curacoa into the Dutch service, and sailed with a Spanish trader to the coast of New Spain several voyages. In the last he made, they were chased ashore by a couple of French; sloops, one of which was commanded by a Dutchman, named Lawrence, who, with his comrade, took possession of their vessel and rifled her. The crew of the prize called to them, and asked if they would give them good quarters which they promised; took them all on board, and used them very handsomely.

The French gave the prisoners a small sloop they took a while after, and they returned to Curacoa.

He having now forgot his resentment, returned to Jamaica, and went on board and cruised in a Spanish barcalonga, of 10 guns, commanded by Capt. Lovering, born at Jamaica. They cruised three months in the West-Indies, and making but a small hand of it, they steered for Newfoundland, to try their fortune on the banks. Here they met a man of war, who renewed their commission for six months longer. The first prize they made was a French ketch, with a Spanish pass, and would have passed for a Spaniard, but by strict search, and threatening the men, they discovered her to be what she really was, though she had, as a Spaniard, slipped through the fingers of a man of war before.

They carried their prize into harbour, went again upon a cruise, met with a French letter-of-marque,

a Bristol built ship, called the Pelican, of 18 guns, and 75 men, half laden with fish. This ship stood them a long argument; they clapped her on board, and two of their men entered, but missing lashing, the barcalonga fell astern, and the two men were made prisoners. However, they came up with her again, clapped her on board a second time, and carried her into the same port where they had left the ketch.

They after this put to sea again, and being discovered by the French settlement ashore, they went into St. Mary's Bay, where they fell in with a large French fly-boat, of 800 tons, 80 men, and 18 guns, laden with fish. They chased and came up with her, under French colours. When they were pretty near, the Frenchman hailed, and asked whence they came. A Guernsey-man, at the bowsprit end, answered, *from Petit Guave,* that they had been cruising on the Banks, and were going into the bay for refreshment. The Frenchman bade them come no nearer, but send their boat on board. They keeping on the chase, he fired at them. They did not mind this, but run up alongside and boarded him. The French ran to their close quarters, and disputed the ship three quarters of an. hour, when they ail called for quarters except one man, who would take none, but ran like a madman into the midst of the English, and wounded several, though he was soon despatched by their pistols. They carried this prize to join the others, and turning all the prisoners ashore, except what were necessary to condemn their prizes, they stood, with a fleet of four sail, far Rhode-Island.

Here they condemned the fly-boat and ketch, but found great difficulty in getting the Pelican condemned, the English owners putting in their claim; but, at length, a Scotch lawyer did their business, upon leaving £300 in his hands to bear the charge of any future suit. Capt. Lovering dying here, the ship's company bought the Pelican, broke up the barcalonga, sent her owners their shares, and got a commission for the master to cruise southward as far as the line, and to be valid for 18 months certain, two years allowing for accidents.

They fitted this ship for a long voyage, out of the joint stock of the company; but iron hoops being scarce in New-England, they were obliged to take casks hooped with wood, which I mention, because it proved the ruin of their voyage to the East Indies for a whole year.

Being fitted for sea, they set sail and steered for the Cape of Good Hope, which they doubled in the month of June, made the best of their way to Madagascar, and went into Augustin Bay, where they victualled and watered; but before this was done it was August, which was too late to go to the East Indies; which they proposed to do with design to cruise on the Moors, not intending to pirate among the Europeans, but honestly and quietly to rob what Moors fell in their way, and return home with clean consciences, and clean, but full hands, within the limited time of their commission.

From Augustin they went to Johanna, and the provision they had salted at Madagascar not being well done, it began to spoil. This, and their clothes wanting repair, made them desperately resolve to take the king of Johanna and make him ransom himself; but the master would not take charge of the ship, being unacquainted with the coast. They cruised among the islands, landed at Comaro, and took the town, but found no booty, excepting some silver chains, and checked linen. From hence they went to Mayotta, where they took in a Frenchman who had been marooned there, and maintained by the king. They consulted with him about surprising and taking the town; but he was averse to it, as he owed him the obligation of being preserved. However, he was in their hands, and must do as they would have him. They surrounded the king's house after they had been three days in his town, and took him and all the inhabitants; but the king's son made his way through the thickest of them with his cutlass, though he was shot afterwards. The pretense they made use of for this unjustifiable violence, was, that the king had poisoned the crew of a ship, which was their consort. He denied it, as well he might, for they themselves never heard of a ship of the name they gave this fictitious one. The king they carried on board, the other prisoners they put into a sort of temple, with a guard over them of 6 men.

The alarm being given in the country, the natives came down in a body, of some thousands, and attacked the guard; but the ship hearing the fire, and seeing the hills covered with blacks, discharged several great guns, loaded with partridge, which made a very great slaughter, and obliged them to retire.

The king ransomed himself for some silver chains to the value of a thousand dollars, and for what provision they demanded; and at setting him ashore, swore allegiance to them as masters of the country, and took an oath besides, never to poison any more white men.

After this notable expedition, they stayed here a fortnight, though always on their guard, and then went back for Augustin with about twenty slaves, which they carried away with them for servants, Here a sickness coming among them, they built huts ashore. They lost, notwithstanding all their care and precaution, their captain and thirty men, by the distemper which they contracted; but it abating, they thought of going to sea again, but on examining their water casks, they found the hoops all worm eaten and rotten, so that there was no proceeding; but this defect was repaired by their cooper, who was an ingenious fellow. He went into the woods with the Mayotta slaves, and with withes and other stuff he gathered, fitted them up, and made them tight; in acknowledgment of which service they chose him captain, and North was made quartermaster.

At Augustin they picked up some stragglers, among whom was David Williams, and on a muster they found they had 105 men. They then made their vessel a free ship; that is, they agreed every man should have an equal share in all prizes; and proceeded for the mouth of the Red Sea.

In the night, after they had reached their station they made two ships; one was the Mocha frigate, of 40 guns, commanded by Culliford: she had been an East-Indiaman, under the command of one Capt. Stout; the other ship was called the Soldada, of 16 guns, the captain's name Shivers; they hailed one another, and on both sides gave the same answers, *from the seas,* and upon agreement, they all lay by that night. In the morning they consorted, and agreed to make an equal division of all prizes, which any of the three should take from that time for two months to come.

The Pelican spared wood, water, and some of her hands to Capt. Culliford, and here Williams shifted on board him. About ten days after these three had joined company, a large Moor's ship, on which they afterwards mounted 70 guns, hove in sight.

They all gave chase, but the small ship came first up with the Moor, who exchanged several shot with the Soldada and Pelican; but the Soldada clapped her on board, and before the Pelican could enter a man, the Moors called for quarters. In boarding the Moor, she fired a broadside upon the Soldada, but only two shot hulled her, and killed two men, which was the only loss they had in taking a thousand prisoners, passengers and sailors.

All the money was carried on board the Mocha frigate, and divided between her crew and the Soldada, excluding without other reason than *sic volumus,* the Pelican from any share. The crew of the Pelican expostulated with them, and bid them remember they had spared both wood and water, or the Mocha could not have kept the station. Instead of any answer, they received a command to be gone, or they would sink them. They answered, they could not go by themselves, wanting the water and wood they had spared. The two consorts gave them a thousand dollars, and some water out of the Moor, telling them to buy wood, where they could purchase it, and so left the Pelican to herself, going away for the coast of Malabar, where they put the prisoners and horses they had taken, ashore, sunk the Soldada, and thence went to the Isle of St. Mary's on Madagascar. They shared out of this prize a thousand pounds a man in silver and gold, besides other goods; and the two pirates amounted to the number of 350 men.

The Pelican kept the same station for some days, when a large Moor ship hove in sight. They gave chase, and the Moor not suspecting her for an enemy, did not endeavour to get away. When the Pelican came up, she fired for the Moor to bring to, which made him set his small sails, though with the loss of several men; for the Pelican being close up, brought them down with small arms. When the Moor had, at length, hove out his small sails, the Pelican could not gain upon him enough to boards though she was not a pistol shot astern. Whenever she came upon his lee quarter, the Moor being a tall ship, took away the wind from the Pelican, and she could never get to windward of him. She plyed her fore chase all this while, and drove the Moor's from their stern chase, but could not, as they endeavoured to do, strike the Moor's rudder, or any other way disable him. At length by the fear and bad steerage of the Moor, the Pelican run up alongside of them, but as she missed lashing, she was obliged to shoot ahead. In the mean while the Moor wore round, the Pelican put in stays after him, but not staying, and being all in confusion, wore also; but in this time the Moor had got the start, and setting all the canvass he could pack on his ship's back, wronged the Pelican and got off.

The loss of this ship made the crew almost distracted, and caused for some time, a great division among them; some cursing the ship for a heavy sailor, and proposing to return home; others cursing themselves, and the ill-management by which they missed lashing, and proposed going to Madagascar, and breaking her up, since as she was a single bottom, she must be worm eaten; bat time, which molifi.es the greatest rage, abated these contentions, and put an end to the animosities which sprung from their disappointment.

They now resolved for the Malabar coast, on which they took three Moor ships in a little time. The first they discharged, after taking out 6000 dollars; the second they took for their own use, mounted her with 26 guns, and called her the Dolphin: the third they sold on the same coast for 18,000 dollars. Their own ship they set adrift. From this coast they made for Madagascar, and near the island of Mascarenhas lost all their masts in a hurricane. They put up jury masts, came to St. Mary's and new masted. Here they found Captain Culliford, Capt. Shivers, and their prize, with three merchantmen from America, which had come to trade with them, one of which was the Pembroke, commanded by Samuel Burgess, and belonging to Frederick Phillips, merchant, at New York. The captain of the Dolphin, and some of the men being weary of this life, went home in these merchants ships, and the crew chose one Samuel Inless, who lived on the island, for their captain. They fitted out for the Straits of Malacca, where they made several prizes of Moor ships, but of little value to them. North, on board one of the prizes, was separated from the rest by bad weather, and drove to great distress for water. The Moor merchant, who was on board with him, and whom he had treated very humanely, showed him a draught, by which he came to a small island not far from the Dutch settlement, and watered. The Moor told him that he ran the risk of his life should it be known that he had given him a sight of this draught. In return for this service, when he met with his companions, he got the Moor's ship discharged. After this they steered for Nicobar, near Achen, and, in the way, met a large Danish ship, which they plundered, and hove down by, cleaned, and returned to Madagascar, where they shared their booty, which was, besides goods, between 3 and £400 a man. A month after their arrival, Commodore Littleton's squadron appeared in sight, which occasioned their hauling up the Dolphin; and, as they could not get her so high as they designed, they set fire to her.

Commodore Littleton brought a pardon for such of the pirates as would accept it, and many of them did, among whom were Culliford and Shivers, who went home with merchantmen. North accepted it also, but would not trust to it, finding the time fixed for their -surrender had elapsed before the men of war arrived.

Most of the pirates having left the island of St. Mary's, where the king's ship lay, North thought it not safe for him to stay, and therefore putting all he had into the Dolphin's boat, he designed to join his comrades on the main of Madagascar; but being overset by a squall, all the people were lost except himself, who swam ashore, and a negro woman whom he put on the bottom of the boat.

Being now on the main, and quite naked, he frightened the negroes he met with, as he got out of the water, for they took him for a sea-devil; but one women, who had been used to sell fowls at the white men's houses, had the courage not to run away, and, when he came near, knew him. She gave him some of her own clothing, and calling a negro man who carried her things, and had run into the woods, they helped him to perform his journey to the dwelling of some white men, which was sixteen miles from the place where he came on shore. Being quite exhausted, he was kindly received and clothed by his comrades, whom he remained with till he had recovered his strength, and then went to a black prince of his acquaintance, with whom he tarried till the arrival of Capt. Fourgette, which was full a year.

In this vessel, which I have already said in White's life was taken, he went round the north end to the west side, and came into Methelage, where they surprised the Speaker; the manner of which is also mentioned in the same life; and, after the death of Capt. Booth, was chosen captain's quartermaster, by Bowen, who succeeded in the voyage, and the consequence of it are already set down, for he was in the Speaker till she was lost.

The next voyage he made was in the Speedy Return (taken from Capt. Drummond) in the capacity of company's quartermaster, with design to cruise in the Red Sea; but touching at the island of Mayotta, they consorted with Capt. Howard, whom they met with at the island, as is already said. From thence they went and victualled at Augustin, having promised Capt. Bowen to meet him in two months; accordingly returning thither, and missing him, they went to Mayotta to inquire after him; but hearing that he was gone a voyage, and as the place of rendezvous was off the highlands of St. John's, they steered their course thither, to join him, and lie for the Moor fleet for Mocha.

In their passage they met with a violent storm, in which they were near foundering. It beat in their stern, and obliged them to throw over all their guns (two excepted, which lay in the hold) and forced them into the gulf of Persia, where they took several small vessels, which they ripped up to repair their ship. Being very much in want of water, having staved all their casks, to save themselves in the storm, and meeting with little in the vessels taken, they hoisted out the canoe to chase a fishing vessel, that they might be informed where they should find water. This boat made from them with all their force, but the ship firing, the people all leaped into the water, some of whom were drowned, and the rest got ashore, except one man, whom they came up with; but as soon as they thought to lay hold of him, he dived, and kept them in play near an hour and a half. They would not shoot him, because it did not answer their ends; but at length North, who was in the boat, took the sprit, and struck him as he rose, and broke his jaw. They took him by these means, brought him on board, sent him to the surgeon, and when they despaired of his being able to speak, he asked for a pipe of tobacco, which he smoked, and drank a dram; after which he seemed very hearty. As the pirates had on board several black slaves, who spoke the East-India tongue, one of them was ordered to inquire of him where they might find water, promising him his liberty, if he would direct them. On this promise he carried them to a convenient landing place, where he showed a well, full of dirt, out of which, after a great deal of trouble to come at it, they drew but three buckets of water, which -sufficed those only who went on shore, to the number of thirty. Enraged with this disappointment after so much labour, they threatened their prisoner with death, who told them, if they would have patience till the sun was set, they would have plenty, for the spring would rise, and flow all night; which they found to be the fact, and filled twenty tons of water, and returned on board, carrying the man with them, for whom they made a gathering of some goods, and about 30 dollars. These they gave him, and exacted a promise, that whenever he saw any ship on that coast, which made the same signals they had made, he would go on board and render them what service he could, assuring him he would always meet with civil treatment, and be well rewarded.

After this they cruised in the gulf of Persia some days, in hopes of meeting their consort, not doubting but she had some share in the storm; but the time of their partnership having at length expired, and she not appearing, they steered for the highlands of St. John, near Surat, the place of rendezvous. When they made the land they spied a ship, and immediately making all clear for an engagement, they gave chase. The other ship doing the like, they soon met, and to the great joy of both parties, she proved their consort. Upon inquiry they found the Prosperous had been ten days on this station, and had not met with the storm which had so roughly handled the Speedy Return. On giving an account of their misfortune, viz. their being obliged to throw over their guns, and a quantity of provisions, Capt. Howard spared them some fresh provisions, and expressing great concern for the accident, renewed his consortship for two months longer; that is, they agreed whatever prizes were taken should be equally divided between the crews of both ships. After they had cruised here fourteen days, they spied seven sail of lofty ships, which proved to be the Moors from Mocha. They both gave chase, but the Speedy Return being the better sailor, first came up with one of them, laid her on board and caried her in very little time, with little more damage them the loss of her bowsprit. The Prosperous continued the chase, and having Capt. Whaley on board as a pilot, took another at an anchor, as is related in Capt. Howard's life.

The Speedy Return steered with her prize for the coast of Malabar, where, by agreement, she was to wait ten days for her consort. In six days the Prosperous joined them, but without any prize, having rifled and dismissed her.

Here they made an equal dividend of their prizes burnt the Speedy Return, sunk the Prosperous, went all onboard the Moor's ship, put to sea, and cruised on this coast, where they made several prizes. When they came over against Cachine, some black merchants, goldsmiths, and several Dutchmen, came on board to trade with them, bringing a great many sequins, and other gold coin, to change for Spanish dollars. As many of the pirates designed to knock off and return home, they gave 500 dollars for 200 sequins, for the conveniency of close stowage about them. The goldsmiths set up their forges on board the ship, and were fully employed in making them buttons, buckles, and what else they fancied, so that they had a fair opportunity of putting in what alloy they thought proper. They here also furnished themselves with a good quantity of arrack, provisions and stores, and then leaving the coast, shaped their course for Madagascar, but, in the way, fell in with the island of Mauritius, and put into a port called the North West Harbour. Here they wooded and watered. This port affords great abundance of a poisonous fish called the Red-Snapper, the nature of which was well known to Capt. Bowen, who persuaded his men not to eat of them, but they were in port, and then are all commanders, so that this wholesome advice was thrown away upon them. The captain seeing their obstinacy, and that they could not be dissuaded, eat with them, chosing rather to share the same fate, than be left alone to the mercy of the Dutch, as he was conscious of what he merited. They supped plentifully on the fish, and drank very heartily after it. Soon after they began to swell in a frightful manner. The next morning some planters came on board with fowls, goats, &c. and seeing the pirates in a miserable condition, and some of these fish lying on the decks, asked if they had not eaten of them? Being answered in the affirmative, they advised their drinking plentifully of strong liquors, which was the only way to expel the poison, which had dispatched them all in less time, had they not done it after their unfortunate meal. They readily followed this advice, as the prescription was agreeable, and by this means, with the care of the surgeons, of whom they had several expert in their business, and stocked with good medicines, they all recovered, four excepted, who paid their obstinacy with their lives.

They here heeled their ship, scrubbed; tallowed, and took in what they wanted. When they had been three months in this port, the governor sent and desired them to put to sea, for he expected the arrival of the Dutch East-Indiamen. They accordingly got everything ready, and went out, but left several of their men behind them, as we have related in Bowen's life.

From hence they steered to Madagascar, and in their passage stopped at Don Mascarenhas, where they took in a quantity of hogs, goats, sheep, fowls of all sorts, and green turtle. Captain Bowen here went ashore with 40 of his men, having obtained the governor's protection by the force of presents. These men designed to give over their piracy, and return home the first opportunities offered them. In six months after they landed here, Capt. Bowen was taken ill of the dry belly-ache, a distemper as common here as in the West India Islands, died, and was buried in the highway, for the priests would not allow him holy ground, as he was a heretic.

But to return. When Bowen went ashore, Worth was chosen captain. The ceremony of this installation is as follows:— The crew having made choice of a person to command, either by an unanimous consent, or by a majority of suffrages, they carry him a sword in a very solemn manner, make him some compliments, and desire he will take upon him the command, as he is the most capable among them; that he will take possession oi' the great cabin: and, on his accepting the office, he is led into the cabin in state, and placed at a table, where only one chair is set at the upper end, and one at the lower end of the table for the company's quartermaster. The captain and he being placed, the latter succinctly tells him, that the company having experience of his conduct and courage, do him the honor to elect him for their head, not doubting his behaving himself with his usual bravery, and doing everything which may conduce to the public good; in confidence of which, he, in the name of the company, promises to obey all his lawful commands, and declares him captain. Then the quartermaster takes up the sword, which he had before presented him, and he had returned, puts it into his hand, and says, *This is the commission under which you are to act; may you prove fortunate to yourself and us.* The guns are then fired round shot and all; he is saluted with three cheers; and the ceremony ends with an invitation from the captain to such as he thinks fit to have dine with him, and a large bowl of punch is ordered to every mess.

Capt. North, leaving this island, steered for Madagascar, and came to Cape Dolphin at the south end, where he anchored, and took on board some refreshments, but it blowing hard, he was obliged to put to sea, and leave his boat with 30 men behind him, He ran along the east side of the island, and came to Ambonavoula, in lat. 17 deg. 38m. where they put on shore some of their goods, and settled themselves among the negroes, several living in a house. Here they lived as sovereign princes among the inhabitants.

The Moor prisoners they kept on board, and allowed them sufficient fresh provisions. North privately told the boatswain of the Moors to take advantage of the land breeze in the night time, and go off with the ship, and what goods were left on board, or the pirates would soon haul her up, take everything on shore, and they never see their own country again. Accordingly the boatswain, following this advice, laid hold of the opportunity of a dark night, and communicating his design to the other Moors, whom he did not acquaint with this advice, as North charged him not, till he was on the point of executing his design, they weighed with great silence and stood to sea.

The next morning some of the pirates proposed to go on board and bring off some iron and other things to trade with in the country; but they were strangely surprised when they missed the ship. They alarmed the rest of their comrades, and went in a body to Capt. North, to tell him what had happened. He answered, if the Moors were gone off with the ship, it was their own fault; they ought to have left a sufficient number of hands on board to have secured her; and there was now no remedy but patience, for they had no vessel to pursue with, except they thought the canoe proper.

Some of the pirates thought, as she lay in foul ground, the cable might be cut by some rock, and the ship blown off to sea by that accident. On starting this, some of them ran up to an eminence, and from thence spied the ship as far as they could well see, with all sail set, which was a cruel and convincing proof that their loss was irreparable.

They endeavoured to make themselves easy, since there was no help; and transporting their goods to different abodes, at small distances, they settled themselves, buying cattle and slaves, and lived in a neighbourly manner, one among another, five years, cleared a great deal of ground, and planted provisions, such as yams, potatoes, &c. The natives among whom they fixed, had frequent broils and wars among themselves, but the pirates interposed, and endeavoured to reconcile all differences, North deciding their disputes with that impartiality and strict regard to distributive justice, (for he was allowed, by all, a man of admirable good natural parts) that he ever sent away, even the party who' was cast, satisfied with the reason, and content with the equity of his decisions.

These inclinations which the pirates showed to peace, and the example they set of an amicable way of life, (for they carefully avoided all jars, and agreed to refer all cause of complaint among themselves which might arise,

116

to a cool hearing before North, and twelve of their companions,) gave them a great character among the natives, who were before very much prejudiced against the white men. Nay, in this point of keeping up a harmony among themselves, they were so exact, that whosoever spoke but in an angry or peevish tone, was rebuked by all the company, especially if before any of the country people, though even but a slave of their own; for they thought, and very justly, that unity and concord were the only means to warrant their safety; for the people being ready to make war on one another upon the slightest occasion, they did not doubt but they would take the advantage of any division which they might observe among the whites, and cut them off whenever a fair opportunity offered.

The example they set, and the care they took to accommodate differences among their neighbours, had calmed all the country round them. After they had lived here near three years, Capt. North, and some of his companions, had a mind to visit the country southward, and trade for more slaves and cattle; to which end, taking a considerable quantity of powder and arms, beside what they might use, with 50 whites and 300 natives, he set forward on his journey. When they had traveled about 80 miles southward, they came to a nation rich in slaves and cattle, who inhabited the banks of the largest river on the east side of the island, called Mangora. With these people he trafficked for a great number of slaves and cattle, which he purchased for guns and powder. They being at war when Capt. North came among them, with a neighbouring prince, he was entreated to give his assistance, for which they, the Mangorians, promised him 100 slaves with 500 head of cattle, and all the prisoners they should take. On these conditions he joined them, and marched to a very large town of the enemy's, which was naturally very strong, and esteemed by the natives impregnable, being situated on a high and craggy rock, which could be ascended by the way only leading to the gate, were was kept a strong guard. The blacks in North's army were for leaving this town unattempted, and marching farther into the country, in search of booty; but North told them it was not safe to leave a garrison of enemies at their backs, which would continually infest them by falling on their rear, and which would be an obstacle to their carrying off what plunder they might get together; beside, it would be an asylum for all the country, which would fly thither till they had gathered a body considerable enough to come down and face them in the open field, which the enemy might do with reasonable hopes of success, as their men would be all fresh, while those of his party would be fatigued with marches, perhaps encumbered by plunder, and worn down with the inconveniences of lying exposed in the fields.

The chief of his allies allowed his reasons good, were an attempt on the town practicable, which experience told him was not; for, though several times besieged, it never could be taken, and it would be the loss of a great deal of time, and many men's lives to attempt it. North desired he would leave the management of this siege to him. The chief answered, he should do as he pleased, hut it was against his judgment to attack a town which nature

117

herself had fortified, which God Almighty would never suffer to he taken, and which had, to no purpose, cost the lives of a number scarce to be told, of his countrymen, in the several attempts they had made to be masters of it.

North disposed his army, and invested the rock on every side; then sent word to the town, if they did not surrender, he would -give no quarter to either sex or age. The inhabitants laughed at his message, and told him, that they did not believe he had learnt the art of flying, and till he had, they thought themselves very secure from his putting such menaces in execution.

Out of the white men, North chose 30, whom he set at the head of three companies, consisting of 100 blacks each; and as they had some grenade-shells with them, soon dispersed the guard at the foot of the rock, and made a lodgement. Though the blacks were acquainted with fire-arms, the shells were entirely new to them, and as they saw then? terrible effect, threw down their arms, and gained the middle of the rock, where they had another *corps de guarde,* though not without some loss. Those who were at the bottom of the rock being put to flight, North sent 10 whites and 500 blacks to take that post, and orders to the other whites to mount the rock, and having beat that guard, if possible, to enter the town with them. They accordingly ascended in this order, as the road was so narrow, only three could pass abreast; and as the enemy, when within cast of a dart, threw down a shower upon them, three unarmed blacks with their shields marched before three small shot men, and sheltered them from the enemy's weapons. These were followed by others, with the same precaution, the white men being mixed with those who thus went up, that is to say, one white musketeer to two blacks.

The enemy seemed resolute to defend the pass, but when they had, to no purpose, spent a number of darts, and had lost some men by the shot, they swiftly took to the top of the rock, where, joined with fresh men from the town, they made a stand and show of resistance. North's men followed, and pouring in a volley, put them into confusion, which gave the assailants an opportunity to come near enough to throw in their shells, half a dozen of which bursting with considerable damage, and the slaughter of several men, they thought to shelter themselves in the town, but the inhabitants, fearing the enemy's entering with them, shut the gates against both, so that the blacks of North's army, notwithstanding all the whites could do to the contrary, made a great slaughter; however, they saved some, whom they sent prisoners to the camp, desiring at the same time, a supply of powder to make a petard.

In the meanwhile, the enemy from the town threw a prodigious quantity of darts, which the besiegers received upon their shields, at least, the greater part.

The town was again summoned, but they refused to surrender; wherefore they were obliged to shelter themselves as well as they could, and expect the powder from the camp; though in the mean while the small shot from without being warmly plied, the throwing of darts from the town became less frequent, for no one could show his head but with the greatest danger.

When the powder came, they cut down and hollowed a tree, which they filled with powder, and plugged up very tight, and under the protection of their shields and muskets, got into the gate, under which they dug a hole large enough to receive it, then setting fire to the fuse, it burst with a terrible crack, tore their gate to atoms, and left an open passage, which the besiegers, who had been joined with 500 more blacks, who came up with the powder entered, and began a very great slaughter. The whites protected all they could who submitted but notwithstanding their diligence, the town was strewed with dead and dying men. At length, what with being tired, and what with persuasion, the slaughter ceased, the town was reduced to ashes, and the conquerors returned to camp with 3000 prisoners, whom his allies led to their own quarters, where culling out the old women, children, and useless slaves, they sent them to North, as if by these they thought themselves released from the promise made to induce his assistance.

When North saw the dishonesty of these people, he sent for their prince, and told him, "According to agreement all the slaves belonged to him; nay, according to justice, he alone had a right to them, since he despaired of taking the town, so far as to dissuade his besieging it; and that he not only owed to him their success, but even the safety of his army, and all the plunder they should make in the prosecution of the war, for reasons already given, and by himself allowed to be good. That he thought he had allied himself to a people of integrity, but lie was sorry to say, he found himself quite mistaken in his opinion, since they were so far from making good their treaty, that they sent him out of the slaves taken, instead of all, those only whom they knew not what to do with; that they must not imagine him so blind as not to perceive how disingenuously he was dealt with; or that he wanted either strength or resolution to resent the usage."

He then asked what was become of a number of young and handsome women he had seen among the captives? The prince answered, "that those fee inquired after, were his and his countrymen's relations, and as such, they could not consent to, or could he require, their being made slaves."

This answer made, the chief left him. As it was delivered in a pretty haughty tone, it did not a little nettle both North and his comrades. The latter were for immediately doing themselves justice; but the former begged they would have patience, and rely on him. They followed his advice, and he sent an interpreter, who inquired privately among the women what relation they bore to the people of the river? The prisoners answered, that some of their forefathers had intermarried with that nation.

I must here take notice, that notwithstanding the inhabitants of Madagascar have but one language, which is common to the whole island, the difference of the dialect, in different nations, makes it very difficult for any but the natives, or those who have been a great many years (more than North and his companions had been) among them, to understand them perfectly, which is the reason he made use of an interpreter, as well between him and the chief, as between the slaves and him.

119

When he had received this answer from the prisoners, he went to the prince, and told him, "It was very odd he should make war on his relations however, he should keep them, since he declared them such, till he could prove his right better than the prince could his nearness of blood; that as he had once taken them, he would try if he could not support the justice of his claim, and told him therefore to be upon his guard, for he openly declared, fee was no longer the ally, but the professed enemy of faithless people."

Saying this, he and his blacks separated themselves from the Mangorians, and North divided them into companies, with his white men at the head of each, and ordered them to fire hall over the heads of their late allies. The first volley was a prodigious astonishment to the Mangorians, several of whom ran away, but North firing two more immediately, and marching up to them, brought the prince and the head officers of his army to him, crawling on all fours. They (as the custom of showing the greatest submission is among them) kissed the feet of the whites and begged they would continue their friendship and dispose of everything as they thought proper.

North told him, "Deceit was the sign of a mean and coward soul; that had he, the prince, thought too considerable, what, however, was justly his due, because not only promised to, but taken by him, he ought to have expostulated with him, North, and. told him his sentiments, which might have, it was possible, made no division, for neither he nor his men were unreasonable; but as the prince had not the courage publicly to claim the slaves, he would have basely stolen them by false pretences of kindred, it was a sign he did not think such claim justifiable, as certainly it was not, for all his captains could witness their prince had agreed the prisoners taken should be given to the whites, and his companions, a sufficient title, to mention no other. That he had resolved to show them, by a severe chastisement, the abhorrence those of his colour have to ingratitude and deceit, and what difference there was in fighting on the ground of justice, and the supporting wrong and injury; but as they acknowledged their error, he should not only forgive but forget what was past, provided no new treachery, in his return, which he resolved upon, refreshed his memory." He then ordered them to bring all the slaves, and they punctually complied without reply.

North chose out the finest and ablest among them, and dividing the whole number of prisoners into two equal bands, he kept that in which he had placed the chosen slaves, and sent the other to the prince, telling him, "though neither fraud nor compulsion could wring a slave from him, yet justice, as some of his troops had shared the danger, and a generous temper, had sent him that present, which was half the spoil, though he could not think of going any farther on with the war; that he ought to content himself with. the taking a town hitherto thought impregnable, and blame his own conduct, if he should continue in the field, and hereafter find the want of his assistance."

The prince and his people admired the penetration, bravery, and generosity of the whites, and Sent them word, "he was more obliged to them for the

120

lesson they had taught him by their practice, than for the slaves they had presented him, though he esteemed the present as he ought. That for the future he should have an abhorrence for every mean action, since he had learned from them the beauty of a candid, open, sincere procedure. At the same time, he thanked him for the present, and not suffering his resentment to go farther than the frightening him into his duty; for he was sensible his balls were not fired over their heads, but by orders proceeding from the humanity of the whites, who, he observed, were tender over the lives of their enemies, contrary to the custom of his countrymen, who give quarter to none, the females and infants excepted, that there may hereafter be none to take revenge; and therefore begged he would suffer their submission to get the better of his design to depart." This could not prevail. The whites and their friends, who came with them, turned their faces towards home, taking their slaves and cattle with them; and though the Mangorians were sensibly touched at the obstinacy of North's resolution, yet they parted very amicably.

As the whites were returning home with their company, they fell in with another nation, the Timouses, whose prince joined North, with 500 men, and swore a strict amity with him and his crew.

The ceremony used among the natives, as it is uncommon, so an account of it may, perhaps, be agreeable. The parties who swear to each other., interweave their toes and fingers, so that they must necessarily sit very close to each other. When they have thus knit their hands and feet, they reciprocally swear to do each other all friendly offices, to: be a friend or enemy to the friend or enemy of the party to whom they swear; and if they falsify the oath they make, they imprecate several curses on themselves, as may they fall by the lance, be devoured by the alligator, or struck dead by the hand of God. Then an assistant scarifies each of the contracting parties on the chest, and wiping up the blood with a piece of bread, gives this bloody bread to each of them to cat, that Is, each eats the blood of the other; and this oath, whether it be with equal parties, or with a prince and his subject, where the one promises protection and the other obedience, (which was the nature of that taken between North and this prince) is looked upon inviolable, and they have few examples of its being broken; but where any has been wicked enough to violate this solemn oath, they say, they have been ever punished according to their imprecations.

As this prince had war with powerful neighbours, he left his country, taking with him all his great men, wives, and relations, with a company of about 500 fighting men, followed North, and settled by him, where he remained two years. During this space, being supplied with arms and powder by Capt. North, he made several inroads into the countries of his enemies, and made all he conquered swear allegiance to Capt. North.

At the expiration of two years, Captain Halsey came in with a brigantine, as is related in the life of Capt. White. This crew, having made a broken voyage, where discontented with their captain, and desired North to take the command upon him; but he declined it, saying, Halsey was every way as capable, and that they ought not to depose a man, whom they could not tax with either want of courage or conduct; and for his part, he would never take the command from any one who did not justly merit dismission, which was not Halsey's case.

The crew were not, however; satisfied, and they made the same offer to White, but by North's industry, they were, at last, prevailed on to continue their old commander; and as North and his companions had expended their money in settling their plantations, and wanted clothes, the former, therefore, accepted the quartermaster's post under Halsey, and the others went in the capacity of private gentlemen adventurers, I mean plain foremast men, as may be gathered in the life of that pirate, to which I refer for an account of the expedition they made in the Red Sea. Capt. Halsey on board a prize, left North to command the brigantine they set out in. The two commanders were separated by a storm, but both made for Madagascar. Halsey got to Ambonavoula, but North fell in. with Maratan, where finding the brigantine was very much worm eaten, and made a great deal of water, with one consent, they took ashore all their goods, and laid up their vessel.

The pirates continued here a whole year, when being desirous of going to Ambonavoula, they asked the king's assistance to build a boat, and he, for 1000 dollars, set negroes to work, under the directions of Capt. North, and a vessel of 15 tons was set up and launched with great dispatch. In this boat they went to a river, called Wanangaro, thirty leagues to the northward of Maratan. Here some of their comrades came to them in a boat belonging to the Scotch ship Neptune, and helped to transport their goods to Amhonavoula, where he had before settled, and had a woman and three children.

He had not been long returned before his neighbouring natives reported, that the Timouses, who had followed him from the southward, had a design to rebel against, and murder him and the other whites, which giving too easy credit to, he made war upon, and drove these poor people out of the country.

Some time after he built a sloop, and went to Antonguil, where he purchased 90 slaves, and took in the Scotch supercargo, Mr. George Cruikeshank, with a design to carry him to Mascarenhas; but all his comrades were against it, saying, when he got to Europe, he would prove their destruction. North answered, that nothing could be more cruel, after they had taken the greater part of what the poor gentleman had, than to keep him from his country, family, and friends. For his part, were he his prisoner he should not ask their consent in doing an act of humanity, and the only one they were able, towards making him some reparation, since they could not return his goods, which were parcelled out into so many shares.

On North's saying thus much, they put the affair in question to vote, and there being many who were under obligations to North, and whom he influenced in favour of the supercargo, 48 out of 54 voted for discharging him. North having gained this point, the pirates asked if he also designed to take with him one John Barnard, a young Scotchman, a great favourite of his, who had been midshipman on board the Neptune, a thorough seaman, and very capable of taking the command in any voyage. He answered, there was a necessity for taking him, since he should want his assistance, as he depended on his knowledge. His companions said Barnard would certainly give him the slip, which would be a loss to them all, as he was an excellent navigator, and therefore his detention was necessary to the common good. To this North answered, that his own security would oblige his taking care that he should not get from him, since no other on board was capable of finding the way back to Ambonavoula.

He went to Mascarenhas, where the supercargo and his negro were put on shore with all the money he had, which amounted to about 1600 dollars; for when the pirates made prize of the Neptune, in the manner already stated, they took none of the money they themselves had before paid for liquors, &c. either from the captain, supercargo, or any other on board; for that they looked upon abase, as well as dishonest action; but to the ship and remaining part of the cargo, they had a fair title, viz. they wanted both.

North would not suffer Barnard to go ashore. However, to make him amends for his confinement, he gave him four negroes, whom he sold for 300 dollars, and took care that he should live plentifully and well on board. North's business at this island, was to get leave to carry his children there to be educated in the Christian faith, which, after some rich presents made the governor, he obtained, and returned to Madagascar. In the voyage, as Barnard was very greatly in his favour, and his confidant, he told him, his design was to leave his children at Mascarenhas, and place fortunes for them in the hands of some honest priest, who would give them a Christian education (for he thought it better to have them papists, than not Christians) and would then go back to Maratan, and endeavour, by his penitence, to make atonement for his former life and never more go off the island on any account; that he would give his sloop to Barnard, with 200 dollars, that he might find some means to return home, since he very wisely refused to join with the pirates.

When he came on the Madagascar coast, he heard a French ship had touched there, and left some men behind; upon which account North ran to the southward 100 leagues out of his way, to inquire after and assist these people.

He found but one man, whom he took home with him, clothed and maintained him. When he came back to Ambonavoula, he found the country all in an uproar, and the rest of his companions preparing for a war with the natives; but his arrival restored their former quiet. After four months stay at home, he fitted his sloop to go out and purchase slaves at Antonguil; but finding few there to his mind, for in two months he bought but 40, he returned to his settlement. He designed now to carry his children to Mascarenhas, but being dissuaded by Barnard on account of the season, he went to Methelage on the west side of the island to trade for samsams. Having purchased a considerable quantity of them, he went to Johanna, thence to Mayotta, and returned again to Madagascar; but not being able to get round the north end, on account of the current, he put for Mayotta again. On the west side of this island he put into a port, called Sorez, where some time before, came a ship from England to trade, commanded by one Price, who going ashore with his doctor was detained (as was also Lis boat's crew) till lie redeemed himself and surgeon, with 200 barrels of powder and 1000 small arms; but was forced to leave his boat's crew, not having wherewithal to ransom them, though the demand was only two small arms for each man. These poor creatures were afterwards sold to the Arabians. In revenge, North and his crew landed, burnt a large town, and did all the damage they could. From Mayotta he went again to Madagascar, were a king of his acquaintance told him the whites and natives were at war at Amhonavoula. He bought 30 slaves, refreshed his crew, and went home. On the news of his arrival, the natives sent to conclude a peace, but he would not listen to them; on the contrary, raised an army, burnt a number of towns, and took a great many prisoners.

This success brought the natives to sue in a very humble manner for a cessation of arms, that a general peace might follow. This he agreed to about four months alter his arrival.

His enemies, having now the opportunity, corrupted some of the neighbouring natives, and in the night surprised and murdered him in his bed. His comrades, however, being alarmed, took to their arms, drove the treacherous multitude before them with great slaughter, and to revenge North's death, continued the war seven years, in which time they became masters of all the country round, and drove out all who did not swear allegiance to them.

North had his will lying by him, which directed Barnard to carry his children to Mascarenhas, in his sloop, which he left to him. He was at the charge of fitting her up, and laid out the greater part of the money North bequeathed him; but the pirates would not suffer him to stir while the wars lasted, fearing he would not return, having never joined them in any piracies; and therefore, by one consent, setting fire to the sloop, they detained him several years.

An Account

...Of the piracies and cruelties of John Augur, William Cunningham, Dennis Mackarthy, William Dowling, William Lewis, Thomas Morris, George Bendall, and William Ling, who were tried, condemned, and executed at Nassau, (N. P.) on Friday, the 10th of December, 1718. Also, some account of the pirates, Vane, Rackham, and others.

About the 20th of July, 1718, Mr. Woodes Rogers, Governor and Vice-Admiral of the Bahama Islands, being sent from England with the king's proclamation and pardon for all pirates who had surrendered by a time specified in the said proclamation, arrived at Providence. It was evening when the fleet came off the town of Nassau in the said island, when Richard Turnley, the pilot, did not judge it safe to venture over the bar that night, wherefore it was resolved to lay by till morning.

In the meantime, there came some men on board the fleet from off a little island, called Harbour Island, adjacent to Providence. The advice they brought was, that there were near a thousand pirates on shore upon the island of Providence, waiting for the king's pardon which had been long expected. The principal part of their commanders were Benjamin Hornygold, Arthur Davis, Joseph Burgess, Thomas Carter and they were all in or about the town of Nassau; that the fort was extremely out of repair, there being only one gun mounted, a nine pounder, and no accommodation for men, but one little hut or house, which was inhabited by an old fellow, whom the pirates, in derision, called Governor Sawney.

The fleet was seen from the harbour, as well as the town, so that Capt. Charles Vane, who had no design of surrendering, but, on the contrary, had fitted out his ship with a resolution of attempting new adventures, took the advantage of the night to contrive his escape; and though the harbour was blocked up, and his ship drew too much water to get out by the east passage, he shifted his hands, and things of most value, into a lighter vessel, and charging all the guns of the ship he quitted, with double, round and partridge, he set her on fire, imagining that some of the ships, or their boats, might be sent near him, and he might do some mischief when it should burn down to them.

Those in the fleet saw the light, and heard the guns, and fancied the pirates on shore were making bonfires, and firing guns for joy that the king's free pardon had arrived; and Capt. Whitney, commander of the Rose man of war, sent his boat with a lieutenant on shore, which was intercepted by Vane, who carried the crew on board and stripped them of some stores they had in the boat. He kept them till he got under sail, which was till day-break, when there was light enough for him to see how to steer his way through the east passage; which was no sooner done but he hoisted a black flag, and fired a gun, and then let the lieutenant and boat's crew depart and join the fleet.

The fleet got safe into the harbour, and as soon as the lieutenant arrived on board, and related what had passed, the Buck sloop was ordered to chase Vane. She made what sail she could through the east passage after him, having a recruit of men well-armed sent to her from the other ships; but being heavily laden with rich goods, Vane had the heels of her, which the commodore observing, made a signal for her to give up the chase and return, which she did accordingly.

They immediately fell to mooring and securing their ships, which took up the time till night. Next morning the governor went on shore, being received at his landing by the principal people in the government of the place, viz. Thomas Walker, Esq. Chief Justice, and Thomas Taylor, Esq. President of the Council. The pirate captains, Hornygold, Davis, Carter, Burgess, Currant, and Clark, with some others, drew up their crews in two lines, reaching from the water side to the fort, the governor and other officers marching between them. In the mean time, being under arms, they made a running fire over his head.

Having arrived at the fort, his commission was opened and read, and he was sworn in governor of the island, according to form.

The next day the governor made out a commission to Richard Turnley, the chief pilot, to Mr. Salter, a factor, and some others, to go on board and examine all suspected ships and vessels in the harbour, to take an inventory of their several ladings, and to secure both ships and cargoes for the use of the king and company, till such time as a Court of Admiralty could be called, that they might be lawfully cleared or condemned by proving which belonged to pirates, and which to fair traders.

The day following a court-martial was held, in which a military discipline was settled, in order to prevent surprises, both from Spaniards and pirates, till such time as the fort could be repaired, and put into a condition of defence. For this purpose the governor was obliged to make use of some of the pardoned pirates, such as Hornygold, Davis, and Burgess, to whom he gave some commands: and George Fetherston, James Bonney, and Dennis Mackarthy, with some other pirates of a lower rank, acted under them as inferior officers.

Soon after, the civil government was also settled, some of the principal officers being appointed justices of the peace; others of inferior degree, constables and overseers of the ways and roads, which were overgrown with bushes and underwood, ail about the town of Nassau; so that if an enemy had landed in the night, they might lie in ambuscade in those covers, and surprise the town; wherefore, several of the common pirates were employed in clearing them away.

The governor, with some soldiers, guarded the fort, and the inhabitants, who were formed into trained bands, took care of the town; but as there was no sort of accommodation to lodge such a number of people, they were forced to unbend the sails, and bring them on shore, in order to make tents, tilt they had time to build houses, which was done with all possible expedition, by a kind of architecture altogether new.

Those that were built in the fort were done by making six little holes in the rock, at convenient distances, in each of which was stuck a forked pole; on these, from one to the other, were placed cross poles or rafters, which being lathed at top, and on the sides, with small sticks, were afterwards covered with Palmata leaves, and then the house was finished; for they did not much trouble themselves about the ornaments of doors and windows.

In the meantime, the repairs of the fort were carried on, and the streets were ordered to be kept clean, both for health and convenience, so that it began to have the appearance of a civilized place. A proclamation was published for the encouragement of all such persons as should be willing to settle upon the island of Providence, by which every person was to have a lot of ground of a hundred mid twenty feet square, anywhere in or about the town of Nassau, that was not before in the possession of others, provided they should clear said ground, and build a house tenantable, by a certain time therein limited, which might be easily done, as they might have timber for nothing. This had the effect proposed, and a great many immediately fell to work, to comply with the conditions, in order to settle themselves there.

Many of the pirates were employed in the woods in cutting down sticks to make palisadoes; and all the people belonging to the ships, officers excepted, were obliged to work four days in the week on the fortifications, so that in a short time a strong entrenchment was cast round the fort, and being well palisadoed, it was rendered tolerably strong.

But it did not much suit the inclinations of the pirates to be set to work; and though they had provision sufficient, and had also a good allowance of wine and brandy to each man, yet they began to have such a hankering after their old trade, that many of them took opportunities of seizing periaguas and other boats, in the night, and making their escape, so that in a few months, there was not many of them left.

However, when the Spanish war was proclaimed, several of them returned back again of their own accord, tempted with the hopes of being employed upon the privateering account, for that place lying near the coast of Spanish America, and also not far from the Gulf of Florida, seemed to be a good station for intercepting the Spanish vessels going to old Spain.

They were not mistaken in this supposition; for the governor according to the power vested in him, did grant commissions for privateering, and made choice of some of the principal pirates who had continued upon the island, in obedience to the pardon, for commanders, as being persons well qualified for such employments, who made up their crews chiefly of their scattered companions, who were newly returned upon the hopes of preferment.

About this time a fishing vessel, belonging to the island of Providence, brought in the master of a ship and a few sailors, whom she had picked up at sea in a canoe. The said master was called Captain King, who sailed in a ship called the Neptune, belonging to South-Carolina, laden with rice, pitch, tar, and other merchandise, bound for London.

The account he gave of himself was, that he was met with by Charles Vane, the pirate, who carried him into Green Turtle Bay, one of the Bahama islands, by whom he was plundered of a great part of his cargo, which, consisting chiefly of stores, was of great use to them; that afterwards they cut away part of one of the masts of the ship, and fired a gun down her hold with intent to sink her; that they took some of his men into their service, and when they were sailing off, gave him and the rest a canoe to save themselves; that with this canoe they made shift to sail from one little island to another, till they had the good luck to meet the fishing boat which took them up; and that he believed Charles Vane might still be cruising thereabouts.

Upon this intelligence, the governor fitted out a ship which was named the Willing Mind, manned with 50 stout hands, well-armed, and also a sloop with 30 hands, which he sent to cruise among those islands, in search of Vane, the pirate, giving them orders also to endeavour to recover the ship Neptune, which Capt. King told them had still goods of considerable value left in her.

They went out accordingly, but never saw Vane. However, they found the Neptune, which was not. sunk as the pirates intended; for the ball they tied into her stuck in the ballast, without passing through. They returned with her about the 10th of November; but an unlucky accident happened to the Willing Mind, occasioned either by the ignorance or carelessness of the pilot, which bilged in going over the bar.

In the meantime, Vane made towards the coast of Hispaniola, living riotously on board, having an abundance of liquor, and plenty of fresh provisions, such as hogs, goats, sheep, and fowl, which he got upon easy terms; for touching at a place called Isleathera, he plundered the inhabitants of as much of their provision as they could carry away. Here they cruised to about February, when, near the windward passage of Cape Mase, they met with a large rich ship of London, called the Kingston, laden with bale goods, and other rich merchandise, and having several passengers on board, some English, and some Jews, besides two women. Towards the north end of Jamaica, they also met with a turtle sloop, bound in for that island, on board of which (after having first plundered her) they put the captain of the Kingston, -some of his men, and all the passengers except the two women, whom they detained, contrary to their usual practice.

The Kingston they kept for their own use; for now their company being strengthened by a great many recruits, some volunteers and some forced men out of the Neptune and Kingston, they thought they had hands enough for two ships. Accordingly they shifted several of their hands on board the Kingston, and John Rackham, alias Calico Jack, (so called, because his jackets and drawers were always made of calico) quartermaster to Vane, was unanimously chosen captain of the Kingston.

The empire of these pirates had not been long thus divided before they had like to have fallen into a civil war among themselves, which must have; ended in the destruction of one of them. The fatal occasion of the difference between these two brother adventurers, was this, It happened that Vane's liquor was ah out, who sending to his brother captain for a supply, Rackham accordingly spared him what he thought fit; but it falling short of Vane's expectation, as to quantity, he went on board of Rackham's ship to expostulate with him, so that words arising, Rackham threatened to shoot him through the head, if he did not immediately return to his own ship; and told him likewise, that if he did not sheer off, and part company, he would sink him. Vane thought it best to take his advice, for he thought the other was bold enough to be as good as his word, for he had it in his power to be so, his ship being the largest and strongest of the two. Accordingly they parted, and Rackham made for the island of Princes, and having great quantities of rich goods on board, taken in the late prizes, they were divided into lots, and he and his crew shared them by throwing dice, the highest cast being to choose first. When they had done, they packed up their goods in casks, and buried them on shore in the island of Princes, that they might have room for fresh booty. In the mean time it happening that a turtle sloop, belonging to Jamaica, came in there, Rackham sent, his boat and brought the master on board of him, and asking him several questions, the master informed him that war with Spain had been proclaimed in Jamaica; and that the time appointed by the general pardon for pirates to surrender, in order to receive the benefit thereof, had not expired.

Upon this intelligence Rackham and his crew suddenly changed their minds, and were resolved to take the benefit of the pardon by a speedy surrender; wherefore, instead of using the master ill, as the poor man expected, they made him several presents, desiring him to sail back to Jamaica, and acquaint the governor they were willing to surrender, provided he would give his word and honour they should have the benefit of the pardon; which, extensive as it was, they apprehended they were not entitled to, because they had run away in defiance of it at Providence. They desired the master also to return with the governor's answer, assuring him he should be no loser by the voyage.

The master very willingly undertook the commission, and arriving at Jamaica, delivered his message to the governor, according to his instructions; but it happened that the master of the Kingston, with his passengers, having arrived at Jamaica, had acquainted the governor with the piracies of Vane and Rackham, before the turtle got thither, who was actually fitting out two sloops, which were now just ready, in pursuit of them, so that the governor was very glad to discover, by the turtler's message, where Rackham was to be found.

The two sloops, well-manned, accordingly sailed out, and found Rackham in the station where the turtler had described him, but altogether in disorder, and quite unprepared, either for sailing or fighting, most of his sails being on shore, erected into tents, and his decks lumbered with goods. He happened to be on board himself, though most of his. men were ashore, and seeing the two sloops at a distance, bearing towards him, he observed them with his glass, and fancied he saw on board something like preparations for fighting. This was what he did not expect, for he looked for no enemy, and while he was in doubt and suspense about them, they came so near that they began to fire.

He had neither time nor means to prepare for defence, so that there was nothing to be done but to run into his boat, and escape to the shore, which he did accordingly with the few hands he had with him leaving the two women on board to be taken by the enemy.

The sloops seized the Kingston, manned her, and brought her into Jamaica, having still a great part of her cargo left. When she arrived, the master of her fell to examining what part of the cargo was lost and what left; he searched also for his bills of lading and cockets, but they were all destroyed by Rackham; so that the ship being freighted by several owners, the master could not tell whose property was saved, and whose lost, till he had fresh bills of parcels of each owner from England. There was one remarkable piece of good luck which happened in this affair; there were, amongst other goods, sixty gold watches on board, and thirty of silver; the pirates divided the silver watches, but the gold being packed up amongst some bale goods, were never discovered by them, and the master, in searching, found them all safe.

In the meantime, Rackham and his crew lived in the woods, in very great suspense. what to do with themselves. They had with them ammunition and small arms, and also some of the goods, such as bales of silk stockings, and laced hats, with which, it is supposed, they intended to make themselves fine. They had also two boats and a canoe.

Being divided in their resolutions, Rackham, with six more, determined to take one of the boats, and make the best of their way for the island of Providence, and there claim the benefit of the king's pardon, which they fancied they might be entitled to, by representing, that they were carried away by Vane, against their wills. Accordingly they put some arms, ammunition, and provision, into the best boat, and also some of the goods, and set sail. They first made the Island of Pines, from thence got over to the north side of Cuba, where they destroyed several Spanish boats and launches; one they took, which being a stout sea boat, they shifted themselves and their cargo into her, sunk their own, and then stretched over to the island of Providence, where they landed safely about the middle of May, 1719, where demanding the king's pardon, the governor thought fit to allow it them, and certificates were granted to them accordingly.

Here they sold their goods, and spent the money merrily. When all was gone, some engaged themselves in privateers, and others in trading vessels. But Rackham, as captain, having a much larger share than any of the rest, his money held out a little longer; but happening about this time to form a criminal acquaintance with one Ann Bonny, a married woman, he became very extravagant, and found it necessary, to avoid detection and punishment, to abscond with his mistress.

For this purpose they plotted together to seize a sloop which then lay in the harbour, and Rackham drew some brisk young fellows into the conspiracy. They were of the number of the pirates lately pardoned, and who, he knew, were weary of working on shore, and longed to be again at their old trade.

The sloop they made choice of was between 30 and 40 tons, and one of the swiftest sailors that ever was built of that kind. She belonged to one John Haman, who lived upon a little island not far from Providence, which was inhabited by no human creature except himself and his family. His livelihood and constant employment was to plunder and pillage the Spaniards, whose sloops and launches he had often surprised about Cuba and Hispaniola, and sometimes brought off a considerable booty, always escaping by a good pair of heels, insomuch that it became a bye-word to say, *there goes John Haman, catch him if you can.* His business to Providence now, was to bring his family there, in order to live and settle, being weary, perhaps, of living in that solitude, or else, apprehensive, if any of the Spaniards should discover his habitation, they might land, and be revenged on him for all his pranks.

Ann Bonny was observed to go several times on board this sloop. She pretended to have some business with John Haman; but always went when he was on shore, for her true errand was to discover how many hands were on board, and what kind of watch they kept, and to know the passages and ways of the vessel.

She discovered as much as was necessary. She found there were but two hands on board, and that John Haman slept on shore every night. She inquired of them whether they watched; where they lay; and many other questions; to all which they readily answered her, as thinking she had no design but common curiosity.

She acquainted Rackham with every particular, who resolved to lose no time, and therefore, acquainting his associates, who were eight in number, they appointed an hour for meeting at night, which was 12 o'clock. They were all true to the roguery, and Ann Bonny was as punctual as the most resolute, and being all well-armed, they took a boat and rowed to the sloop, which was very near the shore.

The night seemed to favour the attempt, for it was both dark and rainy. As soon as they got on board, Ann Bonny, having a drawn sword in one hand, and a pistol in the other, attended by one of the men, went straight to the cabin where the two fellows lay who belonged to the sloop. The noise awaked them, which she observing, declared that if they pretended to resist, or make a noise, she would blow their brains out.

In the meantime, Rackham and the rest were busy heaving in the cables, one of which they soon got up, and for expedition sake, they slipped the other, and so drove down the harbour. They passed pretty near the fort, which hailed them, as did also the guard-ship, asking them where they were going. They answered, their cable had parted, and that they had nothing but a grappling on board, which would not hold them immediately after which they set a small sail, just to give them steerage way. When they came to the harbours mouth, and thought they could not be seen by any of the ships, on account of the darkness of the night, they hoisted all the sail they had, and stood to sea; then calling up the two men, they asked them if they would be of their party; but finding them not inclined, they gave them a boat to row themselves ashore, ordering them to give their service to Hainan, and tell him they would send him his sloop again when they had done with her.

Rackham and his paramour both bore a great spleen to Richard Turnley, who was gone from Providence, turtlings before they made their escape, and they knowing what island he was upon, made to the place. They saw the sloop about a league from the shore, and went on board with six hands; but Turnley, with his boy, by good luck, happened to be ashore salting some wild hogs they had killed the day before. They inquired for him, and hearing where he was, rowed ashore in search of him.

Turnley, from the land, saw the sloop boarded, and observed the men afterwards making for the shore, and being apprehensive of pirates, which were very common in those parts, he, with his boy, led into a neighbouring wood. The surf being very great, so that they could not bring their boat to shore, they waded up to the arm-pits, and Turnley, peeping through the trees, saw them bring arms on shore. Upon the whole, not liking their appearance, he, with his boy, lay snug in the bushes.

When they had looked about and could not see him, they called him aloud by name; but he not appearing, they thought it time lost to look for him in such a wilderness, and therefore returned to their boat, but rowed again back to the sloop, and took away the sails, and several other things. They also carried away with them three of the hands, viz. Richard Connor, the mate, John Davis, and John Howel, but rejected David Soward, the fourth hand, though he had been an old and experienced pirate, because he was lame, and 'disabled by a wound lie had formerly received.

When they had done thus much, they cut away the mast, and towing the vessel into deep water, sunk her, having first put David Soward into a boat to shift for himself. He, however, got ashore, and after some time, found Turnley.

From thence, Rackham stretched over to the Bury Islands, plundering all the sloops he met, and strengthening his company with several additional hands, and so went on till he was finally taken and executed at Port Royal, Jamaica.

About this time, the governor, in conjunction with some factors then residing at Providence, thought fit to freight some vessels for a trading voyage. Accordingly the Bachelor's Adventure, a schooner, Capt. Henry White, commander; the Lancaster, sloop, Capt. William Greenway commander; the May, sloop, Capt. John Augur, commander, of which last David Soward was owner, (she having been given him by some pirates his former associates) in which he also sailed this voyage, were fitted out with a cargo of goods and merchandise, bound for Port Prince, on the island of Cuba.

The governor thought it advisable, for the benefit of the inhabitants of Providence, to settle a correspondence with some merchants of Port Prince, first, in order to procure fresh provisions, there being scarce any upon the island at the governor's first arrival; and there being at Port Prince great plenty of cows and hogs, he proposed to get a sufficient number of each, to stock the island for breed, that the people for the future might have fresh provision of their own.

They set sail on Sunday, the 5th of October, 1718. The next day they arrived at an island known by the name of Green Key, lying S. S. E. from Providence, iii lat. 28 deg. 40 m. being distant about 25 leagues. Here they cast anchor, in order to wait for morning to carry them through some rocks and shoals which lay in their way, and some hands went ashore to try to kill something for supper before it should be dark. They expected to meet some wild hogs, for some time before, one Joseph Bay and one Sims, put two sows and a boar on said island; for they living at that time at Providence, and being continually visited by pirates, were" always plundered of their fresh provisions, wherefore they thought of settling a breed upon Green Key, that they might have recourse to in time of necessity.

This island is about nine miles in circumference, and about three miles broad in the widest place. It is overgrown with wild cabbage and Palmata trees, and has a great variety of other herbs and fruits, so that there is plenty of food for the nourishment of such animals; but the trees growing so close together, makes it bad hunting, and they killed but one hop-, which, however, was of a monstrous size.

The hunters returned on board their ships again before seven, having first divided the hog, and sent part on board each vessel for supper that night After supper, Capt. Greenway and Capt. White came on board of Capt. Augur's sloop, m order to consult together what time to sail, and being all of opinion that if they weighed anchor between the? hours of 10 and 11, it would be day before they would come up with the shoals, they agreed upon that hour for setting sail, and so returned to their own vessels.

Soon after, Phinehas Bunch, and Dennis Mackarthy, with a great many others, came from White's sloop, on board of Augur's. Their pretence was, that they came to see Richard Turnley and Mr. James Carr, who had formerly been a midshipman on the Rose man of war, under Capt. Whitney, and being a great favourite of Governor Rogers, he had appointed him supercargo of this voyage. They desired to be treated with a bottle of beer, for they knew Mr. Carr had some that was very good in his care, which had been put. on board, in order to make presents of, and to treat the Spanish merchants with.

As it was not suspected they had any thing else in view, Mr. Carr readily went down, and brought up a couple of bottles of beer. They sat upon the poop with Capt. Augur in their company, and were drinking their beer; before the second bottle was out, Bunch and Mackarthy began to rattle, talk with great pleasure, and much boasting of their former exploits when they had been pirates, crying up a pirate's life to be the only life for a man of any spirit. While they were running on in this manner, Bunch on a sudden started up, and swore he would be captain of that vessel. Augur answered him the vessel did not want a captain, for he was able to command her himself, which seemed to put an end to the discourse for that time.

Soon after Bunch began to tell what bright arms they had on board their sloop; upon which, one of Augur's men handed up some of their cutlasses which had been cleaned that day. Among them was Mr. Carr's silver-hilted sword. Bunch seemed to admire the sword, and asked whose it was Mr. Carr made answer, it belonged to him. Bunch replied it was a very handsome one, and drawing it out, marched about the poop, flourishing it over his head, and telling Mr. Carr he would return it to him when he had done with it. At the same time he began to vapour again, and to boast of his former piracies, and coming near Mr. Carr, struck him with the sword. Turnley bid him take care what he did, for Mr. Carr would not take such usage. As they were disputing upon this matter, Dennis Mackarthy stole off; and, with some of his associates, seized upon the great cabin, where all the arms lay. At the same time several of the men began to sing a song with these words. *Did you not promise me, that you would marry me* — which it seems was the signal agreed upon among the conspirators for seizing the ship. Bunch no sooner heard them, but he cried out aloud, *that I will, for I am parson,* and struck Mr. Carr again several blows with his own sword. Mr. Carr and Turnley both seized him, and they began to struggle, when Dennis Mackarthy, with several others, returned from the cabin with each a cutlass in one hand, and a loaded pistol in the other, and running up to them, said, *What! do the governor's dogs offer to resist?* And beating Turnley and Carr with their cutlasses, threatened to shoot them, at the same time firing their pistols close to their cheeks, upon which Turnley and Carr begged their lives.

When they were thus in possession of the vessel, they hailed Capt. Greenway, and desired him to come on board about urgent business. He, knowing nothing of what had passed, jumped into his boat, and with two hands only, rowed on board. Dennis Mackarthy led him into the cabin, and, as soon as he was there, laid hold of him, telling him he was now a prisoner, and must submit. He offered to make some resistance; upon which, they told him all resistance would be vain, for his own men were in the plot; and, indeed, seeing the two hands who rowed him aboard, now armed, and joining with the conspirators, he. thought it was time to submit.

As soon as this was done, they sent some hands on board to seize his sloop, or rather to acquaint his men with what had been done, for they expected to meet with no resistance, many of them being in the plot, and the rest, they supposed, not very averse to it; after which, they decoyed Captain White on board, by the same stratagem they used with Greenway, and likewise sent on board his sloop, and found his men, one and all, well-disposed for the design; and what was most remarkable was, that Captain Augur, seeing how things were goings joined with them, showing himself as well inclined for pirating as the worst of them.

Thus, they made themselves masters of the three vessels with very little trouble. The next thing to be done was to resolve how to dispose of those who were not of their party. Some were for killing Richard Turnley, but the majority carried it for marooning, that he might be starved, and die like a dog, as they called it. Their great spleen to him was, because he was the person who had piloted the governor into Providence.

Accordingly, Turnley, with John Carr, Thomas Rich, and some others, were stripped naked, and tumbled over the vessel's side into a boat which lay alongside. The oars were all taken out, and they left them nothing to work themselves ashore with but an old paddle, which, at other times, served to steer the boat, and so they commanded them to be gone. However, they made shift to get safe ashore on the island, which, as we observed before, was quite uninhabited.

The next morning Dennis Mackarthy, with several others, went on shore, and told them they must come on board again, and they would give them some clothes to put on. They fancied the pirates. began to repent of the hard usage they had given them, and were willing to return upon such an errand; but when they got on board again, they found their opinion of the pirates' good nature was very ill grounded, for they began with beating them, and did it as if it were in sport, one having a boatswain's pipe, the rest beating them till he piped *belay.*

The true design of bringing them on board again, was to make them discover where some things lay, which they could not readily find, particularly Mr. Carr's watch and silver snuff-box; but he was soon obliged to inform them in what corner of the cabin they were, and there they were found, with some journals and other books, which they knew how to make no other use of than turning them into cartridges. Then they began to question Thomas Rich about a gold watch which had once been seen in his possession on shore at Providence; but he protested that it belonged to Capt. Gale, who was commander of the guard-ship called the Delicia, to which he then belonged; but his protestations would have availed him little, had it not been that some on board, who belonged also to the Delicia, knew it to be true, which put an end to his beating; and so they were alt discharged from their punishment for the present.

Some time after, fancying the pirates to be in better humour, they begged for something to eat, for they had none of them had any nourishment that, day or the night before; but all the answer they received was, that such dogs should not ask such questions. In the meantime, some of the pirates were very busy endeavouring to persuade Captain Greenway to engage with them, for they knew him to be an excellent artist; but he was obstinate and would not. Then it was proposed to maroon, him, which was opposed by some, because he was a Bermudian, meaning, that he might perhaps swim away or swim on board his vessel again, for the Bermudians are all excellent swimmers; but as he represented, that he could not hurt them by his swimming, he obtained the favour for himself and the other officers, to be set ashore with Turnley, Carr, and Rich. Accordingly, they were put into the same boat without oars, to the number of eight, and were ordered to make the best of their way on shore.

The pirates, the next day, having examined all their vessels, and finding that' Green way's sloop was not fit for their purpose, shifted everything out of her. Those that were sent on shore could see from thence what they were doing, and when they saw them row off, Greenway swam on board the sloop, it is likely, to see whether they had left anything behind them. They perceived him, and fancied he repented refusing to join with them, and had come to do it now; wherefore some of them returned back to the sloop, to speak to him, but they found him of the same opinion he was in before. However, he wheedled them into so much good humour, that they told him he might have his sloop again, in which, indeed, they had left nothing except an old main-sail, an old fore-sail, four small pieces of Irish beef, in an old beef barrel, and about twenty biscuits, with a broken bucket which was used to draw water in, telling him that he and the rest must not go on board till they had sailed.

Greenway swam ashore again to give notice to his brothers in distress, of what had passed. The same afternoon Bunch with several others went on shore, carrying with them six bottles of wine and some biscuits. Whether this was done to tempt Greenway again, or no, is hard to say; for though they talked to him a great deal, they drank all the wine themselves to the last bottle, and then gave each of the poor creatures a glass a-piece, with a bit of biscuit, and immediately after fell to beating them, and so went on board.

While they were on shore, there came in a turtler which belonged to one Thomas Bennet, of Providence, whereof one Benjamin Hutchins was master. They soon laid hold of her, for she sailed excellently well. Hutchins was reputed an extraordinary good pilot among those islands; wherefore they tempted him to engage with them; at first he refused, but rather than be marooned, he afterwards consented.

It was now the 9th of October, and they were just preparing to sail, when they sent on shore, ordering the *condemned malefactors* to come on board Greenway's sloop, the Lancaster. They did so in the little boat they went on shore in, by the help of the same paddle. They found several of the pirates there, who told them that they gave them that sloop to return to Providence, though they let them have no more stores, than what were named before. They bade them take the foresail, and bend it for a jib, and furl it close down to the bowsprit, and to furl the mainsail close up to the boom. They did as they were ordered, for they knew there was no disputing whether it was right or wrong.

Soon after, another detachment came on board, among whom were Bunch and Dennis Mackarthy, who being either mad or drunk, fell upon them, beating them, and cutting the rigging and sails to pieces with their cutlasses, and commanding them not to sail, till they should hear from them again, threatening if they did, they would put them all to death, if ever they met them again; and so they went off, carrying with them the boat, which they sent them first ashore in, and sailed away.

They left them in this miserable condition, without tackle to go their voyage, and without a boat to get on shore, and having nothing in view but to perish for want; but as self-preservation put them upon exerting themselves, in order to get out of this deplorable state, they began to rummage and search the vessel through every hole and corner, to see if nothing was left which might be of use to them; and it happened by chance that they found an old hatchet, with which they cut some sticks sharp to serve for marlingspikes. They also cut out several other things, to serve instead of such tools as are absolutely necessary on board a ship.

When they had proceeded thus far, every man began to work as hard as he could; they cut a piece of cable, which they strung into rope yarns, and fell to mending their sails with all possible expedition; they also made a kind of fishing lines of rope yarns, and bent some nails crooked to serve for hooks-; but as they were destitute of a boat, as well for the use of fishing as for going on shore, they resolved to make a bark log, that is, to lay two or three logs together, and lash them close, upon which two or three men may sit very safely in smooth water.

As soon as this was done, some hands went on shore, upon one of the logs (for they made two of them) who employed themselves in cutting wild cabbage, gathering berries, and a fruit which the seamen call prickly pears, for food, while some others went a fishing upon another. Those who went ashore also carried the old bucket with them, so that whilst some were busy in gathering things to serve for provision, one hand was constantly employed in bringing fresh water aboard in the bucket, which was tedious work, considering how little could be brought at a time, and that the sloop lay near a mile from the shore.

When they had employed themselves thus, for about four or five days, they brought their sails and tackle into such order, having also a little water, cabbage and other things on board, that they thought it was time to venture to sail. Accordingly they weighed their anchor, and setting all the sail they had, got out to the harbour's mouth, when to their great terror and surprise, they saw the pirates coming in again.

They were much frightened at this unexpected return, because of the threatenings they had used to them at parting, not to sail without further orders; wherefore, they tacked about, and ran as close in to the shore as they could, then throwing out their bark logs, they all put themselves upon them, and made to land, as fast as they could; but before they quite reached it, the pirates got so near that they fired at them, but were too far to do execution. However, they pursued them ashore; the unhappy exiles immediately took to the woods, and for greater security climbed up some trees, whose branches were very thick, and by that means concealed themselves. The pirates not finding them, soon returned to their boat, and rowed on board the deserted sloop, whose mast and bowsprit they cut away, and towing into deep water, sunk her; after which, they made again for shore, thinking that the fugitives would have been out of their lurking holes, and that they should surprise them; but they continued still on the tops of the trees and saw all that passed, and therefore thought it safest to keep their posts.

The pirates not finding them, returned to their vessels, and weighing their anchors, set sail, steering eastward. In the meantime, the poor fellows were in despair, for seeing their vessel sunk, they had scarce any hopes left of escaping the danger of perishing upon that uninhabited island, where they lived eight days, feeding upon berries, and shell -fish, such as cockles and periwinkles, sometimes catching a stingray, a fish resembling mead or thornback, which coming into shoal water, they could wade near them, and by the help of a stick sharpened the end, which they did by rubbing it against the rocks, (for they had not a knife left among them) they stuck them as if it had been with a spear.

It must be observed, that they had no means of striking a fire, and therefore their way of dressing this fish was, by dipping it in salt water, then laying it in the sun, till it became both hard and dry, and then they ate it.

After passing eight days in this manner, the pirates returned, and saw the poor fugitives ashore, who according to custom made to the woods; but their hearts began to relent towards them, and sending ashore, they ordered a man to go into the woods single, to call out to them, and promise them upon their honour, if they would appear, that they would give them victuals and drink, and not use them ill any more.

These promises, and the hunger which pinched them, tempted them to come forth, and accordingly they went on board, and they were as good as their word, for they gave them as much beef and biscuit as they could eat, during two or three days they were on board, but would not give them a bit to carry on shore.

There was on board one George Redding, an inhabitant of Providence, who was taken out of the turtle sloop, and who was a forced man. Being an acquaintance of Richard Turnley, and knowing that he was resolved to go shore again, rather than engage with the pirates, and hearing him say, that they could find food to keep them alive, if they had but fire to dress it, privately gave him a tinder box with materials in it for striking fire, which, in his circumstances, was a greater present than gold or jewels. Soon after, the pirates put the question to them, whether they would engage, or be put ashore. And they all agreed upon the latter: upon which a debate arose among the pirates, whether they should comply with their request or not; and at length it was agreed, that Greenway and the other two masters should be kept whether they would or no; and the rest, being five in number, should, as the pirates expressed it, have a second refreshment on the varieties of the island.

Accordingly Richard Turnley, James Carr, Thomas Rich, John Cox, and John Taylor, were a second time marooned, and the pirates, as soon as they landed them sailed off, steering eastward, till they came to an island called Pudden Point, near Long-Island, in lat. 24 degrees, where they cleaned their vessels.

In the meantime, Turnley and his companions made a much better shift than they had done before, his friend Redding's present being of infinite use to them, for they constantly kept a good fire, with which they broiled their fish. There were plenty of land crabs and snakes on the island, which they could eat when they were dressed. Thus they passed fourteen days; at the end of which the pirates made them another visit, and they according to custom made for the woods, thinking that the reason of their return must be, in order to force them to serve amongst them. But here they were mistaken, for the anger of these fellows being over, they began to pity them; but going ashore, ana not finding them, they knew they were hid for fear. Nevertheless, they left upon the shore, where they knew they would come, some stores which they intended in this fit of good humour to present them with.

The poor islanders had got to their retreat, the tops of the trees, and saw the pirates go off; upon which they ventured down, and going to the water side, were agreeably surprised to find a small cask of flour, of between twenty and thirty pounds, about a bushel of salt, two bottles of gun powder, several bullets, besides a quantity of small shot, with a couple of muskets, a very good axe, and also a pot and a pan, and three dogs, which they took in the turtle sloop; which dogs are bred to hunting, and generally the sloops which go turtling, carry some of them, as they are very useful in tracing out the wild hogs. Besides all these, there were a dozen horn handled knives, of that sort which are usually carried to Guinea.

They carried all. things into the woods, to that part where they had their fresh water, and where they usually kept, and immediately went to work with their axe; some cutting down bows, and making poles, so that four of them were employed in building a hut, while Richard Turnley taking the dogs and a gun, went a hunting, he understanding that sport very well. He had not been gone long before he killed a large boar, which he brought home to his companions, who fell to cutting it up, and some they dressed for their dinner, and the rest they salted, for another time.

Thus they lived, as they thought, very happy in respect to their former condition; but after a few days, the pirates made them another visit, for they wanted to fill some casks with water. It happened when they came in, that Turnley was gone a hunting, and the rest all busy at work, so that they did not see them, till they came into the wood upon them. Seeing the hut, one of them in wantonness set it on fire, and it was burnt to the ground; and they appeared inclined to do mischief, when Richard Turnley, knowing nothing of the matter, happened to return from hunting, with a fine hog upon his back, as much as he could carry. He was immediately surrounded by the pirates, who seized upon the fresh meat, which seemed to put them into better humour. They made Richard Cox carry it down to their boat, and when he had done, they gave him a bottle of rum to carry back to his companions to drink their healths, telling him, that they might get home if they could, or if they stayed there, they would never trouble them any more.

They were, indeed as good as their word, for sailing away immediately, they made for Long Island, and coming up toward the salt ponds there, they saw at a distance in the harbour, three vessels at an anchor, and supposing them to be either Bermuda or New York sloops, lying there to take in salt, they bore down upon them with all the sail they could make, expecting a good booty. The turtle sloop taken from Benjamin Hutchins, was by much the best sailor; however, it was almost dark before she came up with them, and then corning close along side of one of them, she gave a broadside, with a design to board the next minute, but received such a volley of small shot in return, as killed and wounded a great many of the pirates, and the rest, in great surprise and fright, jumped overboard, to save themselves by swimming ashore.

The truth is, these sloops proved to be Spanish privateers, who observing the pirates to bear down upon them, prepared themselves for action. The commander in chief of these three privateers was one who was called by the name of Turn Joe, because he had once privateered on the English side. He had also been a pirate, and now acted by virtue of a commission from a Spanish governor. He was by birth an Irishman, a bold enterprising fellow, and was afterwards killed in an engagement with one John Bonnavee captain of a privateer belonging to Jamaica.

But to return to our story. The sloop was taken, and on board her was found, desperately wounded, Phinea's Bunch, who was the captain. By and by a second of the pirate sloops came up; she heard the volley, and supposed it to be fired by Bunch, when he boarded one of the sloops; she came also alongside of one of the Spaniards, and received the welcome that was given to Bunch, and submitted as soon. A little after, came up the third, which was taken with the same ease, and in the same manner, as many of the pirates as could swim, jumping overboard to save themselves on shore, there not being a man lost on the side of the Spaniards.

The next day Turn Joe asked them many questions, and finding out that several amongst them had been forced men, he with the consent of the other Spanish officers, ordered all the goods to be taken out of a Spanish launch, and putting some of the wounded pirates into the said launch, with some provision, water, and other liquors, gave it to the forced men, to carry them to Providence.

Accordingly George Redding, Thomas Betty, Matthew Betty, and Benjamin Hutchins, with some others, set sail, and in eight-and-forty hours arrived in the harbour of Providence, They went on shore immediately, and acquainted the governor with everything that had passed, from the time of their setting out; informing him, that Phineas Bunch, who was one of the chief authors of all the mischief, was on board the launch. The governor, with some others, went and examined him, and he confessed all, wherefore there was no occasion for a trial; and as he had been pardoned before, and it was necessary to make some speedy example, it was resolved that he should be executed the next day, but it was prevented by his dying that night of his wounds.

They also informed the governor of the condition of Turnley, Carr, and the rest, who were marooned by the pirates upon Green Key Island; upon which the governor sent for one John Sims, a mulatto man, who had a two-mast boat in the harbour of Providence, very fit for sailing; and putting some provisions into her, ordered him to get five or six hands, and to sail for Green Key, in order to bring off the live men there marooned.

Sims accordingly made the best of his way, and sailing out in the morning, arrived at Green Key the next day towards evening. The poor people on shore saw them, and supposing them to be some of the pirates returned, thought it best to take to the woods and hide, not knowing what humour they might be in now. Sims and his ship-mates carried some provision on shore, not knowing but they might want, and searched about, calling out to them by their names. After wandering about some time, they came to the place where the fire was constantly kept; on perceiving which, they fancied they must be thereabouts, and that it would be best to wait for them there, and accordingly they sat down, laying the provisions near them. Turnley, who had climbed to the top of a tree just by, saw them, and observed their motions, and fancied they were no enemies who were bringing them provisions, and looking more earnestly, he knew Sims, the mulatto, whom he was very well acquainted with at Providence; upon which he called him, who desired him to come down, telling him the comfortable news, that he was come to the relief of him and his companions. Turnley made what haste he could to the bottom, and as soon as he was down, summoned his comrades, who had climbed to the top of some neighbouring trees, being in haste to communicate the glad tidings to them. Being all together, the mulatto related to them the history of what had happened to the pirates.

That night they supped comfortably together upon the provision brought ashore; but so strange an effect has joy, that scarce one of them slept a wink that night, as they declared. The next day they agreed to go a hunting, in order to get something fresh to carry off with them, and were so successful, that they killed three fine hogs. When they returned, they made the best of their way on board, carrying with them all their utensils, and set sail for Providence, whither they arrived in three days; it being now just seven weeks from the time of their being first set on shore by the pirates.

The governor, in the meantime, was fitting out a sloop to send to Long-Island, in order to take those pirates who had saved themselves near the salt ponds there, which sloop was now ready to sail, and put under the command of Benjamin Hornygold. Turnley and his companions embarked on board of her, and care was taken to get as many men as they could, who were entire strangers to the pirates.

When they arrived at the said island, they run in pretty near the shore, keeping but few hands on deck, that it might look like a trading vessel, and those men that were quite unknown to the pirates.

The pirates seeing them, came only two or three of them near the shore, the rest lying in ambush, not without hopes of. finding an opportunity to Seize the sloop, which sent her boat out towards the shore, with orders to lay off at a little distance, as if she was afraid. Those in ambush seeing the boat so near, had not patience to stay any longer, but flocked to the water side, calling out to them to come on shore, and help them, for they were poor shipwrecked men, perishing for want. Upon which the boat rowed back again to the sloop.

Upon second thoughts they sent her off again with two bottles of wine, a bottle of rum, and some biscuit, and sent another man, who was a stranger to those ashore, with orders to pass for master of the vessel. As soon as they approached them, the pirates called to them as before, begging them, for

God's sake to come on shore; they did so, and gave them the biscuit, wine, and rum, which he said he thought ashore on purpose to comfort them, because his men told him they were cast away. They were very inquisitive to know where he was bound. He told them, to New York, and that he came in there to take in salt. They earnestly entreated him to take them on board, and carry them as passengers to New York; they being about sixteen in number, he answered, he was afraid he had not provision sufficient for so great a number; but that he would go on board and overhaul his provision, and if they pleased, some of them might go with 'him, and see how his stock stood; that at least he would carry some of them, and leave some refreshment for the rest, till they could be succoured another way, but that he hoped they would make him some recompense when they should arrive at New York.

They seemed wonderfully pleased with his proposal, and promised to make him ample satisfaction for all the charges he should be at, pretending to have good friends and considerable effects in different parts of America. Accordingly he took several of them with him in the boat, and as soon as they got on board he invited them into the cabin, where, to their surprise, they saw Benjamin Hornygold, formerly a brother pirate; but what astonished them more, was to see Richard Turnley, whom they had lately marooned upon Green Key. They were immediately surrounded by several with pistols in their hands, and clapped in irons.

As soon as this was over, the boat went on shore again, and those in the boat told the pirates, that the captain would venture to carry them with what provision he had; at which they appeared much rejoiced, and so the rest were brought on board, and without much trouble clapped in irons, as well as their companions.

The sloop had nothing more to do, and therefore set sail, and reaching Providence, delivered the pirates all prisoners into the fort. A Court of Admiralty was immediately called, and they were all tried, and nine received sentence of death, viz. John Augur, William Cunningham, Dennis Mackarthy, William Dowling, William Lewis, Thomas Morris, George Bendall, William Ling, and George Rounsivel, which last was finally reprieved and pardoned. The other seven were acquitted, it appearing that they were forced.

The following is the sentence pronounced upon the prisoners: —

THE COURT having duly considered of the evidence which hath been given both for and against you the said John Augur, William Cunningham, Dennis Mackarthy, William Dowling, William Lewis, Thomas Morris, George Bendall, William Ling, and George Rounsivel; and having also debated the several circumstances of the cases, it is adjudged, that you the said John Augur, William Cunningham, Dennis Mackarthy, William Dowling, William Lewis, Thomas Morris, George Bendall, William Ling, and George Rounsivel, are guilty of the mutiny, felony, and piracy, wherewith you and every of you stand accused. And the Court doth accordingly pass sentence, that you the said John Augur, William Cunningham, Dennis Mackarthy, William Downing, William Lewis,

Thomas Morris, George Bendall, William Ling, and George Rounsivel, be carried to prison from whence you came, and from thence to the place of execution, where you are to be hanged by the neck till you shall be *dead, dead, dead;* and God have mercy on your souls. Given under our hands this 10th day of December, A. D. 1718.

(Signed)

Woodes Rogers, Wingate Gale, William Fairfax, Nathaniel Taylor, Robert Beauchamp, Josias Burgiss, Thomas Walker, Peter Courant.

After sentence was passed upon the prisoners, the governor, as president of the court, appointed their execution to be on Friday next, the 12th inst. at 10 o'clock in the morning.

Whereupon the prisoners prayed for longer time to repent and prepare for death; but the governor told them, that from the time of their being apprehended, they ought to have accounted themselves as condemned by the laws of all nations, which was only sealed now, and that the securing them hitherto, and the favour that the Court had allowed them in making as long a defence as they could, wholly took up that time which the affairs of the settlement required in working at the fortifications; besides the fatigue thereby occasioned to the whole garrison in the necessary guards, set over them by the want of a gaol, and the garrison having been very much reduced by sickness and death since his arrival; also, that he was obliged to employ all his people to assist in mounting the great guns, and in finishing the present works, with all possible despatch, on account of the expected war with Spain; and there being many more pirates amongst these islands, and this place left destitute of all relief from, any man of war or station ship, joined to other reasons, too long to enumerate in court, he thought himself indispensably obliged, for the welfare of the settlement, to give them no longer time.

The prisoners were then ordered to the place of their Imprisonment in the fort, where leave was given them to send for any persons to read and pray with them.

On Friday morning each of the prisoners was called in private, to know if they had any load upon their spirits, for actions committed as yet unknown to the world, the declaring of which was absolutely required to prepare themselves for a fit repentance; but they each refused to declare anything, as well as making known to the governor, if they knew of any conspiracy against the government.

Wherefore, about 10 o'clock, the prisoners were released from their irons, and committed to the charge and care of Thomas Robinson, Esq. commissioned Provost Marshal for the day, who, according to custom in such cases, pinioned them, &c. and ordered the guards appointed to assist him, to lead them to the top of the rampart, fronting the sea, which was well guarded by the governor's soldiers and people, to the number of about 100. At the prisoners' request, several select prayers and psalms were read, in which ail present joined. When the service was ended, orders were given to the Marshal, and he conducted the prisoners down a ladder, provided on purpose, to the foot of the wall, where a gallows was erected, and a black flag hoisted thereon, and under it a stage, supported by three butts, on which they ascended by another ladder, where the hangman fastened the cords. They had three-quarters of an hour allowed under the gallows, which was spent by them in singing psalms, and some exhortations to their old consorts, and the other spectators, who got as near to the foot of the gallows as the marshal's guard would suffer them. When the marshal was ordered to make ready, and all the prisoners expected the launch, the governor thought fit to order George Rounsivel to be untied, and when brought off the stage, the butts having ropes about them, were hauled away; upon which, the stage fell, and the prisoners were suspended.

A Short Account of the Prisoners Executed.

First, John Augur, being about 40 years of age, had been a noted shipmaster at Jamaica, and since among the pirates; but on his accepting of His Majesty's act of grace, and recommendations to the governor, he was, notwithstanding, entrusted with a good vessel and cargo, in which, betraying his trust, and knowing himself guilty of the indictment, he all along appeared very penitent, and neither washed, shaved, or shifted his old clothes, when carried to be executed; and when he had a small glass of wine given him on the rampart, drank it with wishes for the good success of the Bahama Islands, and the governor.

The second, William Cunningham, aged 45, had been gunner with Thatch, the pirate, who, being also conscious of his own guilt, was seemingly penitent, and behaved himself as such.

The third, Dennis Mackarthy, aged 28, had also been formerly a pirate, but accepted of the king's act of grace; and the governor had made him an ensign of the militia, being recommended as a sober, discreet person, which commission he had at the time of his joining the pirates, which very much aggravated his other crimes. During his imprisonment, he behaved himself tolerably well; but when he thought he was to die, and the morning came, without his expected reprieve, he shifted his clothes, and wore long blue ribands at his neck, wrists, knees, and cap; and when on the rampart, looked cheerfully round him, saying, *He knew the time when there were many brave fellows on the island, who would not have suffered him to die like a dog;* and at the same time pulled off his shoes, kicking them over the parapet of the fort, saying, *He had promised not to die with his shoes on;* so descended the fort wall, and ascended the stage, with the agility and address of a prize-fighter. When mounted, he exhorted the people, who were at the foot of the walls, to have compassion on him; but, however willing, they saw too much power over their heads to attempt anything in his favour.

The fourth, William Dowling, about 24 years of age, had been a considerable time among the pirates, of a wicked life, which His Majesty's act of grace did not reform. His behaviour was very loose on the stage, and after his death, some of his acquaintance declared, he had confessed to them, that he had murdered his mother before he left Ireland.

The fifth, William Lewis, aged about 34 years, as he had been a hardy pirate and prize-fighter, affected an unconcern at death; but heartily desired liquors to drink with his fellow-sufferers on the stage, and with the standers by.

The sixth, Thomas Morris, aged about 22, had been a very incorrigible youth and pirate, and seemed to have very little anxiety of mind by his frequent smiles when at the bar. Being dressed with red ribands, as Mackarthy was with blue, he said, going over the ramparts, *We have a new governor, but a harsh one;* and a little before he was turned off, said aloud, *he might have been a greater plague to these islands, and now he wished he had been so.*

The seventh, George Bendall, aged 18, though he said, *he had never been a pirate before, yet he had all the villanous inclinations the most profligate youth could be infected with.* His behaviour was sullen.

The eighth, William Ling, aged about 30, not taken notice of before the last attempt, behaved himself as became a true penitent, and was not heard to say anything besides replying to Lewis, when he demanded wine to drink, *that water was more suitable to them at that time.*

It was observed that there were but few (besides the governor's adherents) among the spectators, who had not deserved the same fate, but pardoned by His Majesty's act of grace.

A Correct Account of the Late Piracies Committed in the West-Indies; and the Expedition of Commodore Porter

THE public mind has been much agitated by the depredations of these enemies of all law, human and divine. It is strange, that in this enlightened age, when the principles of civil liberty are so well understood, and when the doctrines of the rights of man are gaining so many adherents both in this country and in Europe, that there should be found men so lost to every good principle, as to pursue such a predatory warfare against defenceless people; and with the slightest pretext, butcher those unfortunate fellow creatures who may fall hi their way. And it is no less astonishing, as piracy does exist, that all civilized governments have not combined to suppress this horrid practice, and teach these refractory and deluded men, that the arm of justice is not shortened, nor the rulers of the earth asleep.

Our government has taken a forward step to arrest these freebooters in their blood-thirsty projects, and no doubt the expedition which was under the command of that gallant officer, Commodore Porter, has done much towards putting down this nefarious practice in the West-India seas.

Piracies, &c.

Mutiny on Board the British Ship Kate

The crew, 8 in number, of the ship Kate, Captain Purdy, landed in the island of Guadaloupe, on the 24th of January, 1821. They slept on the beach that night, and next morning a planter in the neighbourhood came to them, and brought them to the house. Their story was uniform, all said they belonged to the American ship Retrieve, Capt. Jacob Hawes, belonging to Messrs. Suydam & Wyckoff merchants, of New-York; that after 6 weeks boisterous weather, not being able to keep the ship free, she being very leaky, the Captain had given orders to get the boat in readiness, and that they were doing it, and getting into the boat about 10 o'clock at night, when the Captain's son, about 10 years old, fell overboard in trying to get into the boat, and that the Captain threw himself into the sea to save him, but both perished, and the ship went down; that after one night and two days in the boat, they reached the beach near the Mole, with great hazard of their lives.

They were afterwards escorted to Point Petre, where they were examined by the Judge, and persisted in the same story; except one French lad, who privately disclosed the truth to the attorney general.

They had with them all their baggage, and considerable money. Among the baggage was a Bible, With the label, "Presented by the Merchants' Seamen Auxiliary Bible Society, to the ship Kate, of London— Gravesend, 11th May, 1818." This, the mate, Thomas Murdock, said was given to him by a fellow lodger in New-York. The Judge, however, availed himself of this circumstance to interrogate them a second time. Calling on Murdock, he said — "There is the Bible belonging to the ship Kate, of London, Capt. George Purdy, and upon that very same Bible you swear to tell the truth, and nothing but the truth." Murdock, much embarrassed, said in broken words, that he was not accustomed to 48wear on the Bible, and resisted some time, when the Judge observed to him, that if he would not answer to the questions, he would pronounce him guilty immediately; for to refuse answering the questions of the Court was declaring himself guilty. Murdock then kissed the Bible. "Since I have taken an oath, (said he,) on the Bible, I will speak the truth," and related the real story, in substance —

"That they belonged to the ship Kate, of London, Capt. George Purdy, which ship had been chartered in August last, at Halifax, for a voyage to Berbice and back to Halifax. The ship took a cargo of fish, beef, and some lumber. They reached Berbice, where the cargo was sold for cash. The proceeds were put on board in two boxes iron hooped, containing 5600 dollars. The ship sailed for Halifax in ballast. The mate had been discharged at Berbice, after having some quarrel with the Captain. Six weeks after sailing, finding constant head winds, and in want of provisions, the water nearly consumed, the crew asked the Captain what he intended to do — the Captain told them, he had still some coffee which lie would give them for their support, and that he would try to get to Bermuda; but after 24 hours, the winds against them, they tried for New-York, but without success. On the morning of the 8th of January, three of the crew went and seized the Captain, as he was walking on the deck, and tied him. They said that he and those that lived in the cabin, must either jump overboard, or go into the jolly boat alongside. They then embarked the Captain, who wished and asked to go into the cabin for his cloak and boots, but he was not allowed. They begged earnestly for a compass; his lady also went on her knees and begged for a compass, but this was refused also. His lady with their two children, one a boy two years old, the other a girl four years old, Mr. Robert Meredith, a passenger, and a mulatto boy named William, steward in the cabin, were then forced into the boat, with 20 lbs. of bread, two trunks of the Captain's and Mr. Meredith's trunks and two oars, were sent adrift. The crew were ignorant of their then latitude. After ten days sailing for the West-Indies, Deseada was the first land he made. They had rigged the long boat as a sloop, put in their baggage and money, which had been equally divided among them, excepting the two lads, who had a share between them, when two of the crew went below and scuttled the ship."

Afterwards the rest of the crew confessed their crime. About 1400 dollars were found and lodged at the Register's office — Murdock said he buried in the yard of the tavern at the Mole 450 dollars, but the money could not be found. He had an American protection, said he was born in New-Brunswick, (N. J.) and had papers from the grand and private lodges of New-York. The cook was a negro, from Philadelphia, from whence he went in a schooner to Halifax; his name was Philip Fisher; he stuttered. One was a French lad; one a London boy, one Welshman, an Irishman, and two Scotchmen.

LIST OF ATROCIOUS PIRACIES AND BARBARITIES

BOSTON, NOV. 6, 1821.

The brig Cobbessecontee, Capt. Jackson, arrived yesterday from the Havana, sailed thence on the morning of the 8th ult. and on the evening of the same day, about four miles from the Moro, was brought to by a piratical sloop, containing about 30 men. A boat from her, with ten men, came along side, and soon after they got on board commenced plundering. They took nearly all the clothing from the Captain and mate — all the cooking utensils and spare rigging — unrove part of the running rigging — cut the small cable — broke the compasses — cut the mast's coats to pieces — took from the Captain his watch and four boxes cigars— and from the cargo three bales cochineal and six boxes cigars. They beat the mate unmercifully, and hung him up by the neck under the maintop. They also beat the Captain severely — broke a large broad sword across his back, and ran a long knife through his thigh, so that he almost bled to death. Capt. Jackson saw the sloop at Regla the day before.

Capt. Jackson informs us, and we have also been informed by other persons from the Havana, that $his system of Piracy is openly countenanced by some of the inhabitants of that place— who say that it is a retaliation on the Americans for interfering against the Slave Trade, and for allowing Patriot privateers to refit in their ports. The pirates, therefore, receiving such countenance, grow more daring — and increase in number from the success which has attended this new mode of filling then; pockets.

Capt. Bugnon, who arrived yesterday from Charleston, spoke on the 2d inst. off the S. Shoal of Nantucket, the brig Three Partners, from Jamaica for St. John — had been robbed, off Cape Antonio, by a piratical vessel, of about 35 tons, and 17 men, of clothing, watches, &c. and the captain was hung up by the neck to the fore-yard arm, till he was almost dead.

Capt. Bourn, who arrived yesterday, from Cape Haytien, spoke on the 26th ult. lat. 33, lon. 78, brig Sea Lion, 36 days from Cape Haytien for Belfast, Ireland, which had been plundered by a pirate in the Gulf.

The brig Harriet, Capt. Dimond, from St. Jago de Cuba for Baltimore, arrived at Havana on the 16th ult. having been robbed of all her cargo of sugar, and $4000 in specie, off Cape Antonio, by a boat with 15 men, having two schooners in co. Capt. D. was hung up by the neck, and remained senseless for some time after he was taken down.

The Dutch brig Mercury, 77 days from Marseilles, arrived at Havana on the 16th ult. after having been robbed of $10,000 worth of her cargo, by a piratical schooner and boat, off Cape Antonio.

Fortunately a U. S. vessel has arrived at the scene of these daring robberies, and has already protected two fleets. It is to be hoped some of the villains who have so long preyed with impunity on mercantile property, and been guilty of the most savage acts, will speedily be caught and brought to justice.

Piracies in the U. S. Brig Spark

A letter from a gentleman belonging to this vessel, dated St. Barts, Nov. 3, 1821, says—

"We arrived here, after a rather rough passage, in eighteen days from Boston, all well. We expect to sail again in two or three days. We found here the piratical ship which robbed the Orleans Packet. She is now in possession of the Swedish government. She came into their possession in the following manner: — The crew landed her cargo on a small island near this, from whence it was taken by a schooner to St. Thomas;— they then run the ship into Five Island Harbour, where all the crew, except two men, deserted her. — The government hearing of her being there, sent a guard and took possession of her, brought her into this harbour, and confined the two men found in. her as pirates. — It is said, Capt. Elton has requested the Governor to allow him to take them to the United States for trial. This piratical ship was originally the U. S. brig Prometheus, which was condemned two years since, and was then sold."

A letter from on board the Hornet, dated at Cape Maise, 31st. October, says, "The pirate which we took yesterday mounted two long four pounders, and her crew consisted of twenty gallows-looking scoundrels."— After the capture of the Hornet, spoke three merchant brigs, which probably would have fallen into the hands of the pirates;— and were very happy at their escape.

Piratical Forts. — Capt. Sisson, from Havana, reports, that seventy of the Pirates belonging to the vessels captured and destroyed by the Enterprize, have erected two forts on Cape Antonio, for their defence.

--

From the American Monthly Magazine, of Feb. 1824.

PIRACY.

In the early part of June I sailed from Philadelphia in the schooner Mary, on a voyage to New-Orleans. My principal object in going round by sea was the restoration of my health, which had been for many months declining. Having some friends in New-Orleans whose commercial operations were conducted on an extensive scale, I was charged with the care of several sums of money in gold and silver, amounting altogether to nearly eighteen thousand dollars. This I communicated to the captain, and we concluded to secure it in the best manner our circumstances would admit. A plank was accordingly taken off the ribs of the schooner in my own cabin, and the money being deposited in the vacancy, the plank was nailed down in its original place, and the seams filled and tarred over. Being thus relieved from any apprehension that the money would be found upon us in case of an attack from pirates, my mind was somewhat easier. What other articles of value I could conveniently carry about with me, I did so. I had also brought a quantity of bank notes to the amount of fifteen thousand dollars. Part of these I caused to be carefully sewed in the left lappel of my coat, supposing that in case of my being lost at sea, my coat, should my body be found would still contain the most valuable of my effects. The balance was carefully quilted into my black silk cravat.

Our crew consisted of the Captain and four men, with a supply of livestock for the voyage, and a Newfoundland dog, valuable for his fidelity and sagacity. He had once saved his master from a watery grave, when he had been stunned and knocked overboard by the sudden shifting of the boom. I was the only passenger on board. Our voyage at first was prosperous, and time went on rapidly. I felt my strength increase the longer I was at sea, and when we arrived off the southern coast of Florida, my feelings were like those of another man.

It was towards the evening of the fourteenth day, two hours before sun-set, that we espied a sail astern of us. As twilight came, it neared us with astonishing rapidity. Night closed, and all around was impenetrable darkness. Now and then a gentle wave would break against our bow and sparkle for a moment, and at a distance behind us, we could see the uneven glow of light, occasioned by the foaming of the strange vessel. The breeze that filled our canvass was gentle, though it was fresh.

We coursed our way steadily through the night; though once or twice the roaring of the waves increased so suddenly, as to make us believe we had passed a breaker. At the time it was unaccountable to me, but I now believe it to be occasioned by the bark behind us, coming rather near in the darkness of the night.— At midnight I went on deck. Nothing but an occasional sparkle was to be seen, and the ocean was undisturbed. Still it was a fearful and appalling darkness, and in spite of my endeavours I could not compose myself. At the windlass, on the forecastle, three of the sailors, like my self, unable to sleep had collected for conversation. On joining them, I found our fears were mutual. They all kept their eyes steadily fixed upon the unknown vessel, as if anticipating some dreadful event. They informed me that they had put their arms in order and were determined to stand or die.

At this moment a flash of light, perhaps a musket burning priming, proceeded from the vessel in pursuit, and we saw distinctly that her deck was covered with men. My heart almost failed me. I had never been in battle, and I knew not what it Was. Day at length dawned, and setting all her canvass, our pursuer gained alarmingly upon us. It was evident that she had followed us the whole night, being unwilling to attack us in the dark. — In a few minutes, she fired a swivel and came along side. She was a pirate. Her boat was lowered, and about a dozed hideous looking objects jumped in, with a commander at their head. The boat pushed off, and was n earing us fast, as we arranged ourselves for giving her a broadside. Our whole stock of arms consisted of six muskets and an old swivel used as a signal gun, belonging to the Mary, and a pair of pistols of my own, which I carried in my belt. The pirate boat's crew were armed with muskets, pistols, swords, cutlasses, and knives; and when she came within her own length of us, we fired five of our muskets and the swivel into her. Her fire was scarcely half given, when she filled and went down with all her crew. At this success we were inclined to rejoice, but looking over the pirate schooner, we observed her deck still swarming with the same description of horrid looking wretches. A second boat's crew pushed off, with their muskets pointed directly at us the whole time. When they came within the same distance as the other, we fired, but with little, if any effect. The pirate immediately returned the fire, and with horrid cries jumped aboard of us. Two of our brave crew were lying dead upon the deck, and the rest of us expected nothing better. French, Spanish, and English, were spoken indiscriminately, and all at once. The most horrid imprecations were uttered against us, and threats that fancy cannot imagine.

A wretch whose black, shaggy whiskers covered nearly his whole face, whose eyes were only seen at intervals from beneath his bushy eye-brows, and whose whole appearance was more that of a hellhound than of a human being, approached me with a drawn cutlass in his hand. I drew one of my pistols and snapped it in his face; but it flashed in the pan, and before I could draw the other, the pirate, with a brutality that would have disgraced a cannibal, struck me over the face with his cutlass, and knocked me down. I was too much wounded by the blow to resist, and the blood ran in torrents from my forehead. In this situation the wretch seized me by the scalp, and thrusting his cutlass in my cravat, cut it through completely. I felt the cold iron glide along my throat, and even now the very thought makes me shudder. The worst idea I had ever formed of human cruelty seemed now realized, and I could see death stare me in the face. Without stopping to examine the cravat, he put it in his pocket, and in a voice of thunder exclaimed *"levez vous?"* I accordingly rose on my feet, and he pinioned my hands behind my back, led me to the gunwale of the vessel, and asked another of the gang, m French, whether he should throw me overboard. At the recollection of that scene I am still staggered. I endeavoured to call the prospects of eternity before me, but could think of nothing except the cold and quiverless apathy of the tomb. His infamous companion replied, "Il est trop bonne hetire l'envoyer au diable," and led me to the foremast, where he tied me with my nice to the stern of the vessel. The cords were drawn so tight around my arrng and legs, that my agony was excruciating. In this situation he left me.

On looking round, I found them all employed in plundering and ransacking every thing we had. Over my left shoulder one of our sailors was strung up to the yard arm, and apparently in the last agonies of death; while before me our gallant Captain was on his knees and begging for his life. The wretches were endeavouring to extort from him the secret of our money; but for a while he was firm and dauntless, Provoked at his obstinacy, they extended his arms and cut them off at the elbows. At this, human nature gave way, and the injured man confessed the spot where we had concealed our specie. — In a few moments it was aboard their own vessel. To revenge themselves on our unhappy captain, when they had satisfied themselves that nothing else was hidden, they spread a bed of oakum on the deck before, and after soaking it through with turpentine, tied the captain on it, filled his mouth with the same combustibles, and set the whole on fire. The cries of the unfortunate man were heart-rending, and his agonies, must have been unutterable; but they were soon over. All this I was compelled to witness. Heart-sick with the sight, I once shut my eyes, but a musket discharged close to my ear, was a warning sufficient to keep them open.

On casting my eyes to the stern of the vessel, I discovered that the boatswain had been nailed to the deck through his feet, and the body spiked through to the tiller. He was writhing in the last agonies of crucifixion. — Our fifth comrade was out of sight during all this tragedy; in a few minutes, however, he was brought upon the deck blindfolded. He was then conducted to the muzzle of the swivel, and commanded to kneel. The swivel was then fired off, and his head was dreadfully wounded by the discharge. In a moment after, it was agonizing to behold his torments and convulsions — language is too feeble to describe them. I have seen men hung upon the gibbet, but their death is like sinking in slumber when compared with his.

Excited with the scene of human butchery, one of those wretches fired his pistol to the captain's dog. The ball struck his shoulder and disabled him; he finished him by shooting him again, and at last by cutting out his tongue! At this last hell-engendered act, my blood boiled with indignation at such savage brutality on a helpless, inoffensive dog! But I was unable to give utterance or action to my feelings.

Seeing that the crew had been every one despatched, I began to think more of myself. My old enemy, who seemed to forget me, once more approached me; but shockingly besmeared with blood and brains. He had stood by the side of the unfortunate sailor who suffered before the swivel, and supported him with the point of his bayonet. He drew a stiletto from his side, placed its point upon my heart and gave it a heavy thrust. I felt its point touch my skin; but the quilting of my bank bills prevented its further entrance. This savage monster then ran it up my breast, as if intending to divide my lungs, and in doing so, the bank bills fell upon the deck. He snatched them up greedily, and exclaimed, "Ah! laissez mois voir ce que reste." My dress in a few moments, was ripped to pieces at the peril of my life. He frequently came so near as to tear my skin and deluge me with blood; but by the mercy of Providence, I escaped from every danger. — At this moment a heavy flaw struck the schooner, and I heard one of the pirates say, "Voila un vaisseau!" They all retreated precipitately, and gaining their own vessel, was soon but of sight

Helpless as I now was, I had the satisfaction of knowing that the pirates had been frightened by the appearance of a sail, but it was impossible for me to see it. Still tied to the foremast, I knew not what was my prospect of release. — An hour or two had elapsed after they left me; and it was now noon. The sun played violently upon my head, and I felt a languor and debility that indicated approaching fever. My head gradually sunk upon my breast, when I was shocked by hearing the water pouring into the cabin windows. The wretches had scuttled the vessel, and left me pinioned to go down with her. I commended my Spirit to my Maker, and gave myself up for lest. I felt myself gradually dying away, and the last thing I remembered was the foaming noise of the waves. This was occasioned by a ship passing by me. I was taken in, restored to health, and am now a poor, ruined, helpless man.

The ship Liverpool Packet, Ricker, of Portsmouth, N. H. was boarded on the 16th off Cape St. Antonio, Cuba, by two piratical schooners; two barges containing thirty or forty men, robbed the vessel of everything moveable, even to her *flags,* rigging, one boat which happened to be afloat, and having a boy in it which belonged to the ship. They held a consultation whether they should murder the crew, as they had done before, or not— in the meantime taking the ship into anchoring ground. On bringing her to anchor, the crew saw a brig close alongside, burnt to the water's edge, and three dead bodies floating near her. — The pirates said they had burnt the brig the day before, and *murdered all the crew!* —and intended doing the same with them. They said "look at the turtles, (meaning the dead bodies) you will soon be the

152

same." They said the vessel was a Baltimore brig, which they had robbed and burnt, and murdered the crew as before stated, of which they had little doubt. — Capt. Ricker was most shockingly bruised by them. The mate was hung till he was supposed to be dead, but came to, and is now alive. They told the captain that they belonged in Regla, and should kill them all to prevent discovery.

Brig Dover

Extract from the Log-Book of the brig Dover, Capt. Sabins, from Matanzas for Charleston.

Jan. 16, 1822, sea account, at 1 P.M. — Pan of Matanzas bearing S. saw a boat coming to us from a small drogher, which came out of Matanzas the night before us, with five Spaniards, armed with Song knives, pistols, cutlasses, &c. When they got within hail, they fired a musket at us, cheered, and came on board. They were the most villainous looking rascals that any one had probably ever beheld. They immediately drew their weapons, and after beating us severely with their cutlasses, drove us below. They then robbed us of all our clothes except what we had on, our watches, and everything of value. We were afterwards called up singly. Four, men with drawn knives stood over the captain, and threatened him if he did not give up his money, they would kill all hands and burn the vessel. After robbing the people they commenced plundering the brig. They broke open the hatches, made us get out our boat and carry their plunder to their vessel. They took from us one compass, five bags coffee, one barrel sugar, nearly all our provisions, our colours, rigging, and cooking utensils. They then ordered us to stand to the north, or they would overhaul us, murder the crew and burn the vessel. We made sail, and shortly after were brought to by another boat of the same character, which fired into us, but left us upon being informed that we had been already robbed.

The Porpoise, Capt. Ramage, arrived at Charleston from his successful cruise against the Pirates, having recaptured a Baltimore schooner which had been in their possession three days, destroyed three of their establishments on shore, 12 of their vessels, besides two on the stocks, and brought in four prisoners, against whom it is supposed there is strong evidence.

It is stated, that a Pirate Captain and his mate quarrelled on the question of putting to death all captives,— they fought a duel with muskets, the Captain was killed, and the Mate (who was the advocate of mercy) succeeded to the command.

The schooner Jane, of Boston, was taken the 24th Jan. by a pirate schooner. — They were carried into a place where were three more of the same trader. The captain and crew were threatened, beat, and the vessel plundered of much property; after which they were released.

153

If the Spanish Government is unable to drive the Pirates from their strong holds in Cuba, the Baltimore Chronicle suggests the necessity of occupying the island with American forces for that purpose, as robbers and pirates have a right to enjoy no protection whatever; and in this case all civilized powers are warranted in carrying the war into the enemy's territory.

Pirates Captured

Charleston, Feb. 12. — The four pirates brought into this pert by the United States Porpoise, were landed yesterday from that vessel, and committed to prison. Three of them are Spaniards, the other a Portuguese; two of the former father and son, the son being only about 18 years of age.

Charleston, Feb. 14, 1824.— The United States schooner Grampus, Lieut. Gregory, from a cruise of 4 months in the West-Indies and along the Spanish Main, arrived at our port yesterday morning, last from Santa Martha. She has brought in three Pirates, viz. James Maxfield, one of the crew that robbed the Orleans, of Philadelphia, and Charles Owens and James Ross, who robbed a Portsmouth schooner of $2600 in the Bite of Leogane. One of these daring freebooters was delivered up to Lieut. G. by the Governor of St. Barts, and the other two by the President of Hayti, for trial by the United States. The G. has boarded several privateers during her cruise, and traversed a space of 9000 miles, spreading terror among those wretches whose impotence is equal to their atrocity, and who only require active pursuit to frighten them out of visible existence.

Mobile, June 1, 1822. — Capt. Carter of the schr. Swan, arrived yesterday from Havana, reports that on his outward passage from this port, on the 27th ult. at 8 o'clock, A. M. being then within 30 miles from Havana, he was boarded by an open boat from the shore, manned with nine men, who all appeared to be Spanish, armed with muskets, pistols, cutlasses, and knives, who plundered the vessel of everything they could carry off. They also robbed the captain and crew of their clothing, even stripping the jackets from their backs, and the shoes from their feet.

The villains would not even spare the property of a Spanish Priest, passenger on board, but they robbed him also of his clothes, money, and plate, the value of 800 dollars; they however afterwards, returned his gown.

A sail heaving in sight, they left the schooner with orders to steer E. N. E. and not go over three leagues from shore, under pain of death. From their conversation while on board, it appeared that they intended to board the schooner again in the evening, run her ashore and burn her, but she escaped by the darkness of the night.

Lieut. Allen's Victory and Death

Extract of a letter from Matanzas, dated November 11, 1822.

"The gallant **ALLEN** is no more! — You witnessed the promptitude with which he hastened to relieve the vessels which I informed him had been captured off this port. He arrived just in time to save five sail of vessels which he found in possession of a gang of pirates, 300 strong, established in the Bay of Lejuapo, about 15 leagues east of this. He fell, pierced by two musket balls, in the van of a division of boats, attacking their principal vessel, a fine schooner of about eighty tons, with a long eighteen pounder on a pivot, and four smaller guns, *with the bloody flag nailed to the mast.* Himself, Capt. Freeman of Marines, and twelve men, were in the boat, much in advance of his other boats, and even took possession of the schooner, after a desperate resistance, which nothing but a bravery almost too daring could have overcome. The pirates, all but one, escaped by taking to their boats and jumping overboard, before the Alligator's boats reached them. Two other schooners escaped by the use of their oars, the wind being light.

Capt. Allen survived about four hours, during which his conversation evinced a composure and firmness of mind, and correctness of feeling, as honourable to his character, and more consoling to his friends than even the dauntless bravery he before exhibited."

The Surgeon of the Alligator in a letter to a friend, says, "He continued giving orders and conversing with Mr. Dale and the rest of us, until a few minutes before his death, with a degree of cheerfulness that was little to be expected from a man in his condition. He said he wished his relatives and his country to know that he had fought well, and added that he died in peace and good will towards all the world, and hoped for his reward in the next."

Lieut. Allen had but few equals in the service. He was ardently devoted to the interest of his country, was brave, intelligent, and accomplished in his profession. He displayed, living and dying, a magnanimity that sheds lustre on his relatives, his friends, and his country.

Pirates Entrapped

The British schooner Speedwell arrived at Nassau N. P. in November, bringing in 18 pirates, who had been captured by the Speedwell and her consort. The schooner had been disguised as a merchantman, and the pirates, taking her to be an easy prize, came carelessly along side of her, for the purpose of boarding, when she gave them a hot fire, and threw them into confusion. Many jumped overboard and were drowned; and with these and those killed, the loss of the pirates was about 15 or 16. The remainder of them, 18 in number, were taken prisoners and carried into Nassau.

Sailing of Commodore Porter

Baltimore, Jan. 17, 1823.

Yesterday Commodore **PORTER** left this port in the steam galley Enterprize, to join the squadron fitted out at Norfolk, for the purpose of suppressing piracy on the coast of Cuba. Every friend of humanity must wish that the efforts of the distinguished officer who has been selected to this command will be crowned with success. The means adopted are certainly the best calculated to effect the object. Frigates and sloops of war are totally inadequate, by means of their great draft of water; but the vessels which have been selected by Commodore Porter, are precisely calculated to ferret the banditti. from their lurking places. The aid of steam we think a most valuable addition to the squadron, and from the manner in which the Enterprize has been fitted out, we have every reason to believe she will completely answer the expectations formed. Commodore Porter has been indefatigable since he came here, and several of our citizens conversant in steam affairs, volunteered their services to aid him in the necessary equipments for that department. We learn that she is provided with duplicates of every piece of machinery wiiich might be carried away in action, and that able and experienced engineers were also procured for her.

In a very short time we hope to hear of the Commodore's arrival at his cruising ground, and we doubt not he will soon put an end to the ravages of those lawless barbarians.

Execution of the Pirates

Ten of the pirates captured by the British sloop of War Tyne, were executed at Kingston, Jamaica, on Friday, the 7th of February, 1823.

About a quarter of an hour before day dawn, the wretched culprits were taken from the jail, under a guard of soldiers from the 50th regiment, and the City Guard. On their arrival at the wherry wharf, the military retired, and the prisoners, with the Town Guard were put on board two wherries, in which they proceeded to Port Royal Point, the usual place of execution in similar cases. They were there met by a strong party of military, consisting of 50 men, under command of an officer. They formed themselves into a square round the place of execution, with the Sheriff and his officers with the prisoners in the centre. The gallows was of considerable length, and contrived with a drop so as to prevent the unpleasant circumstances which frequently occur.

The unfortunate men had been in continual prayer from the time they were awakened out of a deep sleep till they arrived at that place, where they were to close their existence.

They all expressed their gratitude for the attention they had met with from the Sheriff and the inferior officers. Many pressed the hands of the turnkey to their lips, others to their hearts, and, on their knees, prayed that God, Jesus Christ, and the Virgin Mary, would bless him and the other jailers for their goodness. They all then fervently joined in prayer. To the astonishment of all, no clerical character, of any persuasion, was present. They repeatedly called out, "Adonde esta el padre," (Where is the holy father.)

Juan Hernandez called on all persons present to hear him — he was innocent; what they had said about his confessing himself guilty was untrue. He had admitted himself guilty, because he hoped for pardon; but that now he was to die, he called God, Jesus Christ, the Holy Ghost, the Virgin Mary, and the Saints, to witness that he spoke truth — that he was no pirate, no murderer — he had been forced. The Lieutenant of the pirates was a wretch, who did not fear God, and had compelled him to act.

Juan Gutterez and Francisco de Sayas were loud in their protestations of innocence.

Manuel Lima said, for himself, he did not care; he felt for the old man (Miguel Jose.) How could he be a pirate who could not help himself. If it were a Christian country, they would have pardoned him for his gray hairs. He was innocent — they had both been forced. Let none of his friends and relations ever venture to sea — he hoped his death would be a warning to them, that the innocent might suffer for the guilty. The language of this young man marked him a superior to the generality of his companions in misfortune. The seamen of the Whim stated that he was very kind to them when prisoners on board the piratical vessel. Just before he was turned off, he addressed the old man — "Adios viejo, para siempre adios." — (Farewell, old man, for ever farewell.)

Several of the prisoners cried out for mercy, pardon, pardon.

Domingo Eucalla, the black man, then addressed them. "Do not look for mercy here, but pray to God; we are all brought here to die. This is not built for nothing; here we must end our lives. You know I am innocent, but I must die the same as you all. There is not any body here who can do us any good, so let us think only of God Almighty. We are not children but men, you know that all must die; and in a few years those who kill us must die too. When I was born, God set the way of my death; I do not blame any body. I was taken by the pirates, and they made me help them; they would not let me be idle. I could not show that this was the truth, and therefore they have judged me by the people they have found me with. I am put to death unjustly, but I blame nobody. It was my misfortune. Come, let us pray. If we are innocent, so much the less we have to repent. I do not come here to accuse any one. Death must come one day or other; better to the innocent than guilty." He then joined in prayer with the others. He seemed to be much reverenced by his fellow prisoners. He chose those prayers he thought most adapted to the occasion. Hundreds were witnesses to the manly firmness of this negro. Observing a bystander listening attentively to the complaints of one of his fellow wretches, he translated what had been said into English. With a steady pace, and a resolute and resigned countenance, he ascended the fatal scaffold. Observing the executioner unable to untie a knot on the collar of one of the prisoners, he with his teeth undid it. He then prayed most fervently till the drop fell.

Miguel Jose protested his innocence.— "No. Re robado, no he matado ningune, muero innocente." — (I have robbed no one, I have killed no one, I die innocent. I am an old man, but my family will feel my disgraceful death.)

Francisco Miguel prayed devoutly, but inaudibly. His soul seemed to have quitted the body before he was executed.

Breti Gullimillit called on all to witness his innocence; it was of no use for him to say an untrutb, for he was going before the face of God.

Augustus Hernandez repeatedly declared his innocence, requested that no one would say he had made a confession; he had none to make.

Juan Hernandez was rather obstinate when the executioner pulled the cap over his eyes. He said, rather passionately — "Quita is de mis ojos." — (Remove it from my eyes.) He then rubbed it up against one of the posts of the gallows.

Miguel Jose made the same complaint, and drew the covering from his eyes by rubbing his head against a fellow sufferer.

Pedro Nondre was loud in his ejaculations for mercy. He wept bitterly. He was covered with the marks of deep wounds.

The whole of the ten, included in the death warrant, having been placed on the scaffold, and the ropes suspended, the drop was let down. Nondre being an immense heavy man, broke the rope, and fell to the ground alive. Juan Hernandez struggled long. Lima was much convulsed. The old man GullimiLlit, and Miguel, were apparently dead before the drop fell. Eucalla (the black man) gave one convulsion, and all was over.

When Nondre recovered from the fall and saw his nine lifeless companions stretched in death, he gave an agonizing shriek; he wrung his hands, screamed "Favor, favor, me matan sin causa. O! buenos Christianos, me amparen, ampara me, ampara me, no hay Christiano en asta, tiara!" (Mercy, mercy, they kill me without cause — Oh, good Christians, protect me, protect me, Oh, protect me. Is there no Christian in this land.)

He then lifted his eyes to Heaven, and prayed long and loud. Upon being again suspended, he was for a long period convulsed. He was an immense powerful man, and died hard.

Pirates Captured

The famous pirate, La Cata, was captured, off the Isle of Pines, about the 1st of March, 1823, by the British cutter Grecian, after a smart action. The cutter had 50 men — the pirate 100, and 8 guns; it was believed that about 30 of the crew of the latter were killed, but only three prisoners were made, the rest making their escape on shore. Considerable quantities of goods were found on board the prize.

The Grecian conveyed the prisoners to Jamaica, where, it seems, there is more law to reach cases of piracy than in the United States.

Lafitte, The Noted Pirate, Killed

A British sloop of war fell in with and captured a piratical vessel with a crew of sixty men, under command of the famous Lafitte. He hoisted the bloody flag and refused quarter, and fought until nearly every man was killed or wounded — Lafitte being among the former.

The schooner Pilot, of Norfolk, was captured by the pirates off Matanzas, and her crew much abused; but they were put ashore, and the wretches went on a cruise in the prize, and captured and robbed two vessels, *within two miles of the Moro castle,* Havana. A few days after, the U. S. schooner Jackall fell in with her and made a re-capture, Securing, however, only one of the pirates; but several of them were killed in the action, fighting desperately. Several captures were made about the same time by Com. Porter's squadron, which was actively employed.

Battle with the Pirates

Almost every day furnished accounts evincing the activity of Commodore Porter, and the officers and men under his command; but for a long time their industry and zeal was rather shown in the *suppression* of piracy than the *punishment* of it. At length, however, an opportunity offered for inflicting the latter, as detailed in the following letter, dated Matanzas, July 10, 1823.

"I have the pleasure of informing you of a brilliant achievement obtained against the pirates on the 5th inst. by two barges attached to Commodore Porter's squadron, the Gallinipper, Lieut. Watson, 18 men, and the Musquito, Lieut. Inman, 10 men. The barges were returning from a cruise to windward; when they were near Jiguapa Bay, 13 leagues to windward of Matanzas, they entered it — it being a rendezvous for pirates. They immediately discovered a large schooner under way, which they supposed to be a Patriot privateer; and as their stores were nearly exhausted, they hoped to obtain some supplies from her. They therefore made sail in pursuit. When they were within cannon shot distance, she rounded to and fired her long gun, at the same time run up the bloody flag, directing her course towards the shore, continuing to fire without effect. When she had got within a short distance of the shore, she came to, with springs on her cable, continuing to fire; and when the barges were within 30 yards, they fired their muskets without touching boat or man; our men gave three cheers, and prepared to board; the pirates, discovering their intention, jumped into the water, when the bargemen, calling on the name of "Allen," commenced a destructive slaughter, killing them in the water and as they landed. So exasperated were our men, that it was impossible for their officers to restrain them, and many were killed after orders were given to grant quarter. Twenty-seven dead were counted, some sunk, five taken prisoners by the bargemen, and eight taken by a party of Spaniards on shore. The officers calculated that from 30 to 35 were killed. The schooner mounted a long nine pounder on a pivot, and 4 four pounders, with every other necessary armament, and a crew of 50 to 60 men, and ought to have blown the barges to atoms. She was commanded by the notorious Diableto or Little Devil. This statement I have from Lieut. Watson himself, and it is certainly the most decisive operation that has been effected against those murderers, either by the English or American force.

"This affair occurred on the same spot where the brave Allen fell about one year since. The prize was sent to Thompson's Island."

A British sloop of war, about the same time, captured a pirate schooner off St. Domingo, with a crew of 60 men. She had 200,000 dollars in specie, and other valuable articles on board. The brig Vestal sent another pirate schooner to New-Providence.

Capture of a Piratical Station in Cuba

The U. S. schooners of war Greyhound and Beagle left Thompson's Island, June 7, 1823, under the command of Lieuts. Kearney and Newton, and cruised within the Keys, on the south side of Cuba, as far as Cape Cruz, touching at all the intermediate ports on the island, to intercept pirates. On the 21st July, they came to anchor off Cape Cruz, and Lieut. Kearney went in his boat to reconnoitre the shore, when he was fired on by a party of pirates who were concealed among the bushes. A fire was also opened from several pieces of cannon erected on a hill, a short distance off. The boat returned, and five or six others were manned from the vessels, and pushed off for the shore, but a very heavy cannonade being kept up by the pirates on the heights, as well as from the boats were compelled to retreat. The two schooners were then warped in, when they discharged several broadsides, and covered the landing of the boats. After a short time the pirates retreated to a hill that was well fortified. A small hamlet, in which the pirates resided was set fire to and destroyed. Three guns, one a four pounder, and two large swivels, with several pistols, cutlasses, and eight large boats, were captured. A cave, about 150 feet deep, was discovered, near where the houses were, and after considerable difficulty, a party of seamen got to the bottom, where was found an immense quantity of plunder, consisting of broadcloths, dry goods, female dresses, saddlery, &c. Many human bones were also in the cave, supposed to have been unfortunate persons who were taken and put to death. A great deal of the articles were brought away and the rest destroyed. About forty pirates escaped to the heights, but many were supposed to have been killed, from the fire of the schooners, as well as from the men who landed. The bushes were so thick that it was impossible to go after them. Several other caves are in the neighbourhood, in which it was conjectured they occasion ally take shelter.

Pirates Taken and Executed

A piratical vessel, and her crew of thirty-eight men were captured off Matanzas on the 16th May, 1825, by a British cutter and a steamboat fitted out at that place. Several of the pirates were killed, and the rest sent to Havana for trial. It was ascertained that some of them had assisted in capturing more than twenty American vessels, whose crews were **murdered!!**

An additional gang of pirates was hung at the same period, at Porto Rico—Eleven at once.